TRAUMA TO DHARMA

TRAUMA TO DHARMA
TRANSFORM YOUR PAIN INTO PURPOSE

AZITA NAHAI, PH.D.

BOOKS

Published in Los Angeles, California, by AnR Books.

Edited by Monica Mitchell
Cover Photo by Ricardo Rico
Cover Design by Lisa Schiavello
Illustrations by Dorothy Boyd

ISBN: 0692066837
ISBN-13: 978-0692066836
Library of Congress Control Number: 2018901656
LCCN Imprint Name: AnR Books, Los Angeles, CA.

DEDICATION

To all of those who have experienced trauma,
to those who have held our hands and guided us through,
and to my future daughter
who will benefit from our pioneering courage...

This place where you are right now
God circled on a map for you.
—Hafez

TRAUMA

A highly stressful event or experience that disrupts your world and the way you have come to make meaning of it, leaving you feeling helpless, immobilized, disconnected, and stuck.

DHARMA

Living a life of purpose, mission, and meaning, where your authentic way of being meets the world's deepest need.

TABLE OF CONTENTS

FOREWORD

When I first met Azita she was hiding from her light. She had been brought to me for guidance by those who loved her dearly and were desperate to help her. Arms crossed and scowling, she came kicking and screaming, and looked at me as someone she could trick into believing everything was fine. In order to connect with this feral creature, I went along with her antics for well over a year . . . all the while inviting her to feel comfortable.

But then we started to dig below the surface of what it means to be "fine," and through the darkness, ignorance, and falsities of nice, we began to uncover the wounds that contributed to her traumatized life. There were defining traumas as well as smaller dramas that added up to become traumas of their own. We had to navigate through the pain, shame, and secretiveness – all the components that surround a traumatic experience – while at the same time unpacking the memories, microscopic measure by microscopic measure so as not to expose too much too quickly. It was a slow and committed process that began to reveal the light that exists on the other side of trauma. That light is known in the language of the ancient mystics and masters as dharma – the ability to project from pure spirit, pure soul.

I found Azita masterful at reaping the lessons her traumas held, and the more she learned, the more she realized that it had never been about tricking me but, rather, about tricking herself into ignoring a feeling deep down within that something more than being nice and fine has always existed. She longed for a life that she began to believe was possible, and this opened the dharmic transition of fulfilling who she is as a person, as a teacher, and as a master. This was opening her to her destiny.

Dharma is an ancient word that means the projection of light, and the ability to project light into a world of darkness is something that gives our lives fulfillment, mission, and mastery of the mystery. Azita's dharmic light was always there, shining from deep inside and the darkness in her past led her back to it. That's what darkness can do, if you let it. I have witnessed Azita along this sacred path, as she braved from kicking and screaming, to kicking with purpose and screaming with meaning. This book is a deep study in how anyone can follow this path. Because Azita is not unique. Everybody in this world has micro and major traumas, micro and major dramas. The pages that follow give you the skills and tools to be able to face these situations that are prevalent in today's world and come out in a meaningful way, living a more purposeful existence.

If you're drawn to this book for any reason let me say that *Trauma to Dharma* is going to be one of those masterpieces that lives in history as a document of how to deal with the 21st century. None of us are immune to what is going on in this world and a call to action exists in each of us. Every one of us has a mission on this planet to make a difference, not just a living, and that difference is your dharma.

Trauma to Dharma is a path from the A to Z of life, no matter where you live, how you live, what you're doing, or when you're doing it. It is a map to a life of fulfillment and purpose, birthed from the gifts of giving and receiving. Because you cannot give without receiving, and you cannot receive without giving. Azita has given us a masterful gift in *Trauma to Dharma* and I welcome you to the next chapter of your life, as you open up the chapters of this book.

Guru Singh, DD MSS

INTRODUCTION

There is a crack in everything.
That's how the light gets in.
—Leonard Cohen

God bless Leonard Cohen. Those words saved my life. Because not only did I crack, I broke. Years back, this stirring sentiment made sense to me during a time when nothing else did, and it truly is the Trauma to Dharma anthem. Yes, life will inevitably crack you open. And yes, that's how the light gets in. But what if those cracks are also personal invitations to let your own light out? What if those harrowing ruptures are life's way of opening us to the hidden gifts beneath the traumas that have cracked us open?

Historically, psychology has focused on the whys and the hows of what breaks us. But standing on the shoulders of the giants in my field, I am more interested in what those breaks open in us. This book is about those raw and real openings we are thrown into after the break—and how to lean into the loss and fear that accompany them. It is about discovering how those cracks can offer us tender entries to our deepest purpose and how we can use them as perfectly imperfect offerings to reach one another.

I am not an "everything happens for a reason" person. That is not what this book is about. We're not here to Pollyanna our traumas to death—this is not about putting a scoop of ice cream on a piece of crap. There is no candy-coating our reality. If life has taught me anything, it's that we must simply keep moving and connecting through our pain and all the things we spend so much energy trying to find a reason for.

Trauma to Dharma is about just that: movement and connection. I do not believe that our minds alone are capable of reasoning with the unreasonable and nonsensical adversities and atrocities of life. Trauma isn't to be reasoned with. As George C. Scott said, "The human spirit is stronger than anything that can happen to it." I know that if that Spirit of ours were a muscle within our human mess of flesh and bone, it would be the strongest muscle we've got. Trauma to Dharma has been my way of connecting to that strength of Spirit.

If you're reading this, then you or someone you know has been pained. None of us leave this life unscathed. We have all been hurt. We have all been pained. How many of us continue to carry the hurt and hate, the anger and rage, like defensive coats of armor? That armor has its place, but left on too long, it hardens and stiffens. It desensitizes us. It constrains us. No longer serving as protection, it becomes a self-induced prison, keeping us shackled to pain that begs to be transformed and holding us captive in our very old and stale stories. Oh, the stories—they can trap us or free us.

Chapter One
MY STORY

Sometimes a person needs a story
more than food to stay alive.
—*Barry Lopez*

It was an early weekday morning in January 2009. I had reluctantly driven myself downtown in LA's famed rush-hour traffic to make it to this "waste of my time" appointment. Here I was, a PhD candidate (and feeling pretty cocky about it), and I was now nervously preparing for a third-grade–level US history exam. You remember those? *What day is Flag Day? Who's the eighteenth president? Who wrote the Declaration of Independence?* I mean, seriously? My ego wasn't having it. But I had no choice: after living in the States for more than thirty years, I'd finally been granted an interview for my US citizenship. So there I sat in the waiting room of the Immigration Office of the Federal Building, listening for my name to be called. And I don't know if you've ever been to an immigration office, but take your last frenetically stressful visit to the DMV and quadruple it.

This tension-filled room was packed with nervous people dressed to impress. Everyone there was waiting to prove themselves worthy of being accepted into the land of the free, the home of the brave. And I was right there with them in my Theory pants and J.Crew button-down. Now, if you knew me, you'd know I never dress like this, but I was well aware of how I needed to "fit in." So there I sat with my fellow citizens-to-be, desperately hoping to make the grade, to literally get that *A* for *American.* The door swung open, and we all anxiously turned to see a tall, broad, and ridiculously intimidating immigration officer. She towered over us all with a name tag that screamed, "This is who I am, and this is who you're *not.*" Claiming her space in the entirety of the doorframe, she called out my name.

My fear grew, and I felt myself shrinking with every step I took toward her. She motioned me into the hallway, and I followed her to her office and sat down. The American flag was to my left, a portrait of George W. hung to my right, and Officer Intimidation sat right in front of me. And thus we began "my trial."

She started to move through the trajectory of my life in the United States: "So you attended elementary and high school in Beverly Hills. And I see you attended university in San Diego and graduated in 1996. Okay. Hmm. You were employed as a teacher here and then ran a business back here...but wait, there's a discrepancy. A huge gap. A hole in your path." Her voice began to rise, laced with an "Aha! I knew I'd find something!" tone of suspicion and distrust. "August 2002. Where were you? You appear to have all of a sudden gone missing in August 2002. There are no records of your whereabouts. August 2002—answer me! Where were you in August 2002?"

I felt a deep, guttural pain surge through my body as my hands began to sweat, my chest began to tighten, and my heart began to race.

Oh please, don't go there. I struggled to grab on to the chair and hold on to a breath—anything to keep me from heading where I was headed.

She provoked me some more, saying, "Answer me! August 2002—where were you?"

In August 2002, I was twenty-eight years old, and I was running from my life for my life. I had been entangled in an abusive relationship for six years. Living a caged existence, I was immobilized by fear and barely existing under the physical blows, mental anguish, and emotional terror of my boyfriend. August 2002 is when I woke up.

But let me back up for a second. The previous summer, in August 2001, disconnected from my family and friends and far removed from the magic of my life, I caught my domineering boyfriend on a good swing. After years of coercing me to miss my annual family vacation, he—shockingly—encouraged me to join them. Growing up I had counted the days until our family getaway each year. My dad would work hard all year to give us a couple of weeks to travel the world together. So you can imagine the elation I felt after having been "given permission" to go. When I arrived at the airport in France and rolled my suitcase out to greet my eager (and disbelieving) family amid the crowd of travelers, my eye caught on one thing: my dad standing between my mom and brother, holding up a handwritten sign that said "Puppy Love, Come Bouncing Back, Love."

Life will give you signs. Mine was literal. "Puppy Love" was the nickname my dad had given me when I was a girl. Those scribbled words took me back—back to our early immigrant years, when my twenty-something parents, my one-year-old brother, and I (only four years old) tried to find a semblance of normalcy on foreign land after escaping revolutionary Iran. Growing up an immigrant child in 1970s Los Angeles under a climate of prejudice, I was anything but normal. And well, it hurt. I would dodge the sting of my "not-normalness" and the hurt of not fitting in by escaping to the imaginative alleys of my mind. Whenever my dad would find me lost in my head and disconnected from the present, he'd wiggle his way into my view and begin chanting this silly song: "Puppy Love, come bouncing back!" It made no sense, really, but it inevitably worked. It always got something in me to awaken and brought me right back to the present and right back to myself.

And that's exactly what it did outside that airport in France in 2001. It awakened something in me. But it took me a year to realize it—a year of the harshest and darkest of domestic abuse that led me not just to suicidal thoughts but to a suicide plan, a year that ultimately found me locking myself in the bathroom and staring shamefully at myself in the mirror, silently screaming at the hauntingly gaunt and lifeless woman reflected back at me. "What's happened to you? How did you get here? Where have you been? *Where were you?*"

Looking back through my lens of recovery, I've come to understand pain as the distance from *where* we are to *who* we are, and at that moment, the distance had never been greater. *Puppy Love, come bouncing back!* So where was I in August 2002? Good question. And I wasn't the only one who wanted to know.

"August 2002—where were you? Explain this to me. Speak!" Officer Intimidation glared at me. I sat there, staring at her as I felt my defensive coat of arms thicken. All I wanted to do was scream, "*Fuck you, bitch!*"—my way of keeping my protective armor intact and hiding any signs of vulnerability or emotional pain. Yet something in me shifted. I took a pause—I swear, God is in the pause—and in that moment, I softened. I looked up at her and said, "Listen. In August 2002, I was drowning in a secret I could no longer hide. You see, I am an abuse survivor, and that late summer, my six-year hell on earth hit a boiling point of no return. And thank God, with the support of my family and my friends, I was able to run away and get help—without a trail, without a chance of him finding me. I was sent away to a specialized hospital and trauma center to heal and regain my strength, my sanity, and my sanctity."

As I continued to pour my vulnerability out into that cold, stark office, I looked up at Officer Intimidation and took a breath. Her eyes, which just moments before had glared accusatory daggers my way, now welled up with tears. Her tough exterior began to soften, and her jaw unlocked. She looked right into my eyes and said, "Me too. I've been there too."

It gets me every time. I don't know if there are two words in our human lexicon that are more powerful than *me too*. *Me too*—I see you. I hear you. You're not alone. *Me too*—I'm right here. I understand.

Talk about land of the free, home of the brave! In that moment, I experienced how our greatest defense is an open heart. And *we* experienced the miracle of a "me-too moment." Yes, your truth will set you free—if you are brave enough to share it.

So it goes without saying that I passed my test and got my citizenship. She gave me her me-too stamp of approval right then and there (approving of my vulnerability and my humanity). Wiping the tearstains from her cheek, she slowly got up from her desk and walked to the door. We paused for a moment before she swung the door back open and into the tension-filled room where we had first met. I stood before the sea of anxious eyes staring in disbelief as they watched little five-foot-three me rise up on my tiptoes and give Officer Intimidation—

turned–Gentle Giant a big hug. To this day, I can only imagine what they were thinking!

We all have our secret struggles with pain. But we aren't wired to carry that pain alone. Me-too moments remind us of that. They remind us that we're in this together. But here's the catch: I cannot have a me-too moment unless I am willing to connect to *me* and brave enough to expose *me*—unless I am willing to connect to myself and my pain and brave enough to share it

My intention in the pages that follow is to offer you a "me-too" by sharing my own journey back to *me*. But this book is also a map. Because during the six years I spent in that painful relationship, I had gone missing. Those who'd known me could no longer recognize me. I was a shell looking outside of myself to fill the emptiness inside. Someone. Something. Anything. Everything. And nothing seemed to work. It wasn't until I found myself on a tearstained yoga mat in a Kundalini class that I heard a clear and steady voice whisper, "When you feel there is something missing in your life, it's probably you."

So I set out to find that missing piece. My first stop back in August 2002 was an inpatient hospital and treatment center that helped people move through crisis, trauma, and the addictions that ensue because of them. It was the place where the "missing persons" went to stand at the helm of their very own search and rescue.

My intensive weeks of work in the trauma track culminated with a phone call to my abuser to say what I'd been unable to say all those years: "No more. Enough. I am never coming back." It was one of the most significant acts I had taken in reclaiming my voice and self. When I was done, my therapist encouraged me to take a moment to walk around the grounds and take it all in and then meet up with everyone in the dining hall. So I took a walk, not knowing how to identify what I was feeling. Nothing had changed, yet everything had changed. With every step I took, I began to feel a little lighter and less burdened. I felt a weight had been lifted. It was as if I had finally removed the 250-pound gorilla strapped to my back. My steps didn't feel like steps. I almost felt as though I was floating...or no, more like bouncing.

Aha. Yes! Of course. "Puppy Love, come bouncing back!"

With a bounce in my step, I made my way into the cafeteria, where the one hundred-plus residents were already eating. As I walked in, heads turned; eyes rose to greet me; and every single one of them put down their utensils, stood up, and started clapping. They all knew where I'd been, what I'd needed to do, and why that little phone call I'd finally made was bigger than this moment. It was precisely in that moment, as I felt myself being carried and celebrated through a sea of kindred spirits, that everything began to make sense.

I realized I wasn't just doing all this work of grieving, growing, and healing for myself. We all need one another to be reminded: If I can do it, you can do it. In that moment I realized I had taken a significant step in reclaiming myself and living my dharma. In that moment I had come home to *me*. And I suddenly understood this wasn't about bouncing back; this was about bouncing well beyond where I had ever imagined I could go. This wasn't just for me—this was for all the *me toos*! Yes, I did it for me, but I also did it for everyone in that cafeteria. And now I realize I did it for all my clients and my students. And yes, I did it for you too. Because we cannot be what we cannot see, and I want you to see the possibilities that await you on the other side of your pain.

No, I could not change what had happened to me. I could not transform the past, but I sure as hell could choose how it would transform me. I started to wonder where I could harness my inner alchemist and turn that pain of mine into purpose, into a life of meaning and, believe it or not, joy. And the answer to that is this book—my personal map from Trauma to Dharma, lived and designed to lead you first to "me" and then to "me too." Because without *me*, there's no *me too*.

Chapter Two
THE STUDY

After my nine-week stint in rehab, fueled by me-too moments, I felt more encouraged and equipped to take back my life. I was fortunate that my inpatient treatment plan ran the gamut of healing modalities, and when I left treatment, I dove back into my life, which happened to be a master's program and a thesis that was waiting to be written. Or waiting for me to be ready to write it. Because what better topic, I figured, for a master of arts in human development thesis than my own abuse story? I set to work on writing a blow-for-blow, tear-for-tear account of what had led to my own treatment and recovery. In doing that work, I successfully intellectualized my trauma. I literally *mastered* it. My mind made sense of it all, and I moved on to my PhD studies. So I was done, right? Healed?

I might've thought so but for a nagging feeling that there was a missing piece. Despite all my treatment, I was still experiencing triggers and noticing unhealthy patterns. My night terrors and frightening thoughts still haunted me. I was quick to startle and slow to trust. I'd break out into a full-blown panic attack if a man took interest in me at an event or gathering, and I still preferred to keep the shades drawn at home.

These symptoms were textbook post-traumatic stress disorder, and I was *still* struggling with them. Yes, there was definitely a piece missing. And it was in a familiar place that I came to realize what that piece was.

Before going to treatment, I had found my way to Kundalini yoga. It was the place, you will remember, that helped me to see that the "something" that was missing from my life was *me*, and once again, it held a solution. Back then, I was so dissociated from my body that I would go to my teacher Guru Singh's class; take perfectly penned notes; and think, *Oh yeah, conceptually, I get it. These teachings are brilliant. It all makes so much sense in my head.* But I couldn't make sense of it in my body. I couldn't go there yet. It was a minefield of pain. So I was doing what came most easily to me—I was thinking my way through it. Our bodies are designed to protect themselves from feeling the depths of life's pains until we're ready. Our problem is we numb ourselves from sensing when our bodies truly *are* ready. They could be screaming at us to finally feel, but we can't hear them. Or we normalize our pain and carry it around, unaware of the heaviness, afraid to feel. This is how I was going through my Kundalini classes, and this is how I was going through my life.

So upon my return to the yoga mat, to my surprise, the emotions were waiting for me. Barely into my first hour, it was like the floodgates opened. Every feeling I hadn't been ready to feel years prior, every piece of my pain that couldn't be thought or talked about, was there in every fiber of my being. And it was all coming up. I was experiencing all my pain, trauma, and wounds. And beneath the surge and swell of emotions, I felt and heard my body crying out to me. Rumi says there is a voice that doesn't use words and implores us to listen. And what I heard from the wordless language of my body was this: "Thank you for finally giving me your attention. I've been waiting for you." And the more I stayed with it, the clearer the message was: *When you feel there is something missing in your life, it's probably you.*

That really was the missing-piece moment for me. On so many levels. Not only had I been missing from my life during those painful years in my relationship, but I—*my Soul*—was also missing from my recovery!

We humans are body, mind, and Spirit, and in my intensive work to date, I had been managing my recovery only in the safety and familiarity of my head. The mat offered a way for me to reconnect to my body—the scene of crime after crime that I vowed never to return to. It allowed me to finally feel *at home* in my own skin, the very place that once had been a source of my deepest pain and shame. On the mat, I found myself learning for the first time to check in instead of check out. And as a result, I started to soften. I'd spent so much time anxiously tight and closed off that it was not lost on me when I noticed my entire being starting to relax, my eyes making contact with others, and my hugs getting longer. And as I deepened my Kundalini practice, I experienced old residue starting to rise up and—in a new way—release. Without even thinking about it, I started feeling again. I started seeing where I was still numbing myself from what I needed to feel. The practice of Kundalini yoga gave my Self and my life the gift of my attention in a way I hadn't been capable of in my recovery.

Traumas disconnect us from others, from the world, and from our own Souls. But through Kundalini, I was becoming more present and more connected. It was only when I reconnected with my body that I was granted access to my Soul—to my Spirit. I felt free, and my life started to get better. Within and around me, things lightened and brightened. I was learning to trust myself again. I developed a sense of self-love and appreciation I hadn't experienced before. I became more engaged in my life and more present and open to those in it. I was energized with a vitality that had been absent for years. My life was growing not only in ways it never had before but also in ways I never could have imagined prior to the relationship and abuse that had brought me here. It—whatever "it" was—was undeniably working for me.

And researcher that I am, I needed to understand what exactly "it" was. Did I simply drink the Kundalini Kool-Aid, or was there some scientific explanation for the changes I was experiencing? And moreover, were there others experiencing this as well? When I looked around the yoga studio, it was clear that these students kept coming back, but what were they coming back for? Was it possible that they felt what I felt? That they too had been transformed by this practice? That I was not the only one thriving out in the world as a result of the work I was doing in class? These questions nagged me, insisting on being answered. So I started my me-too hunt to find out.

AWARENESS IS HEALING

I dove into what turned out to be a weeks-long mind-numbing and disheartening search. If you're anything like me, when you hear the word *trauma*, you might immediately think of post-traumatic stress disorder. That's because in the early days of trauma research and recovery, all attention was placed on how to manage and cope with the stresses and messes that trauma left behind. But I wasn't interested in the *disorder*. Yes, my mind, body, and life fell into complete disorder, but then...they didn't. Something grew out of that disorder, and that something was me.

And this is where the nerd in me wondered if there was any science out there to support my experience.

My first hit came when I changed my search from key words centered around stress and disorder to ones focusing on resilience, growth, and transformation. This is when I discovered the then relatively new concept of post-traumatic growth and the pioneering work of Tedeschi and Calhoun—and it was radical. I felt like these groundbreaking researchers were singing my heart song. Growth after trauma. Me too! I couldn't believe it. I had found my people in the often sterile science world, and the language they were using validated my experience as a trauma survivor. This was becoming personal. It made everything real and grounded. Yes, they said, trauma *can* be a springboard to transformation. People *can* grow through their painful encounters with adversity. This confirmed that I was onto something—that I was not alone in my experience. Specifically, if others had grown and healed from the committed practice of Kundalini yoga as I had, then perhaps *something* could benefit from what I was ready to further explore. And so, like any good scientist, I set up a study.

I had a good sense that the "why" and "how" of one's healing from Kundalini would be explained by science, but I also wanted to know the "what"—what was it that one experienced on the mat that kept him or her coming back? What exactly was healing and transforming about this practice? I wanted to understand the phenomenon, so I put out a call to study this experience and was overwhelmed by the response.

Once I selected my participants—survivors of traumas ranging from bullying, a cancer diagnosis, and divorce to political asylum, sexual abuse, and the death of a child—we dove into in-depth interviews in which I asked them...well, everything. Who and how they were before and after their trauma. How they learned to cope. How it affected their world, perspective, and relationships—to themselves, to others, and to spirituality. And then we dissected their experience on and off the yoga mat—initially and after having been at it for a dedicated time. And from these openhearted and vulnerable interviews my data emerged.

For the next phase of this process, I retreated to Palm Desert with my trusty research assistant—my dog, Bailey. Doctoral research and data collection is a lonely process. Until it isn't. Over the next five weeks, I swam in my participants' words, letting their descriptions tell me what I needed to know about where a practice like Kundalini fit into healing trauma. And the more I swam, the more I realized how their stories mirrored my own. They described feeling more present and alive in their bodies, more able to notice emotions without running from them, and more connected to spirituality and the meaning and purpose in their lives. I began to feel as though they were describing my exact experience back to me. Every one of my participants who had once felt lost and missing from their lives had described the experience of being on the Kundalini mat as a "feeling of home." Which is exactly what it had been for me: a homecoming.

The word *yoga* means *union*, but for all of us healing from trauma, it served as a *re*union. It made so much sense. I had always quietly referred to Kundalini as the yoga of the Lost and Found, because no matter what gets us there, we inevitably find ourselves on the Kundalini mat. And the truth is, whatever we are searching for is also searching for us. It can't reach us until we first find ourselves, but we can't find ourselves without the gift of **awareness**—and every one of my participants stated that this is exactly what their Kundalini yoga practice gave them.

As I further coded and decoded the data, certain words continued to emerge over and over again—all variations of *acceptance, agency, authority, allowing, appreciation,* and *authenticity.* These six *A*'s, as I later classified them, were the subthemes of awareness—principles that each of the participants expressed, described, and experienced as essential ingredients in their healing journeys. These very principles had also served as my own map to freedom before I'd even had words to assign to them! I sobbed when I discovered this. *Me too*, I whispered to myself. I was not alone. And now no one else had to be.

Through their committed "awareness building" Kundalini practice, my participants began to see themselves and their circumstances with a fresh set of eyes. Through connecting to their bodies, they had literally "come to their senses" once more. They were trusting themselves to feel again, no matter how much it hurt, because their awareness allowed them to feel without losing themselves.

Awareness is like taking the cap off our life binoculars and allowing ourselves to see what we couldn't—or *wouldn't*—see before. And while there's a whole lot of good, there's also the dirt and the muck we were refusing to see. So much of our suffering rests in our refusal to see our pain and the number of ways in which we try to deny and avoid it. For me, awareness brought me face-to-face with my personal coping strategies that were no longer working: lying to others and myself, disassociating from my body and feelings, looking for someone or something else to save me, and buying in to my own story that I was damaged goods. And that same awareness also brought me face-to-face with new approaches that alchemized my pain into purpose and transformed my battered and self-hating little Soul into something powerful, fierce, and phenomenal. Just as it was for my participants, awareness was the key to my healing. And it will be for you too. And *no wonder.* Because Kundalini has been dubbed the "yoga of awareness."

KUNDALINI YOGA AS TAUGHT BY YOGI BHAJAN

Our body is the first thing we disconnect from when we experience trauma—or even discomfort—and yet consciousness, or awareness, begins in the body. So in order to heal, we must first return to the body. The body is our way in. Of course, there are endless ways to get into our bodies, and I'm completely in favor of finding any path that works. But it is essential that this physical practice—whatever it may be—also allow a supportive space to access Spirit/God/Higher Power/Source/the Universe, because one cannot reach the depths of healing from trauma without the Spirit element of the mind/body/Spirit combo of recovery. (Note: It is *not* essential that you believe in "God" to work the Trauma to Dharma program, but it *is* necessary that you be open to the possibility of Something. That openness can come in any shape, including and especially the whisper of a feeling that "there's got to be something more...")

When I was training to become a Kundalini yoga teacher, I remember learning that "if it's not devotional, it's not yoga—it is just exercise." And what I experienced on my Kundalini yoga mat and meditation cushion was more than just exercise. It was a resurrection of and reconnection to that Spirit within me and around me. This embodied practice can be anything that moves you, but for me and for this program, it is Kundalini. And for good reason. It is considered by some to be the fastest way to establish an aligned relationship between the body, mind, and Soul because it is the path of *practical* spirituality. It was designed for the householder, practiced by those with families and jobs. It is for everyone—universal and nondenominational. In other words, we don't have to be flexible human pretzels, hard-bodied athletes, or ashram-visiting meditation masters. That is why Yogi Bhajan brought Kundalini from India to the West in the 1960s. He wanted people to understand that we didn't have to travel to India or Tibet in order to reach our highest consciousness; rather, we have everything we need inside ourselves to have that divinely exalted experience of God.

Multiple studies have confirmed the benefits of a yoga and meditation practice as therapeutic tools in the treatment of trauma. But why Kundalini over the numerous other limbs of yoga? Because Kundalini encompasses the best parts of every branch, all working with the energy of "Kundalini" that sits at the base of the spine. That Kundalini energy is pure vital life force, and it's healing. So if physics can confirm that energy flows where our attention goes, then the moment we stop denying or avoiding our pain and actually focus our attention toward it, that's the moment we become our very own healing balm.

When we step onto a Kundalini yoga mat, we step onto a personal threshold of discovery, healing, and transformation. A perfect blend of spiritual and physical practices, Kundalini yoga incorporates movement, dynamic breathing techniques, meditation, and the chanting of mantras. The goal is to raise complete body awareness; build physical vitality; and increase consciousness in order to prepare the body, nervous system, and mind to handle the stresses of everyday life.

On a personal level, Kundalini wasn't just a compass back to myself. It also happens to merge my two selves, because it is on the mat where the scientist and the spiritual yogi in me can finally agree. While doing my doctoral research, I was surrounded by skeptics in the science world (admittedly, myself included), but I was continually bolstered and eventually won over by the fact that the purpose and value of every one of the breaths, chants, and poses included in a Kundalini practice is supported by science. It truly is a marriage between science and the Soul.

Chapter Three
WHAT TO EXPECT ON THIS JOURNEY

There are two types of people in the aftermath of trauma: those who did not die and those who came back to life. The Trauma to Dharma program is for those of us who have chosen to come back to life. There is no linear way to heal and transform, but our minds are always starving for steps. Through the courageous life stories of my research participants, I uncovered the Trauma to Dharma principles, the map from pain into purpose. This book is that map. It contains the essential concepts, tools, and exercises that I've applied toward my own healing and toward healing others in my workshops, classes, and one-on-one sessions. This method will take you on a journey that will change the way you see and relate to your pain, your Self, and your world. But of course, a map will take you only so far. It can chart out the terrain, but it's on you to actually walk it.

The principles of Trauma to Dharma are divided into eight chapters, each of which invite you into a deeper understanding and exploration of the hallmark principles of living in awareness. These everyday principles will change the way you come to experience your life and help you transform your pain into purpose.

Chapter 4 dives straight into the heart of **Trauma** 101. What is trauma? Why does it stick and keep us stuck? And what are the breakthroughs in the trauma world that are shifting the way we treat our traumatic pain? These shifts are placing power back into our hands in order to heal and transform ourselves, allowing our traumas to become springboards to transformation and a more meaningful way of living.

Having gained a clearer understanding of all things trauma, **chapter 5** offers an invitation to bravely step into **Acceptance**, the first of the principles of moving from trauma to dharma. Transformation must begin with acceptance, which is no more and no less than a surrendered commitment to simply being here with the reality of what's happened. By accepting, we finally connect back to ourselves, to our fears and struggles, and recognize that we must acknowledge our pain in order to feel it. And we must feel it in order to heal it.

Once we've settled into acceptance and are no longer resisting our traumas, **chapter 6** introduces **Agency**, which requires our active participation in our own healing. It is a rediscovery of the most powerful tool we've been gifted: choice. We take ownership of our life back by realizing that while we cannot choose what may have happened, we sure as hell can choose how we will face it. And once we have learned how to respond rather than react to life's disruptions, we can move into our...

Authority. In this third principle, we come to see that, with the power to choose, we actually do have a say in how our story writes itself. **Chapter 7** starts to engage our conscious willingness to step out of the ego's fear-fueled victim story and into the Soul's victorious one.

Now while we've tapped into our authority, it's critical to understand that we're not *the* authority. **Chapter 8** explores the principle of **Allowing**, which reminds us that life will continue to humble us into recognizing that we're not the ones steering the ship. We come to *allow* for that Something greater than us to work its magic. This is the faith piece that helps us connect to the Spirit that surges through us. And when we have experienced that spirited presence within ourselves, we are able to recognize it in others.

That sweet recognition brings us to the principle of **Appreciation**, where we step bravely into shared spaces of vulnerability and me-too moments. It is here in **chapter 9** that we recognize that life happens through human connection. We need others along on this messy journey, and through practicing forgiveness, we give one another permission to be flawed, fallible, and perfectly imperfect.

Chapter 10 is about owning our imperfections. The final principle of **Authenticity** is where we relax and fully embrace all of who we are and what we have been through. It is where we start to show up completely and unapologetically to share all of ourselves. And it is through our authentic living we begin to understand and own why we were born.

And that *why* is our **Dharma**. This **final chapter** is where we realize that our healing has a ripple effect and begin to truly alchemize our pain into purpose.

The close of each chapter will also offer a self-reflective Soul Prescription that supports living and embodying that chapter's particular principle. Each prescribed task is designed to deepen your experience and understanding of these principles and to increase your capacity for living in awareness. I still turn to these principles every day, and the stories, explanations, and self-reflective exercises will help you familiarize yourself with the concepts enough to know that they are always available to you. The purpose of these principles and the exercises that accompany them is to awaken you to the wisdom you already carry—right there inside your wounds.

HOW TO WORK THIS BOOK

There is an organic sequence to the principles, and I recommend moving through them in the order given, designating a week for each chapter. Use the first week to get comfortable carving out a committed time for this transformative work. You can create a morning practice before the day steals you away or make time in the evening once the buzz of the day has settled, but it is more important to do it than not. So do what you can when you can.

Each principle builds upon the one before it, so following the book principle by principle will create an insightful and supportive foundation for what's to follow. Of course, there really is no right or wrong way to apply these principles to your life, so don't let this keep you from diving into another chapter or principle that is calling you. Each chapter offers journal questions and exercises to help you understand and practice that particular principle. Take your time to focus on each principle and explore the transformative exercises. I encourage you to try them all and then choose one of the Soul Prescription meditations that speaks to or inspires you and commit to doing it every day for that week. If you pick up just *one* meditation or exercise from these pages and apply it to your life every day, you *will* experience a shift. You will see and feel the difference.

And a warning: be prepared to come up against some resistance, including a roll of the eyes or other demands on your time, for example. Or if you're anything like me, you'll want to read every concept and skip right past the exercises, but listen, it's true what they say: *it works if you work it*. Our insight requires action. It's not enough to simply know something; we must *do something* with that knowledge. We must not confuse information with transformation. It's like sitting all day watching the Food Network but never actually going to the store, pulling out your pans, and trying a recipe. Transformation doesn't happen in your head; it happens out in the field, actively engaged, ready and willing to put a little skin in the game. That's what the exercises at the end of each section will help you do, if you let them. And the more you let them, the more you'll begin to feel at home again—or perhaps for the first time.

TRAUMA TO DHARMA TOOLS

Mental hygiene is no different from dental hygiene. Think of all the layers of mental muck and gunk we pick up in our days. We ingest serving after serving of opinions, assumptions, and stories that our mind chews on all day, or week, or lifetime, and most of us do absolutely nothing to clean it. That mental junk just sits there and slowly hardens and decays, closing off a once-open and imaginative mind. Gross. We brush our teeth every day, *twice* a day, but not our minds? We spend more time on dental hygiene than mental hygiene! The purpose of working the Trauma to Dharma program is to clean out our decayed ways of thinking that prevent us from living a healthy and happy life. What follows is an explanation of the tools that will aid in that process.

Meditation

I cannot count the number of people (myself included) who have expressed the same words to me at the onset of learning to meditate: *"Who, me? No, I can't meditate."* Or *"I'm doing it wrong! I can't turn my mind off! I'm flooded with thoughts!"* If this sounds familiar, then you're not alone. But **meditation** is one of the most powerful actions we can take for our healing. It is a cleansing process, a way to rebalance and clear out self-defeating thought patterns, attachments, and behaviors. Our brains tend to get stuck in habits or routines, many of which can be destructive when we are carrying around trauma. And meditation's magic is that it helps create new routes in our brain to replace the old, destructive patterns simply by offering our thoughts space to rise to the surface and giving ourselves permission to let them go.

I like to think of meditation as a garbage cleaner, which is to say we want all that thought-fueled trash talk inside our heads to come up, and our job is to let it go—to let all those thoughts pass on through that mental chute. The more we hold on to them, the less space we have for peace and quiet. We need space to see more clearly. An empty mind is an open mind, and an open mind is the breeding ground for healing, possibility, creativity, and innovation. And that is why meditation is my forever medicine.

Breath

Breath work is another form of meditation and the cornerstone of a Kundalini practice. It is a fundamental tool because it's a detoxifier, neutralizer, revitalizer, and stabilizer. Breath is the carrier of **prana,** or life force, and by using a wide range of prana-filled breath techniques known as **pranayamas**, we can use the breath to create and manage different energy states of emotional health and consciousness. Yogi Bhajan would say the mind becomes our monster when it becomes our master, and the key to mastering the mind is mastering the breath. The breath allows us to experience the only freedom a human being requires, and that is the freedom from our own (monster of a) mind. It is our lifeline, what we turn to without even thinking, and what's always there during the high highs and low lows. I always say the breath is our entry point and our exit plan. It's our courageous way into what scares us and our conscious way out. And we literally have a lifetime supply.

Mantra

A **mantra** is a syllable, a word, or a string of syllables or words chanted to invoke the power contained within them. The word *mantra* is essentially a Sanskrit word for *sound tool*. Mantras can be done vocally, sub-vocally (whispering), or silently in the mind.

Many people shy away from chanting, especially in an unfamiliar language, because it feels vaguely (or not so vaguely) religious or they don't see the point of reciting random words they don't understand. I get it. My own skeptic had the same resistance. But the science of mantra is based not in their meaning but in the powerful sound currents underneath them and what those vibrations can do. There's nothing random about it. According to the work of Dr. Shananoff-Khalsa and his colleagues, mantra can regulate certain circuits in the body simply by using sound to evoke movement of physical and emotional energy through stimulation of the nervous system. Chanting can create an event inside the nervous system, which can increase awareness and expand one's emotional state.

Human beings have nerve endings on the tips of our tongues. When we repetitively chant a mantra, these nerve endings tap against acupuncture meridian points on the roof of the mouth and create an electric effect that initiates a chemical reaction via the hypothalamus, which sends messages to the pituitary and pineal glands, the command centers of our bodies. And the pituitary gland happens to be conveniently located right at the midbrow point—the spot yogis refer to as the Third Eye Point, otherwise known as our seat of intuition (what I like to call the GPS of the soul). The more we get our pituitary gland to secrete (through specific breathing, chanting, and moving), the more our Third Eye lens starts to expand, allowing us to stretch beyond our limited perspectives and to begin living in awareness. So the more the pituitary gland secretes, the more we can recognize that we are bigger than our past, bigger than our pain.

Additionally, the sound waves and vibrational frequencies we create when chanting mantras target specific neurotransmitters in the brain, which induce a variety of changes in our physical, emotional, mental, and spiritual states. This also applies to silent mantras, because our thoughts are vibrations. These vibrational waves cut through the negative thought patterns (e.g., *I'm damaged and unfixable, people can't be trusted*, and *I never get a break*) that so often accompany illness and stress disorders and, in doing so, activate our own natural healing.

Remember taking road trips back before there was satellite radio, when all we had to listen to were those old-school radio stations? Driving through certain areas, we'd have to mess around with the dial and hear fragments of a song and then static, and we'd have to keep fiddling until all of a sudden there'd be a clear channel and frequency. Well, that's what mantra does. It clears the static in our minds so we can have a clearer frequency to engage and communicate with ourselves and one another with far less getting lost in translation.

Mudra

We've all seen yogis and monks with their distinctive hand positions, or **mudras**, right? Not just for show, of course. These bodies of ours are sensory databases that deliver and receive constantly. Mudras are another form of neural stimulation. Just like the tips of our tongues, our fingertips hold another electric set of nerve endings that have a direct connection to the neural pathways in our brains. Mudras with the right hand activate the left brain hemisphere, and those with the left hand activate the right brain hemisphere. The action of bringing specific fingertips together into a mudra literally activates the brain in a new way, accessing the frontal lobe, helping recalibrate the hemispheres, and forcing them to work in harmony. Over time, this begins to soften the neural pathways that have long been hardened by way of old, painful memories that keep playing on a habitual loop.

What does this mean for you? It means you can interrupt and replace that episode of your past you keep playing on repeat. It means you'll feel more present and awake to life. You'll be more forward focused on new possibilities. You will begin to notice greater moments of insight, less reactivity, and an expanded view on how everything is beautifully connected. You'll actually experience more moments of peace. As you are probably starting to gather, the combination of mantra and mudra is a powerhouse tool to heal, rewire, and reboot. It's a literal brainwash that results in more neuroplasticity and mental flexibility, which creates space to imagine anew—to move from what's past to what's possible. In other words, change your brain, change your life.

Asana

Asana is a general term for a posture within a Kundalini yoga set. It is a physical pose or exercise targeting specific glands and organs and serves as a meditation linking the mind, the breath, and the body position into "yoga," or union. Asanas help reestablish the body as a safe and supportive space to strengthen and heal. Throughout this book, you will be offered one asana or pose for each principle of awareness. These asanas are representative of their particular principle and will help you embody and experience that principle on a cellular level.

Kriya

A **kriya** in Kundalini yoga is a sequence of asanas (postures), breath, and sound mantra that are woven together or combined to manifest a particular state. The word *kriya* literally means *action*. Let's face it: when staring down fear and the residue of old pain or the fresh sting of new pain, we're more likely to react than to act. This is where our time on the mat holding postures and leaning into what's uncomfortable informs and trains us on how we can consciously show up in our lives through action that supports our well-being rather than hinders it. Especially when we're knee-deep in discomfort. Action is all about connecting movements—just like kriyas—and movement and connection are the two primary pillars of growth.

Journaling

Another way we move and connect is through writing. Writing is a powerful healing tool and cornerstone of the Trauma to Dharma program. In addition to the numerous studies proving the benefits of writing (including decrease in stress, distress, and depression; increase in emotional well-being and overall mood; reduction of PTSD flashbacks and nightmares; relief of mental and emotional pressure and tension; clarity of thoughts and feelings; and more effective problem solving—to name a few), there's another familiar piece of science to back this up. When you're holding a pen, what does the positioning of your fingers remind you of? Yep, a mudra. It is yet another way to activate the brain. The act of writing accesses the left hemisphere of the brain—the rational side that is occupied with analyzing and processing—freeing up the right hemisphere or the creative and feeling side. Writing essentially gives us another gateway into feeling and therefore into healing. The **journaling exercises** in this book are yet another way of discharging those toxic emotions stored in your body.

It's important to be in a mindful state when moving through these journal exercises. Create a sacred space to do them, and get comfy and cozy. Give yourself the time to write and to come back to a question if you're moved to write more. It is essential to write freely, minus all the "shoulds" and perfectionist tendencies that so often prevent us from really diving below the surface. Don't worry about what you are writing—just let yourself explore and feel through the process. The mere act of writing will loosen emotions that have been stuck. If feelings arise during the process, stay with them. There are no right or wrong words. No right or wrong feelings. Just what needs to rise to the surface.

And listen, I know we live in a time of laptops and devices that make tapping on a keypad both convenient and habitual. But while any writing is better than no writing, I really encourage you to grab a pen, buy a journal, and channel this the old-school way. Your brain will thank you for it.

Community

Surrounding yourself with a non-judging **community** that allows you to feel safe and supported in this work is essential. We all need people who understand the realities of our trauma and encourage our recovery, such as therapists, support groups, twelve-step programs, and trusted friends and family. Some of us are fortunate enough to already have these communities. For others, it will take some time to find and build them. Regardless, we can all start by creating that same accepting space within ourselves—*and we must*. We need that safe sense of home both within and without to thrive in this work.

Commitment

Your **commitment** is the last and most essential tool in your Trauma to Dharma toolkit, and it is everything. It is a pledge to your Self, your aliveness, and your mighty purpose, and you will be met with the levels of growth and change that match your level of commitment.

We're blessed to live in an age that affords us access to the world's and history's greatest wisdom and guides. From books, gurus, and healers to life coaches, therapists, and Oprah's *Super Soul Sunday*, we're living in a self-help dreamland, and I'm as susceptible to the promise of every new "solution" as anyone. (Seriously. You should see the stack of books on my nightstand.) But when we spend all our time looking outside ourselves for answers, we move farther and farther away from where they already reside—inside. To get to them, however, to excavate the deeper wisdom within, requires commitment.

Trauma to Dharma is a practical guide to help you reclaim the parts of yourself that have been lost. This is not a map to that holy grail of a pain-free life—there is no such thing. There will always be stumbles and setbacks. But when the darkness comes, these principles are designed to guide you back to the light, as they have for me. I won't lie: there are days when it's a struggle; I don't live every day "trigger-free." But I do know what to do when the pain of my past rears its head or the fear of tomorrow leaves me drowning in a sea of overwhelm, and I can truly tell you that I have transformed my trauma into something quite triumphant. That triumph is what I call living my dharma or being authentically me, wiser for the wounds, more purposeful through the pain, and serving others through the lessons of my struggles.

Chapter Four
TRAUMA

Trauma is not just an event that took place sometime in the past; it is also the imprint left by that experience on mind, brain, and body.

—*Bessel van der Kolk*

WHAT IS TRAUMA?

The word *trauma* derives from the Greek word for *wound*, so really trauma is a metaphor for life events that shake the core of our being, our world, and the way we come to make meaning of it. It's something that disrupts and violates the beliefs and barriers that once protected us, leaving us openly wounded. *And this can be anything.* My definition of trauma is any stressful life event or situation that has completely shaken our world and the way we've come to make meaning of our lives— anything that has left us feeling out of control, helpless, and hopeless. When your life feels like it has been turned upside down, that is trauma. And our traumas live along a broad spectrum.

I think the majority of us shy away from the term *trauma* because we consider it this monster of a word that's associated with war veterans or abuse survivors, but what's important to understand is that trauma is not about the event or occurrence itself—whatever it may be—because people will experience the same event differently. Rather, it is about *your experience* of the event or occurrence. What is traumatic to me won't necessarily be traumatic to you. And vice versa. As Rob Bell says, if it's a big deal to you, it's a big deal. Period. And the truth is, while certainly many people endure the wars and abuse—the wounds and scars—that can be universally recognized as "traumatic," most of us live somewhere in the middle of the spectrum.

Take me, for example. When I finally went into treatment for my abusive relationship, I was placed into Sierra Tucson's specialized trauma program. But even though I had acknowledged I needed help, I was still in denial: *Me? In the trauma program? Me? Traumatized? Nope.*

We normalize our own pain, and our egos step in to compare. It's the nature of the ego to want to compare and make itself less than or greater than. "Oh, well, what I went through isn't as bad as what X survived." Or "I'm not starving in Africa/a Syrian refugee/name your global crisis, so how dare I feel what I'm feeling?" Sound familiar? And this is where it's important to recognize that *there is no such thing as a trauma hierarchy*. There are no one-uppers here. When we continue to make excuses or feel guilty or ashamed about our traumas, we disconnect ourselves even further from them. We armor up, and we carry them like protection, which, counterproductively, disconnects us from the world. And that "protection" becomes more of a prison, keeping us both shackled to and trapped by the pain we continue to deny or resist.

Now maybe you're reading this and you know exactly what I'm talking about—exactly what your traumas are. (And if so, *great*. Your clarity and awareness will serve you well on this journey.) But many of us are walking around in a state of pain and suffering, feeling disconnected from ourselves and others, hopeless, helpless, and lost, and we don't even know *why*. Because the truth is that our traumas—our baggage—aren't always and only earned or collected in the ways that we might expect. And sometimes they're not even ours.

THE THREE RIVERS: YOUR TRAUMA BAGGAGE

We've all got baggage, and some of that baggage is ancient—by which I mean some of it isn't even ours. Let me explain. In the yogic tradition, many of us believe we've got three metaphorical rivers running through us. (Stay with me here—I know.) We've got the cosmological, the genealogical, and the chronological.

Let's start with the **cosmological**. If you believe you are this Soul who's lived other lives and has now come back to the planet to do it again, you may have a new era, new face, and new name, but you've got all your *old* stuff. In other words, you've carried into this life with you some of your Soul's old karmic baggage from the last life (e.g., plane crashes, adultery, suicide, and so on)—karmic crap you've got to move through, live out, and resolve. (Thanks a lot, Soul.)

Next up you've got the **genealogical** river running through your being—literally in your genes. In your body alone, you've got seven generations of your ancestors running through your blood—seven generations currently living in your DNA. That means whatever traumas or tragedies your great-great-grandfather suffered—*if he didn't* *do the work of healing them*—he was kind enough to bequeath to you. Have a fear of water that you could never explain? It's possible someone in your lineage drowned or nearly drowned, and that trauma was genetically passed on to you. Same goes for an irrational fear of flying or of relationships. You get the picture. You actually need to move through and resolve *their* shit in *your* life. Are you beginning to understand how some of what you're forced to face and deal with actually has nothing to do with you? What do they say? *It's not your fault, but it's your turn.*

And now as if that's not enough "junk in your trunk" already, you've still got the **chronological** river running through you. The chronological piece is just the circumstances you've taken on in this one lifetime and this one body. But make no mistake: some of those wounds incurred directly in this river/lifetime can have everything to do with the other rivers. Take it back to that inherited fear of water from Great-Great-Grandpa for a moment. Not only are you carrying around *his* initial fear, but that fear can cause new chronological traumas in your own life—being ostracized at a pool party as a kid and feeling like an outcast because you were too scared to swim, for example. And then *that* trauma of being outcast—if you don't address it—is something that can be passed down to your children and children's children. Which is why this work of healing is so crucial.

We've got these three different sources of traumatic residue and baggage we're carrying and needing to heal. That's some heavy shit. And so lightening that load begins with our first recognizing that it's there and then choosing how we want to address it.

POTENTIAL TRAUMA RESPONSES

We cannot change what has happened (not in this present life and certainly not in the prior lives of our relatives and Souls). But we can choose how those things transform us and our lives. Truly, the only choice we have lies in how we choose to live with what has happened.

Researchers O'Leary and Ickovics developed a categorization system to highlight the difference between individual responses to trauma. This system involved four categories of potential responses:

1. Succumbing: where our ability to function is devastated and we continue on a downward slide.

2. Survival with impairment: where we resume some semblance of "normal," but our ability to function the way we used to is impaired.

3. Resilience: where we recover, carry on, and return to our preadversity level. (This would be considered "bouncing back.")

4. Thriving: where we far surpass our previous level of functioning. (This is our goal of "bouncing forward" or post-traumatic growth.)

The purpose of this book and this work is to move out of succumbing or surviving, past resilience, and into thriving. But before we get to that, we need to understand the biological and neurological effects of trauma.

FIGHT, FLIGHT, OR FREEZE:
STRESS RESPONSE AND TRAUMA

The miracle of the human machine is that it instinctively knows what to do when stress occurs. In the face of pain, our brains and bodies work in concert to numb and shut us down from suffering. We aren't that different from our animal counterparts; we're wired for protection and survival. Our nervous systems and their stress response are on hand to help us when we're in danger: if we hear a noise, we immediately orient ourselves to where we hear it; if we see a bear while on a hike or if a shady character lurks in the dark alley while we walk to our car, we feel at risk for danger...and what do we do? Our heart begins to race, right? Sensing a potential threat to our survival, our body's alarms go off. It begins to secrete adrenaline and cortisol, *creating energy to respond to the stress* we are now experiencing. And that energy needs a place and space to move, to be discharged. If you take away nothing else from the science of this section and how it plays into our healing, understand this: *trauma happens when that energy remains in our bodies.*

Now, much of the time, this isn't an issue. When confronted with a stressful (or potentially life-threatening) situation, most of us are familiar with the common responses of **fight** or **flight**. We mobilize for action (that's our sympathetic response) by either running the hell away (flight) or putting up them dukes to fight. Whichever we choose, we have managed to naturally discharge all that energy, and what follows is our parasympathetic nervous system kicking in and releasing our natural chill pill of dopamine, which helps to relax us back to homeostasis—that balanced state of being.

But. There's also a third option that most of us either don't know about or forget, and that's to **freeze**. And the problem with this response is that after the threat is gone, after "freezing in fear," we *still have all that energy inside us that we haven't discharged. And this is when trauma occurs.*

Let's take a moment and get a lesson from our animal friends. Take the gazelle. It's grazing along the African terrain when it notices a lion come into view. It immediately assesses the situation. Looking around, it realizes the lion is far too close to outrun, and well, it also knows it doesn't stand a chance to fight off its predator. So what does the gazelle do? It freezes. In other words, it slows its nervous system, preparing to calm and numb itself from the pain of this anticipated capture and, best-case scenario, potentially fool its predator by playing dead. (The opossum is another trickster animal known to use this tactic.) If the gazelle is lucky, the lion passes by, either not noticing it or perhaps assuming this dead carcass has been there too long to enjoy. Once that lion is out of sight and the coast is clear, what does the gazelle do? It immediately gets up and begins to shake its body—it shakes, and it runs. What animals like the gazelle intuitively know to do when they use that freeze option is to immediately discharge the energy afterward.

Now humans are an entirely different kind of animal. Unlike our four-legged counterparts out on the savannah, when *we* freeze in fear, we suppress our natural instinctive response to release that energy and instead default to our brain's **frontal lobe**. One of our greatest blessings and curses, the frontal lobe is our analyzer, our critical processor. It's where our storyteller lives. So instead of negotiating that literally nerve-wracking life threat in our bodies, as the gazelle and opossum do, we remain in our heads.

Let me give you an example. You're picnicking with your besties at one of your favorite spots in your local canyon, enjoying the post-hike nature high, when you hear rustling in the bushes. You all stop your chatter and look over. In utter disbelief, you find yourselves staring at a mountain lion. *WTF?* You weigh your options. First you consider fleeing the scene by running your little human ass down the canyon but quickly realize that the lion's far too close; he'll surely outrun you. You reassess. You look around to MacGyver your way into some makeshift defense as you consider taking on said mountain lion and fighting him. Yeah right—there's no winning a mountain-lion battle. So you freeze in fear and pray not to be prey.

Now let's say this mountain lion glares over at all your kale-salad-eating, green-juice-drinking asses sitting there, frozen still in absolute terror, and he loses interest. He turns around and runs the other way. What do you do? Most likely, you all look at one another and begin trying to make sense of it: "Oh my God, can you believe that just happened? Where do you think he came from? I knew we shouldn't have picnicked here. What are the chances? What does this mean? Somebody look up mountain lion totem!" We humans immediately begin to analyze. We try to negotiate threatening events in our heads, attempting to make sense of them when what we need to do is negotiate them in our bodies. Like the gazelle, we need to literally "come to our senses"—to shake, move, and feel our way through it. When we don't resolve or clear the energy, it remains stuck in our bodies. And trauma is when these survival responses are not resolved or cleared.

Which brings us back to the notion that trauma is not about the events that happen to us but, rather, our responses to them. If we don't know how to tap into the tools to discharge it, that traumatic energy gets stuck in our body's nervous system, unresolved and incomplete (as in not completed). This unprocessed event continues to be lived out in our bodies as if it's still happening today. And so, unaware, we begin to harbor and carry around these wounds, oftentimes learning to numb or medicate pain whose origin we can't quite seem to place our finger on in order to cope.

MORE ON THE BRAIN

So now that we're getting how our brains are oriented to look for danger and equipped to protect us through the ability to fight, flee, or freeze, it's important to understand exactly what's happening in our bodies to make those responses possible. The **limbic system** is a complex system of nerves and networks in the brain that controls our basic emotions and drives, stores memory (the good, the bad, and the ugly), and scans for and assesses danger (our fear conditioning). Because of all these duties, you could say the limbic system is our trauma "headquarters," and this department's "head" honcho is the **amygdala**.

Located at the top of the brain stem, the amygdala is the gatekeeper for emotional information, behavior, and response. It is also the smoke detector for the brain. Under normal circumstances, the amygdala passes information to the frontal lobe, where our higher order and conscious thinking takes place. (Remember, the frontal lobe is what differentiates us humans from the gazelle—it's the reason we want to look up the meaning of animal totems after the near miss with the mountain lion.) In a threat or emergency, however, the amygdala bypasses the frontal lobe, informing other areas of the brain to shut down. (Well, it's more of a hijack, actually.) It takes a shortcut straight to the **hypothalamus**, which stimulates the pituitary gland and the release of the stress hormone cortisol into the body (i.e., it fires up the sympathetic nervous system that's in charge of the fight-or-flight response). When this happens, our brain begins making decisions before they've been filtered through conscious awareness (the frontal lobe).

Now when all that cortisol is released, the nervous system is stimulated, including the **vagus nerve**, which is located in the brainstem and extends all the way into the abdomen. The vagus nerve is the pivotal channel between the mind and the body and the connection between the brain and the viscera/internal organs. Acting as a highway of sorts, it wanders all the way down into the belly, spreading fibers to the tongue, vocal cords, lungs, heart, stomach, intestines, and glands and pumping all that cortisol down into our body, creating the racing heart, tingling fingers, and excess saliva we experience in moments of stress or danger.

You gotta love that limbic system—it's the reason for our survival. But while we can't live without it, we do have to learn how to live with it. Because remember the amygdala? That fight-or-flight alarm? Yes, it's the part that keeps us alive when in real danger, but it also holds us back from thriving. You see, it cannot tell the difference between a perceived threat and a real threat, between the risk that will kill you and the risk that will propel you into further growth. Ironically, it keeps you alive, but it can also prevent you from really truly living. So when we've been flooded with that excess fight-or-flight cortisol and danger has passed (or never actually existed), we must calm the amygdala by restimulating the vagus nerve and the parasympathetic nervous system to release dopamine and oxytocin into our bodies and control our relaxation response. And the way to do that is through the *body*. As it happens, 80 percent of our fibers run *up* the body, making the body an input or gateway to the brain. (This gives credence to the philosophy that you can't think your way into right acting, but you *can* act your way into right thinking.) So we can deal with our thoughts and perceptions—and even our physiological responses—by diving into the body and breath. Hence the power of yoga and other body-based somatic practices.

FIRST PARADIGM SHIFT IN TRAUMA TREATMENT: BODY-BASED TREATMENT

So now that we understand the nature of trauma, let's talk about healing it. Think about it: when we're struggling, grieving, mourning, hurting, or aching, what do most of our loved ones advise us to do? Go see a therapist. "You need to talk to someone," they say. For years that's been the commonly accepted healing modality. And yes, there is unprecedented value to talking through our pain. Talk therapy is an essential and integral piece to healing ourselves. We must have access to an unbiased, non-judging, and trusting space to air out the dirt, make sense of the mayhem, and explore who we've been and who we are becoming. But as it turns out, talk therapy is not enough.

As trauma researchers dove into understanding trauma's effect on the body, they began to see the connections or (disconnects!) that were occurring in the traumatized brain. Ahh, our brain on trauma... and I have to admit, this is where the doctoral dork in me had her first "scientific orgasm." (That's a technical term, I swear.)

Here's why. Remember that frontal lobe of ours? That analyzer and processer? The one that dutifully tries to come up with solutions and negotiate everything up there in the headquarters? It turns out that after we've been unexpectedly shaken and sucker punched by life, we disengage from our frontal lobe and just leave it on autopilot. This is why we keep repeating habits and patterns connected to our past traumas. And ever wonder why some people (myself included) spend years sitting on the therapist's couch talking about the same thing over and over again? Well, in an "emergency," when the amygdala shuts down other parts of the brain, that includes **Broca's area**. Turned off. Closed for business. "And what the hell is Broca's area?" you ask. It's a part of the left hemisphere of the brain that just happens to be the language center—the department we report to when we need to translate our painful experiences into words. So what that means is that when trauma occurs, our language center goes on strike, and we actually, biologically, can't just talk our way out of it. It's as though the left (cognitive) side and the right (emotional) side of the brain are disconnected from each other.

Where usually our body, thoughts, and emotions are all connected, trauma separates them. This explains the difficulties people have trying to make sense of what has happened. When the two sides of the brain are not working together, the story will either be chaotic and confused—overwhelming feeling and thought, or superficially logical but lacking any felt emotion. You may have vivid graphic thoughts about what happened but no emotion. Or you might experience intense emotions but without any thoughts or actual memories. The paradox at the heart of trauma is we either see and feel *only* our trauma or we see and feel *nothing* at all.

Enter the groundbreaking trauma work from trailblazers such as Peter Levine, Bessel van der Kolk, and Pat Ogden, among others. With the talk-therapy model proving incomplete, these researchers ushered in what I consider to be the first evolutionary shift in treating trauma by focusing our attention on where we are looking to treat it. They recognized and substantiated the need for body-based modalities in treating trauma, and more and more research has further corroborated and supported bringing the body "back." The body—the somatic piece—is an absolute necessity in recovery because *our issues are in our tissues.* In order to understand our way out of trauma, we need to return to our senses to feel and move our way through. If you've been trying only to wrap your head around what happened and haven't seemed to make any progress, your body is the way back in.

This body piece is what had been missing from my own healing before I found my way to Kundalini yoga. The reentry into our bodies, that minefield of old hurts and wounds, must be done cautiously though... which I say from experience and from a very tearstained yoga mat. It must be done carefully and consciously, one breath at a time. Kundalini offers a safe space to ease back into our bodies that have been neglected, violated, and ultimately shut down. Through a yoga practice, we are able to revisit and reunite with them on our terms. Breath by breath. By starting and stopping as we feel ready; choosing how long to hold a pose and when to release tension; and using our breath alternately as an anchor, as fuel, or as a calming agent, each exercise helps us consciously learn how to embody, once again, what it feels like to be an active and empowered participant in our own lives.

The breath is the gateway to growth and healing, and it's for this reason that body-based, bottoms-up approaches such as yoga are finding a seat at the recovery table. And as I was fortunate enough to discover in my own journey, Kundalini in particular has even more benefits to offer, specifically because of its strong meditation component.

Sara Lazar, another trailblazing scientist out of Harvard, contributed significantly to this shift in trauma treatment with her studies supporting how meditation can reverse the damage that our traumas inflict on our brains. Remember that shutdown? That strike? Well, there's good news. *It can be reversed.* What has been hardened can be softened over time, with committed practice. What had to become inflexible and restrictive to survive can once again be stretched and flexed to imagine life anew. Meditation helps develop neuroplasticity of the brain, which means we can create new neural pathways to replace the old roads back to the past. Since so much of our experience of trauma is the tyranny of the past on our present moments, meditative practices allow us to move from "mind full" of the past to "mindful" of the present, where a new life and opportunities greet us and where we can *create* new possibilities with our own thoughts and imaginations. We can use our imagination to heal ourselves.

IMAGINATION: THE TRAMPOLINE STORY

> *You can't depend on your eyes when*
> *your imagination is out of focus.*
> —*Mark Twain*

All this talk of neuroplasticity and neural pathways is really just another way of saying that our traumas, crises, and aching disappointments impair our mental flexibility—our mind's ability to see beyond what we've experienced: *our imagination.* But what is imagination? There are two definitions I like to refer to when it comes to healing trauma. The first is this: "the process of forming new images or ideas in the mind that have not been previously experienced." And then there's *this* one: "the ability to face and resolve difficulties; the ability to be creative and resourceful."

My God, where would we be without imagination? World-renowned trauma therapist Bessel van der Kolk speaks to this notion, and the healing power of imagination, with a powerful story. He speaks of a little boy named Noam whose school was near the World Trade Center's Twin Towers on 9/11. The little boy saw the first plane crash into the tower and said that—even after time had passed—he could still feel the heat of the impact through the classroom window. That's trauma—the sensation of heat that persists long after the original experience is over. Over a week later, van der Kolk saw a drawing Noam had made about what he had witnessed, which included people jumping out of the towers. Toward the bottom of the drawing was an unclear object, and van der Kolk asked Noam what it was. Noam explained that it was a trampoline, "so that the next time when people have to jump, they will be safe."

As human beings we are blessed with the magic salve of imagination. We learn to build trampolines where there weren't any before. But our traumas and crises impair our ability to imagine and dream. When we avoid new experiences, we prevent ourselves from imagining alternative futures for ourselves and others, from building those trampolines. Fear will naturally condition our brains to squelch our imagination and squash our dreams. But those dreams are one of the many ways our dharma and deeper purpose communicates with us, so it's crucial that we reopen that channel. Our imagination can move us from fear to excitement; it can recalibrate the overprotective and overbearing negative mind with the hopeful, positive mind. The difference is a flip of a coin. And that coin can be flipped with the breath.

SECOND PARADIGM SHIFT IN TRAUMA TREATMENT: POST-TRAUMATIC GROWTH

I mentioned there were two very significant and promising paradigm shifts in the world of trauma recovery that lay the supportive groundwork for the Trauma to Dharma program. The first piece was the somatic (body) piece. The second evolutionary, revolutionary shift came by way of Richard Tedeschi and Lawrence Calhoun in the mid-1990s. While trailblazers like Levine, van der Kolk, and Ogden shifted the focusing to *where* we were looking to treat trauma (from the brain to the body), Tedeschi and Calhoun began to reconsider *how* we were looking at it. And what they found is that we were so busy looking at what was wrong with those suffering traumas that we failed to see what was going *right*.

This shift in focus and understanding falls under the science and philosophy of **post-traumatic growth**, or what I like to call the Spirit piece that was missing from my own recovery. It is through this transformative approach that we shift our perspective on the aftermath of trauma from a lens of pathology to one of possibility. The more researchers began to uncover the positive outcomes that came by way of crises, the more they corroborated a very ancient understanding of our innate capacity to rise like the proverbial phoenix and grow through adversity. Our crises may knock us down, but while down and out, over time, many begin to recognize that there is only one way to go from there: up.

As research in this direction continued, reports of growth experiences outnumbered reports of psychiatric disorders. Tedeschi and Calhoun discovered that 50 percent of trauma survivors reported at least one positive life change in the aftermath of their disruptive life crisis. These findings were also supported by my own study, in which participants reported positive growth at an even higher rate. And one of the most significant and meaningful changes uncovered in these studies was people's experience of spirituality. Somehow, it took being humbly thrown to one's knees to surrender to the potential of an extraordinarily bigger and more brilliant "something" (e.g., God, Spirit, the Universe, etc.) existing around us and within us. Yes, it turns out that for many, their lives were actually becoming *more* meaningful as they continued to grow from their trauma.

This is where trauma started to be understood as a potential catalyst for growth and a springboard for transformation. It went from being exclusively a paralyzing life event to an opportunity to test our human and spiritual mettle; a training ground for resilience, enduring strength, and empowerment; and an evolution of deeper spiritual connection, more authentic relationships, and a more meaningful life. It introduced the kind of thinking like, *Oh my God, I've been pained, but I'm still here. I'm still alive. So what do I do with this gift?*

Don't get confused—this isn't saying there is inherent good in trauma but, rather, that we may be able to get something good out of it. The Positive Psychology movement—a term originated by Abraham Maslow and later reintroduced by Martin Seligman—implores us to redirect our attention from what went wrong and what is wrong to what can go right. It emphasizes an understanding of the interplay of light and dark and allows for the possibility that our richest wellsprings of wisdom and deep learning can be accessed through the portal of our pain.

Post-traumatic stress and growth, the dark and the light, go hand in hand. It's not an either/or but rather a both/and. If anything, the stress is what fuels growth. It's the engine. We just need to catch it before it overheats. I like to illuminate this concept of post-traumatic growth with the analogy of taking a shattered vase and turning it into a beautiful mosaic. We're redirecting our attention from the source of our suffering to what can be transformed through our suffering so it becomes less about what broke us down and more about what that can potentially open us to. And there is so much more. But growth does not occur as a direct result of trauma; it occurs *through the struggle*. Through the getting up and trying again. Through the leaning into the challenge of a new and foreign, unfamiliar day and way. Through the placing and gluing of those old broken pieces into the new work of art.

This requires loosening our white-knuckled grip around our pain, and truth is, most of us still hold on to our traumas for dear life. We treat them like these precious and fragile parts of ourselves that cannot be touched under any circumstance. And there's good reason for that, but while our traumas are tender and painful, I am here to tell you they are not untouchable. They are malleable, and they want us to dig into the clay of our lives, get our hands (and hearts) a little dirty, and create something meaningful and miraculous. And make no mistake—it will be a struggle. But that struggle doesn't have to be sufferable. We must be patient with the process, allowing ourselves time to swim through the sea of emotional storms and the psychological terror, but then we must recognize when it's time to rise up. This isn't meant to be easy. But my God, I promise you it's worth it.

SOUL PRESCRIPTION

Journal Question #1: Trauma Descriptors

Trauma can't be summed up in words, but when asked to describe their experiences, participants in my workshop used the following: *breathless, paralyzing, invisible, lonely, stuck, despair, powerless, abandoned, hopeless, shame, broken, dead, loss, betrayal, numb, empty, isolated, abandoned, vulnerable, scarred, nightmare, victimized, self-loathing, rage, shock,* and *violation.*

What words would *you* use to describe trauma? What's *your* experience of trauma? What overriding theme do you recognize here, and how does that relate to your own experience?

Journal Question #2: Pick a Trauma, Any Trauma

Let's go back to why you picked up this book. Where and when have you felt powerless and helpless? Where and when has life shaken your world and the way you've come to make meaning of it? Pick one of your traumas and go as deep as you're ready and willing to go. What's the pain? What's the source?

How did you feel? How did it impose itself on your way of being, doing, thinking, and believing? And what you've come to think and believe about yourself and your world? What patterns keep showing up in your life because of this?

**Pranayama: Breath for Clarity and Peace of Mind/
Four-Stroke Breath**

It's never fun to go back to the scenes of our life crimes. I am sure that writing exercise unearthed a lot and might have even thrown you emotionally off-kilter. Life will do that. This segmented breath is an effective and easy go-to when we're in the heaviness of sorrow and sadness or feeling anxiety and fear. It's a re-balancer and re-energizer that can deliver us to a space of clarity and peace of mind.

Posture: Sit in easy pose (your legs crossed comfortably at the ankles) or on a chair with your spine straight. Hold your palms together at the heart center in prayer pose with your thumbs pressed against your sternum.

Eye Focus: Close your eyes and focus them at the Third Eye point.

Breath: Inhale through the nose in four equal parts (sniffs), and exhale through the nose in four equal parts. On each of the sniffs, powerfully pull in the navel point.

Continue for three to seven minutes.

To Finish: Inhale and hold your breath. Exhale and relax.

Meditation: Daily Stress Reliever/Eight-Stroke Breath

This eight-stroke breathing technique, while effective at *any* time throughout the day, is my go-to before bedtime. I can't tell you how hard it was for me to fall asleep on the heels of a day full of triggers. This controlled and rhythmic breathing helps release stresses from the day and rocks and lulls you into a restful space.

Posture: Sit in easy pose or in a chair (or on your bed) with your spine straight, chin in, and chest lifted. Place your hands in Gyan Mudra (index finger and thumb are pressed together) and rest them on your knees.

Eye Focus: Close your eyes and concentrate on your breath.

Breath: Inhale through the nose in eight equal strokes. Exhale through the nose in one deep and powerful stroke.

Continue for three to eleven minutes.

To Finish: Inhale deeply and hold the breath. Exhale and relax.

Asana: Pigeon Pose with Breath of Fire

We carry a good amount of our unresolved emotions inside the hips and pelvic bowl. Pigeon pose opens the hips and supports the release of undesirable energy (emotion) stored in our body. Add in breath of fire, and we've got a jet-fueled pranic opportunity to clear, cleanse, and literally burn through the old residue.

Posture: Start on all fours. From your hands and knees, bring your right knee forward between your hands, placing your right ankle near your left wrist. Extend your left leg behind you so your kneecap and the top of your foot rest on the floor. Press through your fingertips as you lift your torso away from your thigh. Lengthen the front of your body. Release your tailbone back toward your heels. Work on sinking your hips into the ground and squaring them off. Tilt your chin up, gazing at the ceiling.

Breath: Begin Breath of Fire (this breath is an even, rapid, and rhythmic inhale and exhale through the nose, similar to a dog pant but through the nose rather than the mouth). Keep inhaling and exhaling evenly.

Continue for one to two minutes.

To Finish: Take a deep inhale and exhale as you gently lower your forehead and torso to the floor. Rest/sink into this position for one minute and then switch sides.

Chapter Five
ACCEPTANCE

Wherever you are is the entry point.

—*Kabir*

And the key to enter is **acceptance**. Yes, the first principle, the first step to living in awareness, to living a meaningful and purposeful life, begins with acceptance. And I'm not gonna lie—it's the hardest step. If Trauma to Dharma is a journey home—a journey back to the you that has been missing—then that journey begins by diving into exactly where you are. And I feel you—there's a reason you haven't been inhabiting where you are. Or maybe you feel like you don't even know where you are. I get it. The majority of us carry old wounds that either steal us back to the past, recycling the pain memory, or have us future tripping about events that haven't even happened yet.

Trauma breaks our internal compass, causing us to lose our sense of direction and purpose. But there's a space between where you were and where you are going, and that's the only space where acceptance can happen. That space is wide-open, and that space is *now*. And it's uncomfortable, to be sure. We confuse open with empty, and we don't like empty spaces. So we fill 'em—with people, with activities, with things, with *more* of whatever it takes to ultimately leave room for less of us. But our life requires all of us, and it's waiting for us. Here. In the now. What do they say? *No now, no life.* So consider acceptance the invitation back into your life. Welcome to the party—*your* party. And your party is the present. Yeah, as in now *and* as in a gift.

But I know for many of us, this "gift" is a ribbon-wrapped pity party, a painful event we'd rather not attend. Listen, life tests us. It breaks us. Bad things happen to good people; good things happen to bad people. It can feel unfair, and frankly, it can *be* unfair. So what does acceptance actually look like, and how do we accept these things that are seemingly unacceptable? It's simple but not easy. And we should start by talking about what acceptance *isn't.*

WHAT ACCEPTANCE ISN'T

Before we continue to entertain acceptance—of what was, what is, and what isn't—we must get clear on what acceptance is not. If you're anything like me, the mere thought of "acceptance" gets you to tense up and shut down. *Me? Accept* that? *Why? When it's unacceptable? Absolutely not.*

The opposite of acceptance is **resistance**. And resistance is a fight or struggle. So when we refuse to accept something, by default we are resisting it. Our resistance is a big, fat *no.* And by saying no to where we are, we can't get to the line of yeses prepared to take us back to who we are. We must go where we grow. And when we resist our growth, we suffer.

Energy flows where our attention goes, which means that when we aren't in acceptance, we are also actively (consciously or unconsciously) putting energy into the exact thing we're trying to get rid of or avoid: our injuries and injustices. And what we focus on gets bigger, so you can see how this method doesn't serve us. It's simply adding more pain to the pot.

Acceptance is not a dismissive and indifferent *whatever*. That feigned apathy of a lost teenager is a defense. And I get it. The "who cares" and "what's the fucking point" are another version of resistance— to feeling, to acknowledging that we're in pain, and to admitting that we're afraid of getting sucked into a chasm of heartache and hurt. Nope. Won't have it. *Whatever*.

Acceptance is also *not* a careless, flippant, submissive, or condescendingly complacent sort of *Oh well, it is what it is*—like we're just going to paint a broad stroke over the mess, label it "untouchable," and move on. *"That's life. We just have to live with the pain."* Listen, it ain't lip service: life is painful. But we can do more than just get by, walking around the wreckage. When we get real, we free ourselves to get into the pain so we can recycle, refashion, and repurpose it. Yeah, maybe, *it is what it is*, but just wait and watch what it can become.

And finally, acceptance is *not* a resignation. It is in no way condoning or forgiving what happened. It is not weakened compliance or passive meekness. It is not rolling over like a doormat. It doesn't mean we're giving up. It means we're giving in to the possibility of something more, to the belief that this isn't all there is. Because the truth is that there is so much more, but we can't see it when we keep looking at the same old shit. So we need to change something.

Everybody wants things to be different, but almost nobody wants to actually change. Sometimes it takes the cold, hard blessing of a rock bottom to bring about the willingness to start doing things differently.

But also—gracefully—sometimes we hit bottom when we choose to stop digging.

ROCK BOTTOM

> *If you fall, I'll be there.*
>
> —*Floor*

I know it elicits a chuckle, but there's something more "grounding" to what Floor is trying to tell us. Rock bottom gets such a bad rap, but it is also the perfect, most solid landing place. We all get thrown into our own emotional tsunamis, spinning out of control, fearing that jarring free fall. But the thing is, that fall is mostly an illusion—we're usually not falling so much as we're *tripping*: head tripping, past tripping, or future tripping. The gift of the fall—real or imagined—is that it's precisely while we are amid those metaphorical plummets (or in their immediate aftermath) that we must pause, breathe deeply, and ask, "Where are my feet?" Aha. Right here, *on the floor*. Rock bottom is where we are rooted. It is home base: a place to regroup, reground, check in, and ask ourselves what worked, what didn't, and what we learned.

My rock bottom wasn't pretty, but it was priceless. Because it got me here. We don't realize how imprisoned we are until we get a taste of freedom. At the onset of the summer of 2002, my boyfriend was forced to travel outside the country on business for a total of three months. That's a twelve-week reprieve I was given from his abuse—roughly ninety days of freedom. And in his absence, I began to get a taste of what I was missing while I was missing from my life. Without him around to bully and stop me, I slowly and cautiously stepped out of my shameful and hidden life long enough to reconnect with friends and family. And oh, the joy. The laughter. The calm. And the space to move!

But of course, just as he left, he returned. And so did my immobilizing fear and helplessness. Yet something remained. Something had stuck: my awareness. I could no longer fool myself or numb myself from the harrowing ache of a life I had been living. The six abusive years of pain and shame I had been hiding and denying had become all-consuming. I was drowning in them.

I'll never forget the night before I finally *accepted*. My boyfriend had been home barely a week, and we'd gone to see a movie followed by dinner at Taco Bell: our version of fine dining. Back then I felt like garbage, so I treated myself like garbage, and I fed myself garbage. After dinner he dropped me back at my parents' house, where I was still living at the time. My parents had already left town for our annual summer vacation, so I stepped into an empty house. There was nothing there to distract me from the screaming noise in my head: *I can't take it anymore. The pain! Someone please stop the pain!* I was sick to my stomach. I couldn't breathe. I desperately wanted out of the pain, but I was so blinded by my situation that I couldn't see any way out. Or any way out other than ending it all. That was my only solution. I figured with no pulse and no breath, I would feel nothing. And then, perhaps, this nightmare would finally end.

My refusal to accept that all-consuming pain prompted a suicide plan. I sat there, restless and rocking on my bed, watching the clock slowly move from 11:00 p.m. to 1:00 a.m. to 3:00 a.m., and with every unbearable minute that passed, my plan to end it all became clearer. *I'll just drive my car off Mulholland.*

The more connected I felt to this idea, the less connected I was to my body. It was as if I was floating above it, as if I'd already left it behind. Until I got the call that brought me back. It must have been 4:00 a.m. when my phone rang. I couldn't imagine who the hell was calling me at that hour, and I picked up the receiver to hear my teacher, Guru Singh, on the other end of the line: "I know what you're thinking. You're either going to surrender and ask for help or die."

Not everyone's call will be so literal, but make no mistake: everyone gets a call, a nagging feeling, an intervention, a moment of clarity. They come in all forms. My saving grace was answering that call—literally, I picked up the phone, and then, more importantly, I finally surrendered. My acceptance of the pain I'd been denying saved my life that early morning, and two days later, instead of driving my car off Mulholland Drive, I was flying to treatment in Arizona and landing in the first day of a new life.

Suicide is another form of resistance. And remember, resistance is the opposite of acceptance. Oftentimes our acceptance requires help, and in that rock-bottom moment, I was willing to stop digging and resisting. I was willing to surrender and accept the help that was being offered to me. White flag flown, I accepted where I was and where I no longer wanted to be.

A lot of people fear rock bottom because they think it's synonymous with failure. But our failures are not what will define us—our engagement with life will. Our willingness to keep moving will. Life is in the trying. Because every so-called failure or mistake is really a step—it's *movement*. And as Albert Einstein says, "Nothing happens until something moves." I invite you to let that something be acceptance.

WHAT IS ACCEPTANCE: THE GPS ANALOGY

So what, then, is acceptance? I love referring to our GPS navigation systems as an analogy. Google Maps, Waze...we know them, we love them, and we can't live without them. And the thing about those systems is that they can work only when we enter and connect to our current location. In global positioning and in life, we cannot move toward our aimed destination—be it a fully actualized Self or the nearest Starbucks—without first connecting to where we are now. That acceptance of where you are is the gateway to where you want to go. *In order to get there, you need to be here.*

Let me say it again: we have to be willing to connect to and accept where we are in order to get to who we are—and who and where we want to be. Acceptance is no more and no less than a surrendered commitment to simply being here with the reality of what's happened. It is a softening, a loosening of our tight grip, and an admission that our wounds are real and no longer work, and neither do our old methods of checking out. Acceptance is checking *in*. It is a supportive inhale and a relieving exhale. It is an acknowledgment of our fears and our struggles to find hope and meaning. It's being honest that there is no life without pain and suffering, but that isn't *all* of life. It's an invitation to something more, beyond what we may be able to see right now, to allow life to greet us once again.

Carl Rogers famously said, "It's only by accepting ourselves as we are that we can change." We can accept what has happened without it needing to define who we are, and it is through that acceptance that we cultivate the power to transcend our circumstances. So back to this concept of the GPS and how to make it work for us. It's kind of like a God

Pause Strategy. (And anyone who knows me knows I believe God is in the pause). So pause. Breathe deeply. Look down. Where are your feet? Enter in your current location. (Yes, first be here.) And then—and only then—ask yourself these questions: (1) Where do you need to be/go? (2) What's the kindest, bravest, and most conscious way to get there?

Acceptance is recognizing that we cannot go back to how it used to be but we can have a hand in where we are headed and how. Our acceptance of the breakage, the wreckage, the maddening mayhem, is where we begin to strengthen that Trauma to Dharma muscle. Instead of trying to put that shattered vase back together exactly as it was (or pretending it isn't actually broken to begin with), we can start learning what we can do with its colorful pieces. How can we use them to build something new? Acceptance is an opening to this possibility; it is a curiosity beneath the fear of the unknown.

And maybe you're nowhere near being willing to open. That's okay too. But can you accept your non-acceptance? That's a completely valid start. Sometimes the next step is not knowing the next step and accepting *that*. When it comes to growth, we must learn to recognize and experience resistance and pushback as validation, as confirmation that this is where we're meant to be. And then we can begin to see it as an opening, an invitation to where we're meant to go.

THE WITNESS AKA THE NEUTRAL MIND

So acceptance is finally acknowledging the elephant in the room we've been ignoring, the monkey on our back we're still attached to carrying. (I can throw in a zoo of metaphors if it'll help. The birdie on our shoulder, perhaps?) All these modes of coping and dealing keep us from the heart of experience, which we default to because we're convinced that to "go there" means to fall into a bottomless chasm of emotion. But what is so important to understand is that this swirl of feeling or thought is not who we are. *The voice in our head is not who we are; we are the one who listens.* The one who sees it all. The one who witnesses it. And what acceptance offers us is access to this non-judging but curious witness also known as the **neutral mind**.

Rather than turning to one of our many tranquilizers of choice, we can instead employ a neutralizer. And Kundalini yoga is (conveniently!) just that. It can be an antidote that brings us back to a conscious state of neutrality. By engaging both the embodied witness (or sensitivity, a.k.a. the body piece) and the conscious participant (or consciousness, a.k.a. the Spirit piece), we are able to feel without being fooled by what we're feeling. I will frequently instruct students, clients, program participants, and readers of this book to "engage the witness," and I want to be clear that this isn't about being a detached witness but rather a sensitive participant in the witnessing.

MOVING FROM THE HEAD INTO THE HEART

So much of our resistance resides in our heads. And those heads house our brains, which I call our "bodyguards" because the brain is designed to protect us—until it doesn't. Until it lazily falls into our default surveillance mode, trapping us from feeling. If we continue to live in our heads, we will keep convincing ourselves to play small as a ploy to stay safe (which is really just a code for staying stagnant and stuck in fear). We get stuck psychologizing and managing our life pains in our head rather than actually feeling them because it is so much safer to stay in the analysis. But we can't think and analyze our way out of these things. Hi, analysis paralysis (which ultimately just leads to emotional paralysis). Part of depression is fearing that if we actually allow ourselves to feel, we'll fall down into a chasm that has no bottom. Acceptance is finding that bottom. It's about surrendering our avoidant detours or escape routes and landing back in the present.

Fear, like any other feeling, just wants a way through. The catch is, it will always get stuck in an infinite loop in our heads. The only way "through" is the body—in feeling what we've been resisting. Healing, thus, lies in moving from a head trip to a heart trip.

Our transformation requires our full participation, our embodied engagement—key word being *embodied*. And the gateway back into the body—which is really just another way of saying back into the *present*, back into awareness—is the breath. Wherever we are, our breath is our entryway and our exit plan, and we can decide whenever we want to take that long, deep breath to invite ourselves back in. Once we're in the body and feeling again, herein lies our opportunity to engage our sensitively embodied witness—the one who leans in enough to feel it (*My heart hurts. My chest feels tight. I'm almost too sad to breathe.*) but back enough to see it consciously, neutrally (*Okay, you just got triggered. Try to breath into it. This won't last. You're going to be okay.*).

The mystery, uncertainty, and ambiguity of life can be painstakingly hard and unfair. And it can hurt like hell. But with the embodied witness, we can choose to not let it harden us but, rather, to let it soften and open us. The participants in my Kundalini yoga study claimed they were happier as a result of their practice—but that happiness wasn't all rainbows shooting out of unicorn's asses. It was love and heartbreak and anxiety and peace. All of it. It was living fully

>>>— ACCEPTANCE   AGENCY   AUTHORITY

and deeply, feeling and swimming in the messy miracle of our aliveness.

Remember when I first sat on my Kundalini yoga mat and felt nothing? Many of us traumatized souls will dissociate from our bodies. The terrorizing memories of my abusive past caused me to shut down. I was afraid to face the pain, and so I went completely numb in order to not feel anything. My thinking was maybe if I shut down from feeling, I'd never get hurt again. That was my way of outrunning the pain. And yet, the more we attempt to outrun pain, the more that pain runs our lives. True healing for me began the moment I stopped running and accepted what had happened. The more I leaned into the hurt I was avoiding (through breathing, feeling, crying, and softening), the more I accessed the power to heal.

Through the practice of connecting to the breath and the body, we can bring ourselves back to the present, where we learn to enter the Kundalini state of **Shuniya**—the zero point of neutrality and awareness, where we can still feel what we need to feel without losing ourselves. Rather than allowing our feelings to take over, we can use them as a gauge on the dashboard of our lives, offering us what we need to experience in order to grow.

One gift of trauma recovery is our rediscovery of and reconnection to the sensing, knowing body. It's important to note that Kundalini yoga is not the only way to get into the body. I used to "Forrest Gump it," for example. When I'd feel those awful feelings, I'd run and move *with* the energy rather than suppress, deny, or avoid it. And movement also doesn't have to look like formal exercise at all. A while back, my best friend, Shelby, and her husband, John, lost their son, Mosley, for a few minutes at Kidspace. Even though they quickly found him in the sea of kids, those few minutes felt like a lifetime, and that "lifetime" was traumatic, having left a toll on Shelby's nervous system. She came home later and, after putting Mosley down for his nap, couldn't stop crying. She called me and said she felt like she was drowning in the haunting weight of what could have been, and she couldn't stop shaking. Her body was trying to do what it's naturally meant to, so instead of talking her through it, I instructed her to get off the phone and keep shaking her entire body—vigorously and intentionally—for five minutes. She texted later, saying that it had calmed her and brought her back to the present and into a surrendered space of prayer and gratitude. She had managed to discharge the energy, and in this very simple, practical way, she was able to engage her witness through her body.

The moral of the story is that instead of pushing away or holding too tightly to our feelings, what if we take the middle path and hold them loosely? Just enough to see them, feel them, and give them permission to move through. Because that's all our feelings need—to move through. And they find their way through when we brave our way in.

FEELING IS HEALING

> *The cure for the pain is in the pain.*
>
> —*Rumi*

One phrase became a running joke in the writing of this book because it came up so often, but it couldn't be truer or more important to healing: *Our feelings don't want to be fixed; they want to be felt.* Most of us do everything we can to avoid or fix our pain. We numb or normalize it, intellectualize or spiritualize it. And yet, the moment we surrender the need to fix our pain and simply feel it, everything shifts. So here is your opportunity to give a shift.

Feeling is healing. But we must acknowledge our pain in order to feel it. We must accept our pain in order to hear its call. We must listen deeply to our pain in order to transform it. Our pain is a messenger. And all it requires is being heard, held, and understood. Once again, this is an undertaking that is simple but by no means easy.

This happens to me often: I'll be doing errands in town, roaming the aisles of Whole Foods, and will run into an old yoga student who I haven't seen in some time. He or she will spot me and, while excited to see me, will begin to uncomfortably dance around why he or she hasn't been to class in a while, ultimately landing on some version of *"I really wanted to come back, but I just couldn't handle all those feelings that came up. It was so uncomfortable; I just didn't want to deal."*

"Didn't want to deal" translates to "didn't want to feel."

We've all been there. Myself included. Hell, I lived numb for more than half a decade. It took all those tears on my yoga mat—*all those feelings*—for it to finally hit me: I had attended to everything *but* my body. Whatever we might forget or ignore, intellectualize or analyze, the body still remembers. And that memory remains until we acknowledge it—until we *feel* it. Whatever we refuse to feel remains. It buries itself inside our bodies. And there you have it: *our issues are in our tissues.* Our bodies hold the memory of everything that has happened to us: what pained us, tore us to pieces, and broke us. It all sits in our cells, tissues, and organs, just waiting to be felt and liberated.

Emotional pain is the exact same as physical pain. Unresolved emotions are emotional pain, and the body and brain process both types of pain in absolutely the same way. We don't question that our body still holds on to old running injuries or tennis elbow from back in college, but when it comes to the heart-wrenching pain of breaking up with our first love or losing our first dog, we impatiently question why we are still feeling this. We sit around lamenting, "I can't believe this still gets to me!" But this is exactly where the painful residue is still locked in our tissues. Those emotional and physical connections endure for years and years, drawing direct links between our past and our current experiences. Unresolved physical and emotional trauma is held in the body, in stasis, until it can be brought to consciousness.

This is why the role of the body in transformation work cannot be overlooked. It can be messy and uncomfortable, but that's exactly why we're here—to get into the mess of life and *feel*. Because feeling is living. And so living—truly living—is healing. We can heal our way through anything if we bravely stay engaged in it and with it.

FEELINGS WE TYPICALLY RESIST

Of course there are some feelings we humans are much more resistant to than others. Some feelings are so powerful and scary that we think the path of avoidance will be less painful. A short list of these commonly harder-to-accept emotions includes grief, depression, anxiety, shame, and joy. (Yes, joy.)

Grief

Grief is an interesting creature. In order to feel the pain of loss, we must simultaneously honor and praise the part of our lives for which we tenderly long and ache (be it a person, a relationship, or a chapter). But what is grief if not one of the deepest expressions of love? Our pain is a reflection of how much we loved. Dostoyevsky said, "The darker the night, the brighter the stars, the deeper the grief, the closer to God." When we can learn to bravely accept life's invitation to dive deep into the reservoir of grief, we can humbly settle in beneath the pain of loss. And it is there that we find love and God.

Grief. Love. God. It's all the same. Semantics, really. Good old Charlie Brown knew what he was talking about with his signature catchphrase "Good Grief"—an age-old euphemism for *Good God*. Yep, grief is good. Grief is God.

And I've grown to appreciate these God moments. I am often reminded of one of Rumi's odes to grief:

I saw grief drinking a cup of sorrow and called out, It tastes sweet, does it not?

You've caught me, grief answered. And you've ruined my business. How can I sell sorrow when you know it's a blessing?

Grief is itself a medicine; that's the blessing. If we don't allow the time and space to truly grieve, we leave no room to naturally express the love we feel for the things we've lost. Teetering on the precipice of pain, we resist the gaping hole of loss because we are frightened by the haunting emptiness it leaves behind. Yet once we step through grief's tender threshold, we wholly (and holy) come alive. We are awakened to our undying connection to everything and everyone we have ever ached for.

And grief doesn't have an expiration date. We like to use milestones to gauge our progress—six months, one year—but grief is a journey that becomes a lifelong companion. Like breathing, we wake up with grief, we brush our teeth with it, and we move through our days and our years with it. I don't know if it lessens or if we grow stronger, more conscious, and more resilient in our ability to carry, incorporate, and include it in our lives. Probably it's both. But there is no "right" way to grieve—there is only *your* way.

Depression

Sometimes we're just not having *any* of it—as in feeling the feelings—so we show our sensitivity the door. *Enough with you—I'm done feeling.* Enter **depression**, a numbing agent that isn't selective. There to free us from feeling the heavy load of our past, depression freezes our ability to feel anything at all. When we can't feel anything, we're left with a whole lot of nothing, and the emptiness that comes from nothingness can get pretty lonely. That's one of depression's strong suits—it alienates us not only from our lives and everyone in them but from ourselves as well. Because in order to numb ourselves from feeling the feelings, we dull our senses and numb ourselves from our own vitality, our own pulsing connection to Spirit.

Depression is a creeper. Its heaviness is immobilizing, trapping us in bed, burying us alongside the host of ghosts from our pained past. Its thick and stagnating fog of despair leaves us lifeless and apathetic, unable to make decisions because when nothing seems to matter, why bother? But I like to think of depression as life stresses that weren't properly pressurized into diamond-like opportunities for growth. Instead they have amassed into a pile of coal, leaving those they bury literally too "petrified" to move.

ACCEPTANCE   AGENCY   AUTHORITY

Those with depression crave love but feel they don't deserve it. So when we feel buried in that depressive pile, it's helpful to treat ourselves the way we would our dearest friend who's having a rough go at it. Perhaps all we need to say is, "I know I can't fix this for you, but I'm here as long as you need me to be," and give it the patience and permission to just be. Depression is asking us to take care of our Self, to offer care in ways we may have never received.

Anxiety

Where depression leaves us too frozen to feel anything, **anxiety** keeps us nervously jacked up and sensitive to *everything*. If depression can be characterized as the regrettable weight of the past and that haunting "what happened?" feeling, then anxiety is our fear-fueled worry about the future and the alarming "what ifs."

We are all guilty of those anxiety-ridden head trips to that make-believe land of tomorrow's misfortunes. We love to catastrophize, weaving our high-drama "what ifs" into our own personal Oscar-worthy tragedies that never actually happen. Mark Twain nailed it when he said, "I've lived a long and difficult life filled with so many misfortunes, most of which never happened." I can't count the number of masterfully crafted misfortunes I've conjured up in my mind and put my poor body through, disasters that never actually came to pass yet still left me with emotional battle scars.

If depression is our apathetic, can't-be-bothered companion, then anxiety is that restless and neurotic but protective friend who loves to pay a worrisome visit. And the moment we can recognize either one of them as just that—a friend—we are better able to step back and see it rather than be it. Because the more we attempt to feed or outrun anxiety, the harder it kicks and the louder it screams. All it wants, however, is a place to land. That place is called now, and the only way back to now is to come to our senses. We cannot abort these head trips (to the future or the past) with the head. The only way to settle back into now is through the body, and the more we do that, the easier it is to uncover the message beneath our mental and emotional mayhem. Our head trips are a trap stealing us from the present, which is the place that matters most, because it's the only place where life can greet us.

Shame

But what good is life if we don't feel worthy of its offerings? Meet **shame**. Shame convinces us that we're not worthy or good enough for anything. Instead of John Cusack adoringly blasting "In Your Eyes" up into our bedroom window, shame is following us around wherever we go with the same boom box blaring, "You're good for nothing. Who the hell do you think you are?" on repeat. Yep, shame is a bully, and it is provoked by trauma. John Bradshaw, a leading voice in how we heal the shame that binds us, spoke of how trauma replaces our self-loving and self-soothing capabilities with inadequacy-fueled shame and regrettable self-blame. ("*This happened because I deserved it.*") It can disrupt and taint the way we come to see ourselves, but no one deserves a life trapped on that self-blaming shame train.

And yet to fall on the other side of the shame tracks is no better. Because to be shameless is to be unrepentant and disconnected, another way of playing God. Just as healthy fear is important because it prevents us from running in front of a moving vehicle, healthy shame is also valuable. But where healthy shame is living with a humble acceptance of our flawed and fallible human limits, toxic shame leaves us believing what limits us is an innate defectiveness on our part. As a result, we reject who we are, falsifying and covering up. And that covering up only feeds shame's growth. Shame is like mold: it thrives when hidden out of sight. And just like mold, it cannot survive when exposed; it cannot survive in the light. So our goal is to let the light in. And remember Leonard Cohen's cracks? Every split and fracture life has gifted us is a perfect opening to air out the shame that no longer serves us.

Foreboding Joy

The more we air out and discard those stale blankets of shame, the more room we have to enjoy life. Because we finally feel deserving of it. But even that comes with its challenges. In *Daring Greatly*, Brené Brown speaks poignantly about the concept of **foreboding joy** and why we often resist joy at all costs. Sometimes, when we get too joyful, we start to feel panicked, terrified that something terrible is going to happen and it's all going to go away. (Sound familiar?) So as a defense strategy, we humans will sacrifice feeling joy on the off chance that it might get swept right out from under us, leaving us facedown in a ditch of disappointment. We try to control our level of disappointment by rehearsing our worst-case scenarios and buzz-killing our way through our own delight.

This further confirms how all feelings can be terrifying—even the good ones. Because feelings are risky; kind of like life, they are uncertain and unpredictable. And yet this is why we are here—to feel it all. Living *is* feeling. Yogi Bhajan used to say that angels are jealous of our human bodies because these bodies of ours are what give us the ability to sense and feel and experience the joyful and dreadful polarities of life and every feeling in between. And all of it is proof of our aliveness.

There's a Spanish proverb that says, "The door to the human heart can only be opened from the inside." The more we shut out the pain—be it grief, depression, anxiety, shame, joy, or any other form—the more we shut out life. The more we try to protect ourselves from the pain, the more it hardens us closed. We armor up and lock the doors of our hearts from life, from love, and from the beauty that still exists beneath and around it all. We cannot deny or move around the pain of life; nor can or do we just "get over it." As I'm fond of saying, the only way out is through, and those doors that only we can open for ourselves exist in our own hearts. So it is essential that we quit waiting for someone or something else to open them for us. We are the miracle we've been waiting for. We hold the key to inviting joy back into our lives. And that key is acceptance.

NUMBING OR AVOIDING BEHAVIORS AND ADDICTIONS

Our pain is a wake-up call, a gauge that change is coming. Usually it begins with a whisper, but most people are so resistant to feeling it or intent on ignoring it that they don't notice. Then it tries to speak sternly and seriously. And when it continues to be ignored, it will yell and scream to get our attention: "Are you listening now?!" (Probably, because you don't have a choice.)

The pain in our lives is like a boiling pot of water on the stove. We go to touch it and realize, *Oh shit, I'm burning. Let me move my hand.* That's exactly pain's purpose—we hit the burning pot, and our body's knee-jerk reaction is to move. Pain is a sign to move. And that movement isn't the running-from-our-lives kind. It's the reassess-what-we've-been-doing-and-change-course-a-bit kind. And no one likes that. Truly, no one. We may *want* to change course, but we sure as hell don't *like* it, because that requires commitment and discipline and stepping into something different. So the majority of people avoid the call by numbing themselves.

A lot of us have been numb for so long that we can't identify our pain anymore, or that we even have any pain in our lives at all. If we're not able to access the pain, it means we've been shielding ourselves in patterns of denial. And the best way to start the uncovering process is to look to our habits. What are we doing? Are we bingeing every night? Finishing that entire bottle of wine after work? Smoking, shopping, packing our schedule to the gills, zoning out on social media? And why are we doing it? What are we avoiding? This line of questioning brings us directly to our addictions—our ways of avoiding, denying, numbing, and resisting the pain in our lives. (The flipside of this is cutting. Sometimes people numb themselves so much that they need to feel *something*, and self-inflicted wounds allow them to feel alive without having to feel their deeper pain.)

God bless the miracle mechanics of our bodies. They have a natural way of numbing themselves from life's pain. It's a brilliant survival response designed to protect us, and it works exceptionally— until it doesn't, and what was originally intended to protect us begins to imprison us. Our fear of the past and pain can hold us hostage. We repress and store, avoid and ignore these tender pieces of our lives in an effort to protect ourselves. But that doesn't change the reality that *is happening*, and all that denial does is disconnect us from our own heart.

Our methods of dealing with our pain have taken us this far, and we must genuinely appreciate them for doing that. But those of us who are lucky—and I do believe we are the fortunate ones—come to a point where these methods can't take us any further. Where before this way of managing the pain was a supportive assistance that allowed us to remain in our lives as best we could, now that old way is keeping us from life. It's gone from a *means of assistance* to a *means of resistance*.

So much of our suffering is born out of our resistance to feeling what is there, and our addictions are our way of avoiding the suffering we create by denying ourselves the permission to feel. Are you tired? Because it takes *a lot* of energy to deaden your aliveness. And you are too alive to be shut down.

HEALING AND WHOLENESS

Healing is not a getting there, it is a being here. Healing is coming into wholeness. *Heal* and *whole* come from the same root. That means, in order to heal, we must integrate *everything*—all the pieces and experiences that make us who we are. In other words, while that past of yours is not all of you, it's still part of you. And it's coming with you. I always say some people run from their past, but me? I wouldn't be here without it.

And that's the point of all of this—to be here. So often life feels like it's all about "getting there." Even healing becomes a version of "getting there," right? How many of us are trying to "do" our way through our healing to-do lists? But healing isn't a destination; it's an integration. And in order to integrate it, we must first accept it.

When we are suffering and in pain, it's because we have convinced ourselves that we are in control of something—or of everything. And whatever we control, we carry. The weight of our guilt, shame, grief, and pain are a heavy burden, and so often we further compound our suffering by denying that we are even carrying these things to begin with. Acceptance starts with acknowledging that we've been lugging this load. From there, we can begin to equip ourselves with how to lighten it. We can assess what's really there, let go of what we're not actually responsible for, and bring in tools to help us carry what remains.

And it's in what remains that the magic of integration really happens. By getting present and clear, we can come to see that the heavy weight we've been carrying—that backpack full of rocks—is actually *food* that can be used to nourish and strengthen us and then *help us with the carrying*. It won't always taste (or feel) good. The things that make us grow often don't; nor does growth itself. But the flipside is to feel nothing, and well...that wasn't working, was it?

INTUITION

Our suffering comes from a lack of understanding. To understand is to stand under, and in order to stand under something, we need to get *into it*. This brings us to **intuition**—that ability to understand things immediately, without the need for conscious reasoning. Understanding doesn't happen just in the mind. We know that integration is a key to healing, and full understanding comes only by integrating all the parts of ourselves—mind, body, and Spirit.

Anyone who's ever "listened to their gut" knows that intuition isn't a mental thought; it's a felt sense. That gut feeling we get is the belly brain, our Soul's GPS and source of intuition. And we can access that only when we can feel. (Is the absolute necessity of being in our bodies and feeling coming together yet?) Intuition is an embodied act, not a detached act.

Our intuition is the command center of our highest nature and our greatest tool for tapping into our Soul's purpose. It is the calm, still voice that comes from the neutral mind, where communication between the Soul and the Self happens. While the voice of fear speaks loudly and harshly, there's calmness to intuition. It states simply and clearly what it needs. Because it is so quiet, so easily drowned out by the noise of fear, it is only by getting "into it" that we can hear our intuition—not by stepping out or checking out. We can see things in a higher light only by getting into the rawness of our humanity. Intuition, thus, is not about detaching or about rising above—it's about leaning back and staying grounded, in and through the body. It's about getting still and silent and going as deep into ourselves as we can. Because depth and clarity go hand in hand. As in the ocean, it is in ourselves: the deeper we dive, the clearer we'll see.

While what Hafez said is true—"The place where you are right now God circled on a map for you"—he didn't mean you have to stay here. You picked up this book because you're uncomfortable. "Here" is no longer where you want to be; you're ready to move. And the good news is you can. The even better news is you can be an active participant in that, and your intuition will direct you. Your acceptance is the gateway to where you want to go, and your intuition is your clearest, strongest guide.

THE INEVITABILITY OF CHANGE

Now a word about change, because (spoiler alert) that's where this is all headed. As human beings, we are wired for change; we are wired to grow. It has everything to do with our vitality. And yet *change* is the one thing we fear the most. (Well, change and public speaking.) We are swimming in a sea of uncertainty that rises and falls with the torrents of change, and we are constantly grasping for certainties. Yet one of the only certainties we have is life's uncertainty; the one constant we can be sure of is change. The universe is not static. Neither are we or our lives.

It's so strange that the nature of life is change but the nature of human beings is to resist change. And yet, it's so understandable. Our traumas are often a sudden change forced upon us without proper warning. And so, as we trek through the aftermath of trauma with our startled and shaken wounds, the last thing we want to experience is more change. *I've already gone through a devastating, life-changing disruption*, we think. *I can't take anymore.* Even if we're miserable and in pain, we're accustomed to it. It becomes our normal, which makes it feel familiar and safe. And many of us would prefer to stay feeling safe and miserable to stepping into the unchartered unknown that accompanies change. Because familiarity is comfortable. Yet comfort is not where we grow. In fact, *we cannot pursue growth and comfort at the same time.*

Change comes from the old word *cambium*, which means "to become." As human beings, change is our currency for growth, and as such, it's meant to feel strange. If it doesn't feel uncomfortable, then we aren't meeting ourselves at our Soul's edge. If we're committed to growth, then we need to embrace change and our "becoming," growing pains and all.

The good news is that real change is seldom a giant step. Usually it's a process that starts with a single, small but deeply real first step. What I love about Kundalini yoga and its strange and stretching poses is how they emulate the pressures of change, preparing us for the strangeness of the unfamiliar that accompanies growth. It teaches us to hold fear and faith at the same time, fueling our steady willingness to cross the bridge of change. In the words of the master shape-shifter/change-maker David Bowie, we must be willing to "turn and face the strange." And as far as I'm concerned, when it comes to our growth, the stranger the better.

And here's something to keep in mind: while unexpected pains and disruptions remind us of life's impermanence, we must remember pain is just as impermanent. It too shall pass. The more we are able to deepen ourselves to accept it, the more we are able to expand ourselves to quell its bitterness. And the great irony of all this is that it's only when we accept things that we can change them.

TRANSFORMATION REQUIRES PARTICIPATION

Everything will be okay as soon as
you are okay with everything.
—Michael Singer

In order for us to change our relationship to pain, we must first be willing to accept it. But transformation requires participation. Once we've acquired knowledge through our acceptance, through our willingness to be present, it's time to look at what we're doing with it. Knowledge gets us only so far. Now it's time to recognize that we can actually do something about it. We have the power and ability to choose how our experiences of life's pains, disruptions, and traumas will transform us. But in order to grow, self-awareness and self-acceptance must be accompanied by new behavior. Trauma to Dharma is about being both the witness—through present-moment experience and somatic awareness—and an active participant. Only then can we transform our pain into purpose.

>>>—   ACCEPTANCE   AGENCY   AUTHORITY

SOUL PRESCRIPTION

Journal Question #1: Resistance

What is your resistance to acceptance? What's your fear around it? What are you afraid will happen if you accept? (For example: if I accept the way I feel about how my body looks now, then I'm going to stop trying, and I'm only going to look and feel worse.)

Journal Question #2: Acceptance

What can acceptance look like and feel like for you? How might your acceptance surprise you in a good way?

Pranayama: Two-Stroke Breath to Connect the Subconscious and the Intuition

We can't have a present-moment experience without engaging the witness, and we can't engage the witness without the body and the breath. When you are solely and completely identified with the voice in your head and the emotions that accompany it, then you've lost yourself. Yet when you are aware that you are thinking, that awareness becomes your gateway back to you and into being. Our thoughts can at best point us to the truth, but they are not *the* truth.

Posture: Sit in easy pose or in a chair with your spine straight. Bend your arms at the elbows. Place your hands in Gyan Mudra (thumb and index finger pressed together) with the palms facing forward.

Eye Focus: With eyes one-tenth open, gaze down at your nose.

Breath: Slightly pucker your lips. Inhale powerfully in two strokes through the mouth (one second per stroke), and exhale powerfully in one stroke through the nose (one second).

Continue for three to eleven minutes.

To Finish: Inhale deeply. Bring your hands together at the center of your chest in prayer pose, hold, and exhale.

Pranayama and Meditation to Release Grief

Our lungs are the seat of our grief and sadness, so our breath is our greatest tool in accessing and releasing those pent-up emotions.

Posture: Sitting down, place your hands at your heart center (right hand over left).

Eye Focus: Close your eyes and focus them on the Third Eye point.

Breath: Inhale through a circled *O* mouth (really sip in that air), and exhale through the nose.

Continue for three to eleven minutes.

Kirtan Kriya: Sa Ta Na Ma Meditation

We can process and rewire how we experience our traumas. This powerful meditation can change the physiology of the brain circuits where those fearful and painful thoughts brought on by trauma originate by helping to stimulate the regeneration of brain cells. It also enables us to let go of old stories and patterns from the past that have been hardwired in our neural pathways so we can accept the present and allow for our future to unfold.

ACCEPTANCE   AGENCY   AUTHORITY

Posture: Sit in easy pose.

Eye Focus: Close your eyes and focus on the Third Eye point.

Breath and Mantra: As you chant each syllable of the mantra **Sa-Ta-Na-Ma**, alternate touching each finger to the thumb. For **Sa,** touch the tip of your index finger to your thumb; on **Ta,** touch the middle finger to the thumb; on **Na,** the ring finger; and on **Ma,** the pinkie.

For two minutes, sing/chant out loud. For two minutes, whisper. For four minutes, be silent. Mentally say the words to yourself while still tapping your fingers. For two minutes, whisper again. For two minutes, sing/chant out loud again.

Continue repeating the sequence, always starting with the thumb tip to the index finger. The pace between each movement is approximately one second per fingertip.

To Finish: Inhale and hold the breath for a few seconds. Focus your eyes upward, exhale, and relax.

Translation: **SA** is the beginning; infinity; and the totality of everything that ever was, is, or will be. **TA** is life, existence, and creativity that manifests from infinity. **NA** is death, change, and the transformation of consciousness. It is letting go/releasing. **MA** is rebirth, regeneration, and resurrection, which allows us to consciously experience the joy of the infinite.

Asana: Painting Your Aura

This is a nervous-system refresher and energy pick-me-up for more presence and focus. It moves the spinal fluid, and a flexible spine makes for a flexible mind.

Posture: Standing up, inhale and stretch your arms up with a bend in the knees. Exhale, fold forward, and swing your arms up behind you.

Repeat this motion and continue for three minutes.

Chapter Six
AGENCY

God, grant me the serenity to accept
the things I cannot change,
Courage to change the things I can,
And the wisdom to know the difference.
—The Serenity Prayer

Once we have actually "accepted" the invitation to be present in our lives again, we begin to realize that we very well might be able to actualize change. Acceptance brings us into the present moment, and through accepting the things we cannot change, we now enter into the conscious space to *change the things we can.* Our acceptance and presence are our first steps away from the sidelines of life and toward suiting up and getting equipped, toward engaging as conscious and active participants in our own healing and growth. And for me, it all comes back to the short but oh-so-powerful Serenity Prayer. No matter where, when, what, why, or how I am, it has been my humbling anchor. It steadies me in my commitment to brave through the only thing I can be certain of: life's uncertainty. It reminds me how, through radical acceptance, we open ourselves to the world we otherwise miss out on through our resistant denial. If we continue to pause and breathe deeply, acceptance becomes a grace period, a space rich with possibility and opportunity to *choose*. And this brings us to **agency**.

WHAT IS AGENCY?

Agency is the capacity, condition, or state of taking action and exerting one's power. Human agency is the capacity for human beings to make choices, and this principle is taking back ownership of our life. The beauty of having moved through acceptance is that we gain access to that built-in "I got this" toolbox we've been carrying with us in these human forms but forgot (or maybe never even knew) was there. This is where we find the only tool we truly need to build our new foundation of recovery and growth, and that tool is **choice**.

Now remember, the root of trauma is an experience of helplessness that involves extreme lack of control, choice, or agency—an inability to take effective action. Think about the traumas we've survived—we feel completely helpless around them, right? Powerless! But there's one power that we *always* have in any situation, and that is our power to choose. We can't necessarily choose events or circumstances, but we can always choose our attitude toward them. When we humbly acknowledge that we don't have control over the world around us, we can begin to redirect our attention to the only thing we can control, which is ourselves—our thoughts, choices, and actions.

While we cannot choose what may have happened or what may still happen, we sure as hell can choose how we will face it. Changing the past is not an option—we cannot choose the past—but we can choose now, and we can choose being here now. And that choice to be present is critical because it aids us in avoiding the pull to replay or repeat our pained past patterns or to catastrophize the future *somethings* that haven't even happened yet. It is only by choosing now that we can choose what's next. We can choose to change our perspective, to take one more step, or to do something differently. And that is where our liberation and our healing lie.

Dale Carnegie illustrates the power of choice perfectly: "Two men looked out from prison bars, one saw the mud, the other saw the stars." We have all been blessed with the freedom of choice, but it is up to us what we do with it. We can make ourselves prisoners by our own choices or use them to find freedom within our own hearts and minds; we can let our circumstances harden us to become more afraid and resentful or soften us to be kinder and more compassionate. Positive thoughts and positive actions bring about positive results. It's literally our choice. And we always have a choice.

Active Participant

Now making these choices and really taking life by the reins in this way demands that we be fully conscious and engaged. This second Trauma to Dharma principle of agency requires us to become **active participants** in our lives. And I understand that this is no small order.

Choosing to be active participants in our lives, in our healing, in our "so now what?" is a game changer. There are countless practitioners and healers offering powerful and effective modalities, and you can be sure that I have benefited deeply from their services. Being able to talk things through with therapists, get cranial sacral massage and acupuncture, and even engage in equine therapy all contributed to my recovery, but every single one of these put me in a passive role, relying on experts who were practicing *on* me. What I really needed was for *me* to be practicing on me. This is what I loved about Kundalini yoga—it was just me and my body. I alone chose how far I went on any given day holding a pose or a breath. *I* determined how fast or slow I moved. *I* decided when I needed to stop, and *I* chose when to keep going. That practice finally put me squarely in the role of active participant in my healing, which gave me a sense of empowerment and control. And that is exactly what we need as survivors of trauma.

You may be deducing that stepping into this role of active participant is going to require you to *take action*, and you would be correct. And action—especially the action of choosing to do something we're not accustomed to—requires courage.

Courage and Confidence

> *Life begins at the end of your comfort zone.*
> —*Neale Donald Walsch*

So many of us wait to take action in our lives until we feel confident—about the action itself or our ability to execute it. And an unfortunate side effect of that is we end up never taking action. How we handle a lack of confidence becomes a critical part of our journeys. When we've fallen victim to life's harrowing disruptions, we lose all sense of trust in life and ourselves. We start to keep our world small and controlled because we want to feel safe. We start to wonder how we can trust life again—or how we can trust *ourselves* in life. But trust—like choice—takes practice.

And the secret here is we won't actually feel confident until *after* we've taken action. So if we're waiting for confidence to precede courage, we'll be waiting forever. Confidence comes only after taking action.

The word *confidence* comes from the Latin word for faith and means "to walk with faith." Those who are waiting until they feel confident enough to take action likely will never get going. Initially, taking action requires courage, not confidence. Courage is when we act even in the face of fear. Confidence, then, comes as a result of stepping out of our comfort zones. With every responsible choice we make, we take effective action to feel more in control and empowered, and we deepen our faith and trust in ourselves.

Everything we want is on the other side of fear. It's trite but true. Think about all the breakthroughs and "firsts" you've had—I'd be willing to bet the ones that were the most rewarding and resulted in the most growth started with the most fear. It's time to start making choices that scare us. It's time to start acting on the things we're afraid to do but know we need to by harnessing fear's energy to bust out of our comfort zones. And all that begins by coming back to the place where everything happens: here in the present. Because one more important note about using our agency (before we all go jumping out of airplanes and moving cross-country and making every manner of life-changing decision): sometimes taking action means *not doing anything*. Presence is action too; it is the action of being. Even when it hurts like hell. Pausing is an action. So as essential as it is to make a choice when the time is right, it is equally critical to sit in stillness of the Self and allow presence to be our guide. It is every bit as courageous to choose to do nothing when nothing is required.

DON'T WASTE A GOOD TRIGGER

Triggers. We all have 'em. Someone says or does something, we hear a song, smell a scent, or pass by the scene of an old crime of the heart, and instantly we feel a tsunami of emotion overtake us. The old memory tape starts reeling in our heads, and the emotional intensity transports us back to that painful moment, person, or situation we have worked so damn long and hard to heal, to forgive, to "love and light" the hell out of. And here we are, practically drowning in it, and we're thinking, *Really,* again*? Still? Haven't I worked through this shit?*

Our triggers pull us under the high tides of old wounds like they occurred yesterday. And that's the rub: they *are* yesterday's wounds in need of the radically loving salve of today's wisdom. Because if a trigger has shown up, it means there are some unresolved emotions we're still carrying. There is more healing left to be done. In these situations, we tend to react with one of the three trauma responses: by taking it head-on and fighting; by fleeing through avoidance, escapism, or just plain ole running away; or by numbing ourselves and checking out (i.e., freezing). Regardless of our choice, the majority of us fall into a spin, being pulled right back to the past. But these triggers have real value, and they present themselves to be both a **gauge** and an **invitation**.

When approached consciously, these triggers are just a light on the dashboard of our lives saying, "Hey, we're a little off-center. Let's pull over for a second and take a look at this before we decide what direction we want to go." They offer us an opportunity to stop and recognize where we used to be, where we are now, and where we are not. This can present us a much-needed reminder of how far we've come and also of the courage and strength we have in our reserves (which we're going to need to endure that which still lies before us).

And that brings us to how our triggers are also an invitation. Our road to recovering ourselves always leads us to and through exactly what we need. And what we need usually comes in the disguise of these perfectly unpleasant triggers. Every trigger is a timely wake-up call inviting us to dive deeper and heal another tender layer or hidden piece of our past experience that remains unresolved. That's the tricky piece to our past traumas: they are multifaceted creatures that expose themselves over time. And we heal them only by not shying away from their tormenting emotional storms and rather, by taking a breath, grounding our feet, and recognizing that *we are no longer where we were.* We heal them only by checking in, not checking out. I always say don't waste a good trigger—they are a personal invitation for **integration**.

An Invitation for Integration

Trauma is caused by stagnant, pent-up energy that got trapped in the body rather than moving through. And we're still carrying this unresolved emotional charge of our past experience around with us. It is archived in our cell tissues, festering and clogging up our circulation and creating disharmony in the body and in how we perceive, receive, and respond to life. And just as old physical injuries can flare up, so too can old emotional injuries. Welcome to a trigger. But we can allow those emotional whirlwind-like visits to inform us rather than consume us, to lead us onto a path of discovery.

Remember how feeling is healing and healing is an integration? Well, since we cannot heal what we cannot feel, life will continue to offer plenty of opportunities to get deeply in touch with that residual pain and the stories attached to it. It will do so in order for us to integrate another layer of that pain and take conscious control of our life back. This does not mean something is wrong with us; it means we are humans and have history. Life is going to be chaotic and triggering—there's no getting around it if we're actually living. Our goal is not to avoid these triggers but to find peace and awareness around them without letting them steal us away from the only thing we truly have: the present moment. Because the truth is these emotions aren't asking us to go back there; they're asking us to be here, begging for our conscious care and attention to heal this next ready layer of our past.

All this trigger talk makes me think about Harville Hendrix and Helen LaKelly Hunt's **Imago Relationship Therapy.** Because what are our relationships if not chock-full of trigger-happy opportunities to get us to dig deeper and get it right? Hendrix and Hunt talk about how when we're emotionally charged—when we're ready to react to a trigger out of fear and anger and hurt—that painful "charge" we're feeling oftentimes is only 10 percent about the present situation. The other 90 percent of our feelings are about some past wounds that are resurfacing and causing pain now.

Whatever we resist persists. It's not news that our core issues arise again and again in our relationships. (Pick a relationship, any relationship—partner, parent, friend, etc.) And for good reason. Not only do we bring our baggage of beliefs and assumptions about love and intimacy to every relationship we enter, but the brain also unconsciously creates an image of a partner to attract into our lives to repeat old patterns in order to heal old wounds. But healing can come only if we pay attention to the sting of the trigger and only if we're willing to do the work. This is the difference between a "wound mate," who supports us in staying exactly the same, and a "soul mate," who's here to help us heal and grow.

The key is bringing awareness to these triggers and moments where emotions come up. Because fighting, fleeing, and freezing are all forms of checking out, of taking the easy way out. But what is really required for our healing is not a way out but a way *through*. That's integration.

And this whole integrating thing...it's gonna take a human minute. So please, let's be patient with ourselves when we lose our shit in the carpool lane or when we snap at the customer-service representative on the other side of the phone. It's in our human nature to react to these triggers. As our awareness grows, we may feel crazy when we can't immediately change our behavior, but these reactions are not pathological—they're primal. The emotional triggers around the people and things we hold dear will always instinctually and physiologically yank our survival chains; it's just on us to notice and pay attention. Because change stems from there. And as far as I'm concerned, that little bit of crazy is exactly what will save us from being insane. The definition of insane, of course, is doing the same thing over and over and expecting different results. And our awareness is the first step in changing that pattern.

Hysterical vs. Historical: The Ninety-Second Rule

> *If it's hysterical, it's historical.*
> —*Melody Beattie*

Hopefully it's clear by now that we all get triggered and that it's no commentary on us as humans other than that we are, in fact, human. There's more to explore, however, in regards to the hysterics around these triggers. Brain scientist Jill Bolte Taylor offers up some revelatory research and a very helpful dose of science behind these emotional responses in her book, *My Stroke of Insight*. (She also has a TED talk of the same name.) Her book, which was based on her firsthand experience of recovering from a massive stroke, clues us in to the physiological mechanism behind emotions. She explains that an emotion such as anger, frustration, disappointment, etc. is an automatic response that is meant to last ninety seconds from the moment it's triggered until it runs its natural course. That means once we are triggered, chemicals in our brain surge through our bodies, creating a physiological experience, and that energy automatically flushes out of our bloodstreams after ninety seconds. *Ninety seconds.* One and a half minutes. *That's all.*

So any time an emotion lasts longer—and when don't they?— it's because we've chosen to fuel it with our thoughts and use it to corroborate some story we're attached to. (*People always disappoint me*, *I'm a burden on others*, *I'm better off alone*, and so on.) Emotions are simply energy in motion (e-motions) with a shifting and changing nature. Only we don't permit them to move naturally when we deny and run away from them or—in this case—when we hold on to them and feed them with story. Her story. His story. History.

Which brings us to the moral of *this* story: if we're hysterical, it's historical. If we're stuck and suffering in a feeling for more than ninety seconds, it's because we're feeding it with our story of woe. And we do this because our storylines give us a false sense of certainty and comfort (even if we're miserable in them). We'd rather be right than happy, and to be "right," in this case, is to feel safe in our familiar stories that are birthed out of our habitual emotional responses—our tendency to get sad, angry, disappointed, or jealous. We become addicted to those responses (the neurological pathways get so well-worn that we just naturally fall into them), and we use our stories to feed these feelings, to get a "hit" of being right because, *Yeah, I knew she'd disappoint me!* The stories themselves aren't even the root of our suffering—the addiction to our response is. If we're programmed for disappointment, for example, we're going to get what we expect, and we will stop at nothing until we do.

The only way to counter our hysterical reactions is—you guessed it—by being present with them. Emotions intensify when we fuel them with words—it's like pouring kerosene on a little ember. So when a not-so-fun emotion rears its head, instead of trying to avoid its discomfort, the goal is to first pause and then open up completely to it—for ninety seconds. No writers, producers, storytellers, or interpreters allowed in the room. We want to simply acknowledge the feeling, giving it our full, compassionate, non-judging attention to feel the sensation rather than feed the story. By doing this, we free ourselves to notice where it's present in our body and to observe if it remains the same for very long or if it shifts and changes. If the body you're in is human, *it will.* Remember, our feelings don't want to be fixed; they just want to be felt. This is how we do that. And I promise it's worth the ninety seconds.

JFK to LAX: Expect Turbulence

An opportunity to test the power of these ninety seconds presented itself to me a couple years ago on an uncomfortable flight from New York to Los Angeles with my good friend Lisa. We had coordinated our individual trips to NYC with the intention of spending time together in one of our favorite cities. The plan was that we'd meet up in between obligations and feed our tummies with good food and our friendship with much needed quality time.

Well, as often happens, plans didn't pan out. We ended up barely seeing each other the entire visit and reconvened at the American Airlines gate at JFK upon boarding our flight back home. Had I known the chill I was stepping into as I approached our gate, I'd have brought an extra jacket and scarf for the flight. She was cold as ice, shut down and shutting me out. Outside of civil pleasantries and a polite "How was it?" she ignored me. I had never in the years of our friendship experienced this with her before, so you can imagine the discomfort in this unchartered terrain of disappointment. And it brought up so much. *Oh my God, I'm a terrible person. I've let her down. She's realized I'm an imposter of a friend, and she's going to unlove and abandon me.*

And once I'd filled my cup of self-blame and unworthiness, I turned it on her. *How could she be so rude? And so cold! I didn't do anything wrong! God, she's so sensitive!* Ah, the workings of the ego. It has to point the gun *somewhere*; it's happy to jump on either side of the better-than or less-than fence, but it will always pick a side. It's either all *your* fault or all *my* fault. If it's your fault, how dare you? Shame on you. If it's my fault, well then...I knew it: I'm damaged and worthless. *How dare I? Shame on me.*

After I went through my how-dare-you/how-dare-I spin cycle, anticipating six hours sitting next to her on this flight back to LA, I wanted nothing more than to hash it out and fix the discomfort. But I could tell Lisa wasn't having it. As I felt the heat rise from my belly (and it was boiling, overcompensating for her icy approach by overheating), I wanted to burn through it all and yell, "Say something!"

And then I remembered the breath. The way in is the way out. My breath granted me access back to the land of Pause—the great spirited God pause, the space between stimulus and response. And in that space, I was reminded of Jill Bolte Taylor's ninety-second rule. *What is truly going on here? How much of this is happening now?* I asked myself. *And how much of this is part of my story? Az, what good is it going to do you and every one of the poor souls on this plane if you lose your shit? If you give your emotions free rein?*

So in that moment, as deeply uncomfortable as it was to not fix this by fighting back, I tapped into my agency to choose...consciously and caringly. I was able to see beyond the emotional storm enough to hold my ground amid the unsteady trigger of fear and its storytellers and say, "Hey, guys. Stop. Take five. We're okay. Emotions have taken flight. This isn't a time to be rewriting history here. Seatbelts on. We can revisit and address this delicate and tender hurt once we all have landed." I knew it would be only from that grounded and conscious place that I could engage responsibly rather than reactively.

Once I quieted the story in my head and allowed the emotions to move as they are designed to, I was able to let go of the need to resist the situation or assist it by adding more fire to it. While the discomfort was still there and I was sitting in the limbo of the unresolved, knowing one of my nearest and dearest was disappointed, I was able to have a silent chuckle about it: *Aha! Here we go! I am not my thoughts and my stories!* I felt a silent victory in that moment, even amid the discomfort, because I recognized that I could engage my witness after all. That I could be an active participant in the crazy flight of life and, over time, learn to feel my feelings instead of doing everything in my power to fix them and those of others I adore.

REACTING VS. RESPONDING

So when something triggers us, when we get emotionally hijacked by way of the amygdala (that internal watchdog/alarm system) and start to spin in our stories, the key to our healing—the key to moving forward versus staying exactly where we have been—lies in the difference between **reacting** to the stimulus and **responding** to it. Yogi Bhajan explains that difference this way: "Reacting comes from emotion; responding comes from devotion."

When we react to a trigger—to a situation or provocation—we let our emotions steer, going straight to our habitual fight-or-flight plan. It's primal, unconscious survival mode. Do or die. And it's 100 percent necessary when jumping out of a burning building, diving into a pool after your child falls in, or screaming for help when someone grabs your purse on the street. But most of the time that's not what's happening.

Where reacting is an out-of-control action, responding comes from a place of control. The definitions of responsibility include "being accountable for one's actions" and "being able to respond." Likewise, *to respond* is to be responsible, conscious, and caring. The devotion that Yogi Bhajan is referring to as the place from which we respond is a conscious engagement of our highest Self. And the way to tap into that is by taking a moment to assess what would really serve us and everyone involved in a given situation when these triggers occur. A *response* arrives on the other side of that moment, that grace period where we (God) pause and come back to that place within ourselves. It is where we see beyond the emotional stir and investigate the root of our current climate of emotions. We root to rise. And our aim is to rise in response and responsibly take action.

So how do we move from an emotional reaction to a conscious response when our day-to-day life can be like walking through a minefield? It shouldn't surprise anyone at this point that the body is the way in, and our awareness is the way through. Our breath is the gateway back into the body, so when we take pause and breathe deeply, we can reground into the moment and ask ourselves, "Where are my feet?" From this sometimes uncomfortable but necessary space between stimulus and response, we get an opportunity to move from our knee-jerk (emphasis on *jerk*) reaction to a place of discernment of what we can and cannot change. And then we can choose how to respond consciously.

The Space Between

The space between your heart and mind,
Is the space we'll fill with time.
—Dave Matthews Band

When it comes to exercising the power to choose between reacting and responding, there is no greater example than the Austrian neurologist, psychiatrist, and Holocaust survivor Viktor Frankl. Frankl knew something about suffering and optimal performance in extreme environments and was the epitome of living a life from Trauma to Dharma. After he saw his father, mother, brother, and wife sent to death in concentration camps, Frankl went on to become an influential psychiatrist. In his work, he defined how **tragic optimism** was a mental framework for turning human suffering into achievement (rise, phoenix, rise!) and translating guilt into self-improvement (what doesn't kill us makes us stronger). All this is predicated, he found, on the ability to extract meaning and purpose from our short lives here on Earth. This means that those of us who truly know who we are and why we are here are likely to adapt to life's artillery better than those who don't.

Frankl explains our way to accessing choice perfectly: "Between stimulus and response there is a space. In that space is our power to choose our response. In our response lies our growth and our freedom." So our gateway to growth and freedom from the tyrannical grip of trauma is accessed through our most powerful tool: choice (specifically, how we choose to respond when life knocks). And that choice awaits us in...that space between. Those spaces between stimulus and response: How many of us truly allow for those? You know the ones: the space between receiving a charged text and our immediate need to reactively text back, or between someone cutting us off on the highway and our hand slamming on the horn or thrusting up a middle finger.

When we allow for those spaces between, we are able to recognize that we have an opportunity to choose how we want to respond to life. We become undeniably aware that it is not our circumstances that define us but, rather, our responses to them. And we afford ourselves the most generous option of using our agency to respond accordingly, instead of reacting unconsciously.

This is exactly why we rely on the breath—in order to take a beat before we defensively beat down what's in front of us, to consciously be a player in the game and not the ball being reactively kicked around. Any mindful, body-based, breath-infused practice will further cultivate this skill, but Kundalini yoga inherently offers us tools to check in, respond, and be actively engaged participants in our lives. Every Kundalini class begins by chanting or "tuning in" with the Adi mantra: *Ong Namo Guru Dev Namo*. This mantra translates to "I bow to the infinite wisdom within me," and it's the perfect reminder to *turn in* in order to *tune in*. *Gu* means *darkness*, and *ru* means *light*, so *guru* is the movement from darkness into light. It is in here that we find Frankl's "space between," and it is here where the Serenity Prayer beckons us to go in order to access "the wisdom to know the difference."

Mommy and Me

It's fair to say my mom is the captain of my cheering squad. Everything I do (poor relationship choices and addictive tendencies aside), she is always there, front and center, to support me. This means she's a fixture in my weekly yoga classes, and you can bet your sweet ass that she was present and sitting on hers, appropriately cross-legged on a yoga mat, for my Kundalini teaching debut in November 2009.

I was nervous to teach, of course. Crazy nervous. Although I had done the yoga teacher training program, I actually had not planned on becoming an instructor. The opportunity had presented itself like so many great callings do: it was thrust upon me. And I guess you could say that having my mama there in those early weeks felt like bringing an extra dose of life support with me, kinda like packing a security blanket for the first day of kindergarten. Or college.

Except for when it didn't feel like that, 'cause let's face it: us humans with mothers know they have direct cords to our trigger buttons. *Nobody* pushes our buttons like our mamas.

So imagine me up there on the teacher's platform, sitting where my teacher Guru Singh sits—where Yogi Bhajan himself sat—in front of a roomful of students. I'm teaching, sharing, riding the nerves, and getting into some semblance of a groove when, in the midst of my lecture, I look over at my mother—again, front and center—dramatically motioning to me the way only a mother can as she mouthed the words "*I can't hear you. Speak up. Use your voice.*"

Oh. My. God. All of a sudden she had turned into a stage mom. I wanted to die. No, scratch that. I wanted to throw the Guru Ganesha statue beside me squarely in her direction. Sure, it wouldn't have been very yogic of me, sitting up there all dressed in my Kundalini whites, but before I could even decide between that Ganesha statue or a framed picture of Guru Gobind Singh, it got worse. Barely a minute had passed before I looked over at her again to witness another extraordinary mat performance. This time, she was hugging her arms around her body and shaking as she mouthed the words, "*It's freezing in here. Do something about the temperature!*"

Now what daughter wouldn't react to that? And believe me: I wanted to. Every fired-up cell in my emotionally charged body wanted to scream at her—or at least shoot an evil eye in her direction. But here's the thing: I didn't. Sure, I was sitting in front of dozens of students, so the prospect of other people's reaction to my reaction helped keep me at bay. But there was more to it than just that. Coincidentally (if you believe in those), it just so happened in that class, I was teaching a pranayama on the "only responsible way out of reacting." So in that very moment, I literally practiced what I preached, and I breathed.

By inhaling through my left nostril and exhaling through my right, I used my breath to calm myself and to move the energy into motion (e-motion—it just needs to move!), rather than allowing the energy/emotion to move me. That was enough to create that space between. And after just three rounds, it hit me: *This annoying woman sitting there motioning and miming is on my team. She is genuinely here to support me and wants me to succeed. Give her a break.*

Now this is a relatively benign example, but we all struggle with life's challenges—sometimes bigger, sometimes smaller: fights with loved ones, disputes at work, conflicts within ourselves. The external challenges we experience are a natural part of life and create an inconvenience, sure. But whether they turn out to be internally disruptive or supportive has everything to do with the meaning we attach to them. When we are willing to sit in the uncomfortable spaces long enough to move through our emotional reaction, we eventually arrive at a place where we can respond to life with courage and consciousness. And from there we can alchemize almost any situation into an opportunity for healing and growth. Because *we*—not our circumstances—determine who we are and what we will be.

Can I Get a Witness: Engaging the Witness

Have you ever noticed the reason most people complain—especially here in the United States? If they're unhappy, it's because of stress. If they're overweight, it's because of stress. If they come off as unavailable, it's because of stress. We see headlines calling out stress as the culprit behind all our ailments. "STRESS IS A KILLER!" screams at us from magazines, the news, and our doctors' mouths. And yet, how soon we forget that we live in this binary universe, this push and pull of opposites. It's part of the natural order of our world—our evolution—to experience stress, pressure, tension, and friction. It's designed to be there as leverage for our growth (like that piece of carbon that turns into a diamond instead of coal, all because of pressure). There is no such thing as a stress-free life, and stress is *not* the killer. Our reaction to it is—our reaction that we now understand can be turned into a healthy and conscious response with the proper tools.

We first explored the embodied, sensitive, and neutral witness in acceptance, when we refamiliarized ourselves with the present moment. The compassionate, nonjudging witness is what allows us to reach a place of calm beneath life's tsunami of emotions. A hundred percent of our emotional pain is attributed to our thoughts, so by tapping into our neutral witness, we give ourselves the power to explore our internal world of feeling and thought from a nonreactive space that can consciously be followed by appropriate action. When we follow the source of these thoughts, we will find it is usually the ego that's the first and loudest to speak—always in fear, either on defense or offense. It is the ego that gets our frontal lobes spinning with done-me-wrong stories, and it will run us ragged. So before we run down that exhausting road, we can instead employ the neutral witness who is *actually* the core of who we are, to take note of who's running the show here and from what part of our Selves we want to be responding.

Worrier vs. Warrior

To steal a phrase from Oprah, here's what we know for sure:

1. There will always be pressure, tension, stress, and friction.

2. We can decide how we take it on and take it in.

When responding to stress, we can choose to make ourselves miserable or strong. The amount of energy we expend is the same, so it is up to us to decide how we want to use it. Do we want to be coal or diamonds? Do we want to be **worriers** or **warriors**? Worriers *react*, entertaining and focusing on all the possible things that can go wrong. Warriors *respond*, staying present to recognize what can and cannot be controlled, conserving their energy so they can act responsibly when the time is right to overcome any potential obstacles that come their way.

The allure of worrying is very strong. But as they say, worrying is like wishing for the thing we don't want to happen. And if we're not worrying about our own stuff, it's all too easy to project this energy on the people around us. I'm a recovering codependent, so I get it. However, it's one thing to have concern for those in our lives, and it's entirely another when that concern moves into obsessive thinking, controlling, or a belief that our own well-being is dependent on another person's behavior.

Excessive worry, preoccupation, and caretaking are, simply put, wasted energy. They steal us from ourselves—the only person we can control—and beyond that, they are illusions. It's hard to believe this when we are still engaged with them, but the reason we humans like to hang out in these worry-filled spaces is because they fool us into thinking we're doing something to solve a problem. But in reality, we are doing nothing.

Now there *is* a place for doing nothing, but it's a different kind of nothing. Moving from worrier into warrior isn't about detaching from those we love; rather, it's about detaching from our controlling over-involvement. We're so quick to say, "Don't just stand there—do something!" But the warrior's cry is instead, "Don't just do something—stand there!" Energy flows where our attention goes, so in order to be warriors, we must become alchemists who transform and redirect that energy, which we do by pausing and tuning in to accept the facts before us rather than the stories in our heads and then choosing how we want to proceed.

Witness Protection Program: The Lion vs. The Dog

There's a Buddhist teaching I love to reference when I teach about reacting versus responding: Throw a stick for a dog; he runs after it. Throw a stick for a lion, and he turns around to see who threw it. The lesson to take from the lion is to look to see who's throwing the stick. When we get distracted or triggered, who's stirring our torrential pot of emotions? Where are those feelings and emotions coming from? Are they rooted in the now? Are they worth chasing?

Lions represent strength and steadiness. They confidently weigh what's really a threat or cause for alarm. The mighty lion holds court from his regal seat, looking around and saying, "I'm king of the effin' jungle, and you ain't disturbing my peaceful catnap unless it's worth it." It would serve us all well to consult with our inner lions before chasing every metaphorical stick thrown in our path.

It is always prudent to engage our inquirer before running off with our spin doctor, and a good question to ask that offers a perfect way to cultivate the necessary space between is, "Is what I'm experiencing a fact or am I spinning a story?" Triggering people and places—even and especially when they're in our own heads—are here to reflect the pieces of us that need a little unearthing. Emotional turmoil reveals an opportunity to explore our inner landscapes. I love to use the ocean as a metaphor for our overly stressed and reactive minds. If we dive deep below the surface of our emotional tsunamis, there is always stillness patiently waiting for us.

The beauty and grace of Kundalini yoga is that it calms the overactive mind and allows us to make those dives into the torrents of emotion rather than simply letting them submerge and overwhelm us. We can use a Kundalini practice or sadhana (daily spiritual practice) as an opportunity to sit and explore our inner landscapes. Within the safety of this space, we can give permission to all the feelings to arise and move as they need. And we can lean in and feel the frenzy of sensations free from any need to interpret them. This is how we transform that worrier into a warrior: by learning to let go and let everything be just long enough to access the truth, by letting things fall apart in order to let better things fall together.

RESPONSIBILITY, FATE, AND DESTINY

I am not my fault. I am my responsibility.

—Unknown

The essence of responding is responsibility—it's recognizing that regardless of what has happened up until now, we are capable of making new choices that can improve our situations moving forward. We can either allow our past to keep interfering with our expression of optimal love and happiness, or we can move forward on the pathway of freedom and joy. It's our choice, and we always have a choice. Being responsible does not mean we caused any of the traumas or tragedies to happen or that they are our fault. Owning our part doesn't make us culpable; it merely makes us accountable for what we're going to do about it—how we are going to utilize our agency.

Guru Singh says, "When you commit to taking on your fate and doing something about it, this fate turns into destiny." We have a choice: to live in our **fate** or our **destiny**. Our fate is the path paved *for* us. It is all the painful circumstances and the shit (and also the blessings and good fortune) we must connect with and accept in order to move forward. Often we get immobilized by life's fated circumstances. Our destiny, on the other hand, is the path paved *by* us. It is where we embrace all the pain, fear, frustrations, and challenges of our lives and use them to lift ourselves from the chaos of our existence toward all that we're meant to be. If pain is the distance from where we are to who we are, then where we are is our fate and who we are is our destiny. And sometimes there can be a lot of pain in between.

The pain in our lives is our disconnection from Self, from our true essence, from our *Sat Nam* (*Sat* is *Truth*, and *Nam* is *Identity*). The trauma and crises in our lives disconnect us from who we are, and it is up to us to reconnect to our truth. Our circumstances don't define us; our response to them does. Fate is the shit, the compost of life; destiny is our birthright to fashion that shit into fertilizer. We have the inherent ability to convert and shape what has been given to us as fate into our destination of choice, getting us from where we are to who we are. And only we have the power to fulfill our destiny. Only we have the power to turn our shit into fertilizer and grow. That's dharma. It's a profound shift, and it is on us as individuals to assert the authority to make it happen.

SOUL PRESCRIPTION

Journal Question #1: Choosing to Take Action

Right before big things happen in our lives, we are forced to make a choice that terrifies us. What's a choice you know you need to make? (Is it time to have that conversation, go to the gym, end the relationship, open your heart again, start your blog, write your book, or ask for help?) If everything you want is on the other side of fear, then what choice can you make that scares you? Go for it. If it doesn't scare you, you're not stretching enough.

Journal Question #2: The Space Between

Reflect on a trigger. Where, when, and how do you tend to react and feel out of control in your life? It could have been this morning, last night, or last year. Who do you tend to react around? What situations? How can you cultivate and access the space between? How could you choose to respond next time?

Pranayama: Alternate Nostril Breathing for Perspective and Emotional Balance

Our yogic and meditative practices help us reclaim ownership of our lives and the one thing we have power over: the power to choose how to respond to life's storms (the majority of which happen between our ears). This pranayama is a great way to rebalance your emotions and cultivate that space between. That way you can see the choices before you and respond instead of react. It is an excellent practice to do before bed to let go of the worries of the day and a powerful technique to establish emotional balance and calmness after being emotionally triggered or while under acute stress.

Posture: Sit with a straight spine or in easy pose in a chair.

Eye Focus: Close your eyes and look up at the Third Eye point.

ACCEPTANCE | AGENCY | AUTHORITY

Breath: Close off your right nostril with your right thumb. Inhale deeply through your left nostril. When your lungs are full, close off your left nostril with your pinkie and exhale smoothly through your right nostril. Your breath should be complete, continuous, and smooth. (An alternative method of closing off the nostrils is using your thumb and index finger.)

Continue with long, deep, regular breaths for three to eleven minutes.

To Finish: Inhale, exhale completely, and hold the breath out. Relax completely.

Asana: Stretch Pose

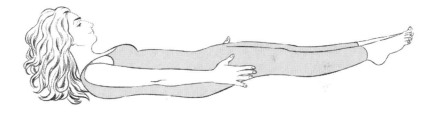

This powerful pose helps us reconnect to our core of personal strength and our seat of action. (Hi, agency!) By working on the third chakra, it boosts resolve and self-esteem, gives that extra grit to make new and scary choices, and adjusts and strengthens the navel point—which is your power center—increasing core energy and willpower. Stretch pose resets the entire nervous system and strengthens the abdominal area, and in conjunction with Breath of Fire, it is calming and rejuvenating and purifies the blood.

Posture: Lie on your back. Start by rooting your lower back down into the ground, then raise your head and heels six inches off the ground. Stretch your toes so they point away from you. Place your arms either above your thighs with your palms facing down but not touching your legs or alongside your legs with your palms facing but not touching your body. (Or you may place your hands underneath your buttocks to support your lower back.)

Eye Focus: Focus your eyes on your toes.

Breath: Breath of Fire. (This breath is an even, rapid, and rhythmic inhale and exhale through the nose, similar to a dog pant but through the nose rather than the mouth.)

Hold for one minute. Work up to three minutes.

To Finish: Relax for a minute, allowing the energy to move and calibrate.

Chapter Seven
A U T H O R I T Y

The two most engaging powers of an author are to
make new things familiar and familiar things new.
—Samuel Johnson

By engaging the witness, we recognize we can be active participants in our lives by accessing the ticket to freedom that is choice. But choice comes with responsibility, and the majority of people shy away from that—the sad truth is we'd rather continue complaining, blaming, and shaming than move out of victimhood. This is where our courage is required. There is courage behind every choice to bravely and humbly recognize the responsibility we bear in any situation. Yes, it is easier to keep scapegoating and passing the buck, but that just keeps us stuck. And we're ready to unstick. So taking on that responsibility means we are willing to take ownership of where we are now and **authority** over where we are going.

WHAT IS AUTHORITY?

Authority, by definition, is the power to give orders or permission and to make decisions. One of my study findings was that, through Kundalini yoga, participants experienced a noticeable shift in how they came to perceive themselves. Their acceptance led them to agency—to making choices toward effective action and change—and with every responsible choice, they began to trust themselves more and feel a sense of empowerment. Of authority.

Once we start making new choices and taking conscious action (*I'm going to actually get up and out of bed today. I might just go outside for a walk, return that phone call, look up that twelve-step meeting, inquire about that therapist, make it to that yoga class I'm terrified to go to...*), we start to feel a sense of authority over our lives again— or perhaps for the first time. In rising to these personal challenges and using our agency and practical tools to cultivate that "space between" to respond rather than react, we reveal our hidden capabilities. And this, in turn, starts to challenge our beliefs that we're not good enough, that we'll never get better, and so on. We realize we are much stronger than we once thought and we actually have the power to do something to feel different. With every healthy choice, we build a stronger sense of self-efficacy and begin to feel more confident about ourselves and our abilities to make a difference in our lives.

Now we can't address authority without pointing out its relation to the word *author*. When we're embracing and standing in our authority, we realize we actually have a say in what happens and how our story writes itself out. This principle begs us to ask, "Who's the author of our story?" Who's the one writing here? Are we still choosing to pen this life script through the lens of the victim, writing out a dramatically pitiful and hopeless Lifetime Movie Channel version of our life? Or have we shifted to a new understanding? Most of us are attached to our old stories and hold tight to them. Those old stories kept us safe and helped us survive. Until they didn't. Until they moved from protecting us to imprisoning us.

BELIEF SYSTEMS

If you believe you can
or if you believe you can't, you're right.
—Henry Ford

Our stories are fueled by our beliefs, and at this point in the process, it's time to start looking at whether these beliefs are hindering or supporting growth. Our belief systems feed the preconceived opinions, assumptions, and labels we bring into an experience before we even have it. They feed our expectations so much that we end up in a relationship with our expectations rather than with life itself.

The Talmud says, "We do not see things as they are. We see them as we are." And though this sounds very esoteric, it's actually grounded in basic biology and neurology. Our brains are wired to protect us by looking for ways to keep us safe, and they have developed an incredibly quick and efficient (i.e., lazy) way of sorting through the thousands of pieces of information they take in each second. Early in our lives, the brain picks up information based on our observations and experiences. Then, out of sheer laziness, as it starts to sift through the vast quantities of new information, our brain picks and chooses to perceive things that are familiar to us—stuff we already know. Because what we already know is familiar. And familiar—if it hasn't already killed us—is safe!

Once our brain decides which bits to let in, it begins building bridges (i.e., shortcuts) between our nerve cells, interlacing nerve fibers to create **neural pathways**. These pathways are based on the routes we've experienced and traveled before, so the map in your brain will differ from the one in mine. The purpose of both, however, is to establish routes that get us from point A to point B—where we input data, memorize, and strategize—as quickly as possible. The neural pathways are worn and hardened habitually, and man, our brains are creatures of habit. Once they figure out how to do something (and have managed to survive it), they will do it again and again and again. Insanity, anyone? Yep. In the wise, wise words of Cypress Hill, "Insane in the membrane. Insane in the brain!"

Those neural pathways basically just play personalized reruns of what we've previously experienced, telling a story about whatever trauma or disruption we've lived through and trying to make sense of it somehow. But we all know by now that we're going to get a big fat *fail* trying to make sense of our lives through our heads—only our bodies give us access to our senses. So those stories about all men being unavailable, or that we're guaranteed to be disappointed, or whatever yours may be based on that one chapter of life you've lived so far, play on a loop in our heads, coloring our expectations of life. We then weave these expectations based on that one painfully disruptive occurrence into our brains as data, and the brain naturally uses that data to start to form more bridges of information and expectation. And then those bridges begin to harden, and well...we get what we expect. This is what it means when we hear, "We are what we think." If we believe what we're thinking, that is.

Biology of Belief

When it comes to beliefs, there's a stale philosophy that our DNA controls our life. The old saying "I'm just wired that way" corroborates this central dogma that we are all a consequence of our genes and can't do anything about it. This genetic determinism—saying our heredity controls us and there's nothing we can do about it—is a popular philosophy among victims looking to remain victims. But what's interesting about this entire notion is that it was merely a hypothesis that was never proven as scientific fact!

Cell biologist Bruce Lipton asserts something quite the opposite, however. In his book *The Biology of Belief*, Lipton says that it's not our genes but our beliefs that control our lives. While genetics may offer us a potential blueprint for our life patterns, he states, we actually construct our lives in response to the circumstances we encounter. And if we look to the science of epigenetics, it becomes clear that we can actually assert a level of control over our genes based on how we respond to life. And our response, as we now know, lies in our belief system. So when we boil it down, our beliefs control our biology.

To add further weight to this argument, there's Masuro Emoto's research on water and resonance. Dr. Emoto wondered if the way water formed ice crystals could be affected by positive or negative thoughts. In order to test this, he froze water and ran experiments by projecting concentrated thoughts or words directly on various containers of water, and then he photographed the ice crystals that formed under a microscope. What he discovered is that water exposed to loving words or thoughts formed brilliant and beautiful symmetrical snowflake patterns, while water exposed to negative and pejorative thoughts and words formed dull-colored, asymmetrical patterns.

What this means, of course, is that *water has memory*. It holds the vibration of our thoughts and stories within it—be they positive, negative, or neutral. And since we human beings consist of 65 percent water, well, the things we think and believe about ourselves have an enormous effect not only on our reality but also on our biology.

Fit In or Be Found Out

Growing up, I felt like I never fit in. I was an immigrant child. The Iranian Revolution had left many Iranians and particularly Iranian Jews with no choice but to flee. So when I was four years old, my family *Sound of Music*-ed our asses out of there and headed to the United States, where we started over.

But imagine the political climate then, with the Iran Hostage Crisis and the looming threat of terrorism. Rather than being welcomed into this new land, I was constantly met with taunts and chants of "Go back home!" I wanted so badly to fit in that I became a chameleon, a people pleaser. I did everything I could to convince people that I was worthy and lovable, because the voice in my head (validated by the ones outside it) told me I was anything but.

That's an exhausting way to live, but I did it. And actually, I did it pretty well. But what I quickly came to realize was that once I did fit in, I spent all my time worrying about being *found out*—found out that I was some imposter, some uninvited outsider who had crashed the party. Those words from my early childhood fed into this learned belief about myself that had a lasting vibration. It left an imprint on my being.

Sticks and stones may break my bones, but words can never hurt me? What a crock of shit that is. Thoughts and words have a vibration we feel all the way into our cells and tissues, and when they're allowed to fester long enough, they become a belief. Our belief waves can create a tsunami of life both internally and externally...which explains the dysfunctional, abusive relationships I got myself into over the years. With the "I'm unworthy, unlovable, unacceptable, and not good enough" tape playing in my head, I found men to mirror those thoughts I had about myself. The good news, however—what I came to understand in my recovery—is that *we* are not the problem. *The way we look at the problem is the problem.* We, in fact, *are the solution.*

And you know what else is a solution? Scientifically speaking? Water.

The human brain is composed of 70 percent water, and the lungs are nearly 90 percent. So imagine the power we can have over our own bodies and beings when we harness the **flexibility** of that element. Back when I was a child, I used that flexibility not to acknowledge my greatness but to accommodate my fear. I molded myself to fit in at the expense of losing myself. But the fact is—*the science is*—we can also feed ourselves the loving, strengthening, empowering messages we need to foster our own healing and recovery, because it is our beliefs that control our lives.

Conscious vs. Subconscious Minds

When it comes to our beliefs, our **conscious mind** (where we are present to what truly is and can be) is constantly duking it out with the

ALLOWING   APPRECIATION   AUTHENTICITY ⟶

subconscious mind (that repository of habitual stimulus/response tapes that fuel our expectations). Neuroscientists tell us that 95 percent of our thoughts are controlled by our preprogrammed subconscious mind—so nearly 100 percent of the time, instead of actually thinking, we're simply projecting a movie of something we've learned in the past onto the present. When we're triggered or our "buttons are being pushed," all that means is we're falling into old, hardwired thoughts or ways that have been hardened in our brains. And that simply needs to be replaced.

This is why mindfulness practices that make us more conscious are so critical for our healing. Our conscious mind is the creative one, the one that conjures up positive thoughts. The subconscious mind, however, is a million times faster and more powerful than the conscious mind. The subconscious mind is our autopilot where the conscious mind is manual control. If a ball is coming at us, for example, the subconscious mind will interpret and respond quicker than the conscious mind will.

One way to think of it is by imagining Los Angeles's famous freeways. Our brain is the sprawling city, and our neural nerve cells and fibers are the many freeways, thoroughfares, and side streets that run through it. Now imagine living with access to all those different roads, and yet the only one we use to get around is the I-10 freeway. Which is great if we only want to travel east to west and experience just one small piece of the greater Los Angeles area the same exact way every single time. (I mean, talk about autopilot.) But think of how much we're missing out on by choosing to take that same route back and forth, over and over again. This is exactly what our brains do, navigating us through life using the same default route (in our case, fight, flight, or freeze). And even though it may be miserable, we prefer to place our faith in the familiar disaster we know or have created. Our minds are slackers that want to take the known route—their version of the easy way—even if it's the more unconsciously painful way. Because we'd rather be safe. Because we'd rather be right.

So these messages programmed in our subconscious mind will undermine our best conscious efforts to change our lives. Hence things like positive affirmations aren't enough to effect change—we have to go deeper to exit the proverbial freeway. The comments we make to ourselves ("I'm stupid," "I won't amount to anything," "I'm unlovable," and so on), our behaviors, and the beliefs and attitudes we observe or experience are downloaded into our subconscious minds like freeways, and they need to be reprogrammed. Our brains need to be rerouted! Enter meditation and yoga pranayamas.

Part of what these practices do is help soften those hardwired bridges to allow for flexibility, creating openings to new paths and possibilities. They also get us into the space of the observer, allowing us to engage our witness (our consciousness) and ultimately step in to override and rewire the self-sabotaging subconscious programming. Unless we are consciously working against it, our subconscious minds are controlling the way we are experiencing the world. Because it's not only *what* we see and perceive but it's *what we believe about what we see* and the meaning we give to it that dictates our belief systems. And those are the belief systems that determine our biology—our health. So to borrow words from Guru Singh, this is where it is incumbent upon us to take on our empowered sense of authority to rewrite the meaning of our world.

Analysis Paralysis

Now these neural pathways aren't the only byproduct of our lazy brains, keeping us stuck on repeat, devoid of any new growth (though certainly they would be enough). Just as we are attached to these old stories, we are also attached to the ideas of our lives more than we are attached to actually living our lives. My animal communicator once told me that my dog Bailey said I spent more time thinking about what I was planning to do than actually doing it. Take as long as you need processing my use of an animal communicator (hey, it's LA), but know that neither she nor Bailey were wrong.

Analysis Paralysis is when we think, analyze, and conceptualize something to the point of immobility. We get stuck in the *idea of life*, no longer allowing life to happen or experiencing it when it does. And this all stems from our need for control. There are benefits to controlling the pieces of our lives that require attention and involvement, but what happens when we attempt to control, plan, and analyze more than the universe requires? Any time we enter something new (a new relationship, a new phase, a new year, a new day) and step into the space of the unknown, we tend to experience fear. And so the fearful control freak inside steps in and tries to take over the mind, feeding us all those old stories we could sing in our sleep.

The difference is that now we're waking up. While once these stories lulled us, now they've dulled us. No longer feeding us, they've left us hungry, starving for new flavors of experiences. And though it can be terrifying to step outside our comfort zones, that is exactly how we expand our way of seeing the world. Each brave step brings us into the depths and the breadth of new experience, into awareness. And with the

ACCEPTANCE   AGENCY   AUTHORITY

cap off our life binoculars, we can see wider than we did before. From this new place, we can and must begin to rewrite our story—rewrite what was. Because so much of our growth is about unlearning what we've known and letting go. We cannot grow if we're always in the know.

GROWTH IS UNLEARNING

> *Maturity is a process of subtraction, not addition.*
> —*M. Chadbourne*

Part of our healing, growth, and transformation involves a humbling practice of **unlearning**. Yes, we have so much to unlearn here. We all love holding on to our belief-fueled problems and stories. On top of being excellent leverage for sympathy and a great way to avoid taking responsibility, they keep us safe from risk by filling us with excuses and reasons for why things should stay the same. But once we've reached the point at which "the same" is no longer how we want things, it's time to change. And self-awareness alone doesn't guarantee that; understanding why we are the way we are isn't enough. True transformation is stepping in and engaging with it all *and then releasing it*. And make no mistake: that can be scary. But we need to be willing to look at where we are attached to the very things we complain about and let them go—even and especially if it's scary as hell. Our spiritual growth is an emptying of ourselves so life can fill us anew.

Old Stories: Our Ten-ish Match

This process of growth and unlearning begins with our old stories, and one of my oldest stories is that I can't trust men because they will always disappoint me. Now if you really want to grow, a great way to speed that along is to order yourself a live-in human mirror (i.e., a relationship, which is really just a fancy word for two people with pained pasts that have colored their individual journeys to each other). My mirror, also known as Ricardo, came with a set of beliefs that he can't be trusted because he always lets people down. Can you imagine a more perfect partner for this work? Here I am with my belief that I can't trust men and they will always disappoint me. (And you'd better believe I show up looking for disappointment—hell, I tee it up because it feels familiar and right, even if it's also miserable.) And here he is, believing he can't get anything right except for disappointing people, which he happily takes on because it's safe, even though it's miserable.

And all that believing and expecting brings us to a Saturday not too long ago. I was teaching a workshop, and he was accompanying me to film it. Power couple, right? We'd made a plan to leave the house at 10:00 a.m. because I needed to get there with ample time to set up so, naturally, I was ready to go and waiting for him at 9:55. Well, 9:55 turned into 10:05, then 10:10, and 10:15 stretched into 10:30, and...man, I wish I could say those pranayamas kicked in, but they didn't. With every minute that passed, I felt my temperature rising and a heat brewing in my belly. And you know what else was brewing? My old beliefs. *This is going to be one disappointment after another. This is a precursor. He doesn't care. What am I doing with him? This is a sign!*

And then finally he strolled in, a half hour late, stepping right into my stewing silence. As we settled into the car ride, there was more silence. (And there's nothing scarier than the thick and heavy silence of a woman sitting next to you!) What ensued was the quintessential he said/she said match. I said, "We needed to leave at ten."

He said, "You never said ten. You said ten-ish."

Ish? "Ish" isn't even a time. Or a word! I never said ten-ish. I *would never say* ten-ish. "Admit that you're late."

Nope.

Now remember, this harmless tit-for-tat is rooted in our fear-filled need to be right. If I'm right about ten, he's disappointed me. If he's right about ten-ish, he's given himself a little space to let me down. So there we sat, holding on to our stories, the perfect wound mates. I'm programmed for disappointment; he's programmed to disappoint. That's my story, and I'm sticking to it. And around and around we go, both of us right. And miserable.

So all this got me thinking (which I had plenty of time for in our silent car ride) about a story of how tribesmen would capture monkeys in Africa. They would cut a hole in a coconut just big enough for a monkey's hand to fit in, and then they'd tie the coconut to a tree. Next, they'd fill the coconut with peanuts and leave a peanut trail that ultimately led the monkey back to the coconut. Upon reaching the coconut, the monkey would plunge his hand into the large fruit and grab as many peanuts as he could and—aha! The hole is too small to withdraw with a fist full of peanuts, so the monkey's hand is trapped. All he has to do is open his fist and let go of them to be free. But of course, the nature of the monkey is such that he would never let go of his peanuts. To let go would mean to lose something he believes he needs. And yet, in holding on to them, he remains trapped.

The nature of our monkey mind is no different. Those "peanuts" are our beliefs: *I am always going to be disappointed. I am always going to let people down.* Those beliefs paint the way we see our world and the stories we tell about it. The more we hold on to our old beliefs, the more we remain captive to living out the same old story. And for what? For *peanuts.* "I did it for peanuts" is synonymous with "I did it for barely anything at all." In other words, it doesn't really pay much. So what is the value of holding on to old beliefs?

We may be trapped, but at least we'd be right! And we'd rather be right than happy. (Is that sinking in yet?) This brings us back to the car ride to the workshop, in the midst of my heated "ten-ish match" with Ricardo. This perfect soul-mirror of mine looked over to me and said, "I'm sorry. You're right. You said ten. I was late." *Fist of peanuts unclenched. Hand free, heart open. Fifteen–love, Ricardo.*

And me? Well, this just didn't compute. It wasn't in the script I knew. You would think I'd have felt better with this admission, this vindication, but no. I realized I was no longer even attached to being right; rather, I was attached to the feeling of disappointment I've grown so accustomed to. And I wasn't ready to let that go. I was still clenching my fistful of peanuts tight.

Using what tools I did have access to in the moment, I settled into a pause and looked at him. And in the grace of that God pause, I remembered some wise words from Tommy LaSorda, famed Dodger GM who Ricardo and I had just gone to see speak the previous night. Sharing some tough-love advice he had once given his team during a terrible losing streak, he said, "Quit playing for the name on the back of your jersey. Play for the name on the front of the jersey."

As I continued to stare at Ricardo, it hit me. *Wait a second... what are we doing here? This isn't a ten-ish match—we're on the same team! We're wearing the same color jerseys!* Yep, it takes teamwork to make the dream work. And I can't be a team player if I'm still gripping that fistful of peanuts. I looked at him again, and my fist of peanuts finally unclenched. Hand free, heart open. That "my way or the highway" approach is one hell of a long and lonely road. And we are not meant to travel this road alone.

It's said if you want to travel fast, travel alone. If you want to travel far, travel together. So we have to look at where our peanut gallery of beliefs is trapping us. Those beliefs are only as real as we make them. Yes, we make-believe. And we all have within us the power and ability to choose beliefs that will free us to be happy rather than trap us into being right. The distance from right to happy is short—all it requires is moving from our head (needing to be right) into our heart (embracing the courage it requires to be happy).

Three Minds

Per yogic teachings, there are three functional aspects of the human mind: the positive, the negative, and the neutral. And all serve a necessary purpose.

The **positive mind** is open and constructive. It seeks fulfillment and possibilities. The positive mind inspires and motivates us forward, searching for what can be useful and beneficial for us. (The danger of the positive mind is that if we rely on it too much, we become careless.)

The **negative mind** is reactive and protective. Wanting to keep us safe, it seeks out danger. The negative mind is developed to preserve our life. (Too much of it, however, makes us overly careful and stuck. Its danger is that it keeps us small.)

The **neutral mind** is the soulful assessor. It is the space we hold after our yogic practice—awake and aware without judgment or stories. The neutral mind is a balancing scale, our in-house, unbiased, calm, and compassionate therapist who looks at all the dueling positives and negatives, assesses them, and finds the implications of each. It's our Soul channel where we access our intuition.

The neutral mind is our ideal default state, but for the majority of us, the negative mind is the channel on which we continue to watch, write, and live out the story of our lives. An overactive, overworked negative mind plays into the dark side of the ego, which is at best suspicious and at worst vicious. We all know the feeling: always under attack, just waiting and wanting to be offended so we can fight back. The negative mind is a gun loaded with fear, and it's looking for targets.

The fear-fed ego fuels the victim in us all, who needs to pass the buck for all our pain, discomfort, and disappointment somewhere. And off we go, stuck on that blame-complain-and-shame train. That negative drain train. And while there is honorable truth to being victims in our lives, that victimhood gets old and stagnant. At some point, the self-pitying victim—that deflated side of the ego—must own up to passing the blame and responsibility on to someone or something else all the time. That ownership is our way to freedom.

REWRITING OUR STORIES

So much of our Trauma to Dharma work involves releasing the hold our past has on us. We all have unique stories of our families, communities, and cultures, but many of those stories do not reflect the truth that we are all deserving of love. In her pivotal research on shame and vulnerability, Brené Brown uncovered that the *only* thing that differentiated people who were living a "wholehearted" life from those who weren't was that the former believed they were worthy of love and belonging. They didn't necessarily receive more love or experience more belonging than the people in the other group; they simply *believed* they were worthy of those things. And there's a powerful message in that. Regardless of the past experiences that have influenced the way we view ourselves and our world, we all have the right and capacity to be happy and loved. And the most authoritative action we can take about the past is to reframe and change our perspective of it.

We see the world we choose to see. This doesn't mean we put blinders on or turn away; it just means that we can shift the way we are looking at it. The gift of living in awareness is it allows us to call out our overactive negative mind (and its understudy, the victim) that's always focusing on what has or could go wrong and discern where our stories are neither protecting us nor supporting our growth. Our stories evolve like we do. They're constantly in need of rewrites and updates. And when we're ready to begin that undertaking, the ego is a good chapter to start with.

The Ego vs. The Soul

> *Soul and Spirit include body, emotions, and mind;*
> *they do not erase them.*
>
> —Ken Wilber

God bless our **egos**—our little (or not so little) protectors. The ego is the first to be awakened and irritated when life sucker punches us. And understandably so. It wants only to keep us safe. Unfortunately, in its efforts to safeguard, it puts up walls and boundaries that, when left unchecked, become prisons that dim the light of possibility and stoke the flames of cynicism and paranoia. Our "the world is out to get me" and "things never go my way" mentalities are the ego's reactive thinking, its prized quality. It will always want to hold on to what's safe and familiar. And it always wants to prove itself right by proving it has been wronged. The ego also thrives on separation, so it keeps holding on to reasons to be better or less than—reasons to "other." That's the play of the ego, creating a separation between us and them, between me and you. Our ego is all black and white, there's no gray. So either it loves or hates the story we use to define ourselves; either we're awesome or awful. But either way, we're different and separate. Better or worse than but never the same.

But despite its bad rap, the ego isn't all bad. It strives to make life harder than necessary only because it needs intensity and challenges to feel important and worthy of accomplishment and fulfillment. So here's where the ego comes in handy: it wants the fight and can never get enough because it's always looking for more and for better. It's looking for a better now. The ego, while seemingly trying to take us down, is also the part of us that will keep striving to improve what is. Even while telling us we're a piece of shit, it will tell us we're the piece of shit around which the whole world revolves. It can make us crazy, but also it can save our lives. If we can transcend it.

To transcend the ego means to include it, not to discard or deny it. We cannot eliminate the ego because we need it—it is the glue between the body and the Soul—so instead we must humble it. Psychologist Ken Wilber explains that "transcending the ego" actually means including it in a deeper and higher embrace. That we "do not get rid of the small ego, but rather, we inhabit it fully, live it with verve, use it as the necessary vehicle through which higher truths are communicated."

In other words, we must recognize our ego as a friend, not a foe. Albeit an irrational, unstable friend. And well...okay, *sometimes* an enemy. But what do we do with our enemies? We keep them close and kill 'em with kindness. And in the ego's case, also firmness. Because all the ego is really looking for—all it really needs to be turned into an ally— are boundaries and direction. With that, the ego can get us to throw up the white flag and surrender; it can get us *here*, to wanting more for our lives and being willing to fight for it. But the ego alone cannot sustain us in the spirited place of Oneness where our recovery lies. That's when the Soul must step in.

A spiritual path is anything that helps us live more fully and grow to our greatest potential. The ego loves to play master of its domain, but it also loves a challenge, and that's when we can use its drive and vigor— once we align it with the heart's intention. See, the ego is a neat freak and control freak, but the Soul is here to get dirty. It's here to get into the human-mess of life because that's where the magic is. So we can employ the ego to do the Soul's work.

The ego wants to play dirty, but the Soul wants to *get* dirty. It wants to get earth all over it. The ego knows no better than to create drama out of trauma. The Soul, however, sees it all as fuel for *dharma*. So the two must be integrated and balanced. A spiritual somatic practice like Kundalini yoga can teach us how to embrace both our sensitivity (the ego lives in the world of senses) and our consciousness (our Soul directs us through our humanness), so we can move from being a victim, running scared (ego), to a victor, living sacred (Soul).

Victim and Victor

You become mature when you become
the authority in your own life.

—Joseph Campbell

Authority involves a conscious willingness to rewrite our narratives by stepping out of the ego's fear-fed victim story and into the story of the Soul. That is the difference between the **victim** and the **victor.** The victim reacts from emotion while the victor responds from devotion. The victim is disconnected from choice while the victor is connected to voice. The victim is stuck in the trauma while the victor is uncovering the dharma. So the first question to honestly ask ourselves in claiming our authority is where we have been coming from: the victim or the victor. And the greatest way to pinpoint our meaning maker is by paying attention to the voice we've been listening to all this time. What question has it been asking? The victim—or ego—is the one who will always ask, woefully and pitifully, "*Why is this happening to me?*"

The victor—the Soul—will refrain and reframe. It will instead ask, engagingly and curiously, "*Why is this happening for me?*" What do I need to learn here? What is the lesson? What hidden talent or strength is this summoning me to unearth and bring to life? That is the question of the victor, of the Soul. While the victim is still stuck in the trauma, reacting to protect and survive, the victor is finding fierce compassion and kick-ass admiration for having gotten this far and is ready to patiently uncover that something more. This inquiry and possibility, this curiosity and care to mine a deeper meaning and to entertain the idea that just maybe there is something valuable and malleable to why certain things happened, is the path of the victor. Our willingness to transform our wounds into a source of power and wisdom is what moves us from being a victim of our circumstance to becoming the hero in our journey.

The victim and victor mine very different meanings from raw experience, and we all have the innate ability to move from the victim story of blaming, complaining, and shaming to living and breathing the victor story of claiming. *This is the authority piece.* And this doesn't mean we are betraying our past: what it held, offered, and did to us. Letting go of our victim story isn't an abandonment of what was; it is a thank you, a fuck you, and an "I acknowledge you and am now ready to be transformed by you in a whole new way."

We become trapped when we've written our way into a victimized and helpless life hole that we cannot seem to get out of, but the minute we reclaim all of our stories, we have the authority—the power—to free ourselves, one step and one word at a time. Like Harold and his purple crayon, we can sit here and forever exhaust ourselves over the many wrongs and rights of our lives, or we can write our way out of where we've been wronged. And this "write" here is where miracles take shape. Because all our traumas and stories created those cracks that Leonard Cohen spoke of, cracks that threatened to break us but that also let the light of possibility in. And these are the very same cracks that will allow our individual light *out*. The thing about recovery is it's all about light. To "recover" is to "shed light." On our patterns and stories. On what has and hasn't served us. That's the work of recovery—retracting and re-patterning, yes, and also reclaiming the light that has always been there.

Now remember, to get where we're going, we must start where we are, so first we must give our victim a voice—it is a part of us and deserves to be heard. It's gotten us this far, after all, so it's critical to give it some real, focused space to scream, cry, and share its experience of the trauma, grief, hurt, and loss. All of it. It's not just okay but necessary to really lean into the "Why did this happen *to* me?" Go to town. Squeeze out every last bit of comfort that might be left in that line of inquiry. Because that's its sole remaining value.

I've said it before, but it's so important that I'm going to bring it up again: we cannot pursue comfort and growth at the same time. We will always have moments when we need comfort, and these old victim stories provided that for a long time. They kept us feeling safe and protected—until they didn't. Even these old go-to comforts don't feel good after a while, because deep down, we feel an ache for something more. We ache to grow. That is why we're here. And these old stories have maxed out their growth support.

It's time to go where we grow, and we do that by taking back responsibility, by recognizing ourselves as authors of our lives and owning whatever version of the story we've been writing until now. This is putting a boundary around the ego and setting its limits. And from this grounded and authoritative land of *now*, we can revisit who we've allowed to pen our way through and where it's time for a rewrite. If the victim's been writing and rewriting all these years (and spoiler alert: it probably has in one area or another), then it's time to call it in, give it a hug, thank it for getting us this far, and free it. Let it know we are now ready to pass the pen on over to the victor, who can refashion our wounds into wisdom.

And then from that fully voiced, fully heard, and fully appreciated place, we can begin to invoke more of the Soul to take over our story. We can't change what happened, but we can choose how it will transform

ACCEPTANCE   AGENCY   AUTHORITY

us. We can choose what happens next. So we must allow the curious and openhearted victor to now ask *its* pressing question: "Why did this happen *for* me?" What are the opportunities and triumphs here? What can come out of this? Where can this story of ours no longer be tragic but triumphant? Where are we willing to give that holy shift, to adjust the lens of how we've come to live and breathe and move through our story? That shift is the hallmark of post-traumatic growth.

Calling Out My Victim

A few years ago, while I was neck-deep in recovery and my spiritual practice, with access to all these tools and more, my victim crept up. Let this be proof that no matter where we are and how hard or long we've done this work, the victim will still want a say. And it will still call in the ego's help, along with its full orchestra, to play our sad song of circumstance.

And my song? I was thirty-nine and single. Longing, praying, and hoping to someday be a mother and feeling the biological and societal pressure of that ticking body clock. Pressure that came by way of my own internal voice and the concerned voices of doctors, family members, and friends, all ringing the same bells: "You aren't getting any younger, Az. A spring chicken you ain't."

Yep, I was continuously reminded of my looming "expiration date," and I had to face the fact that the closer I edged toward it, the less likely it was that I'd be a mama (in the old-school, birthing-a-child-myself kind of way). The pressure kept building, and well, as I've learned through the sutras, "When the time is on you, start, and the pressure will be off." So I made a decision to "start." To do *something*. And that something was freezing my eggs.

So there I was, a thirty-nine-year-old hen pecking through what felt like a dream as I sat in the waiting area of the clinic. Ready to do this. Before I turned forty. I was pumped and excited and, well, totally full of shit. I sat there, terrified, with a clipboard piled high with forms and files and questionnaires requiring my attention.

As I made my way through the stack of paperwork, dutifully providing all the answers to every detailed and intimate question one could conceive, I turned the page to find the one that set off all my triggers and alarm bells: NAME OF SPOUSE.

Immediately I felt my stomach turn. My heart ache. *Fuck. Seriously? I don't have a spouse!* And the spiral began: *Is this really happening? Am I really sitting here alone? My God, this is not at all how I had imagined it to be!* And wouldn't you know who woke up and reared her head? You guessed it: my victim. Poor, pitied, and pitiful Az, fully accompanied by her melodramatic orchestra of melancholic violinists to add the soundtrack to what had now become a pity party.

Look at you—you're still so damaged. Yeah, right, "you've come so far"! Look around, Az...no partner by your side. You're clearly still too unworthy to be loved. Here you are, all by yourself. All alone. Poor, poor pitiful you! And you thought you'd be married by now? With children? Ha. What a joke. A spouse? Nope, no spouse for you. Children? Think again. Take a look around. You're by yourself, sitting alone in this cold clinic, ready to freeze your eggs. In the hopes of what? This cold and lonely feeling? Get used to it.

So you can see where this story is going. Me as victim. And as I was sitting there, practically drowning in this sea of self-pity, I took a deep breath and paused. I cannot say it enough:

ACCEPTANCE   AGENCY   AUTHORITY

God is in the pause.

Because then it hit me. (A God pause will do that.) Who am I listening to right now? Whose voice is shaping and coloring the meaning of this moment and experience? How much longer do I want to let her keep writing and wreaking havoc? And then, just like that, I shifted. I was, all of a sudden, consumed with gratitude. (Yep, the God pause will do that too.) Sitting alone in that cold clinic, I couldn't believe I'd made it this far. After everything I'd been through, I never in a million years would have thought I'd be alive today to even consider motherhood as a possibility.

There is a time and place for pity, regret, and all the appropriate feelings we need to experience as we move through our traumas, grief, and loss. That is part of healing. Until we wake up one morning and choose to redirect our attention from all that was missing to all that is there. Enter gratitude. Gratitude is the way back to the victor.

So right then and there, with gratitude as my editor, I reclaimed authorship and handed that authority back to my Soul—to my victor: *Wait just one sweet second, my dear Az. Can you see what's happening here? Look at how far you've come. If you had asked yourself ten years ago whether you'd feel healthy and strong enough to be here now, filling out this form, you'd have said, "No way in hell!" God bless the resources, teachings, technology, community, and support. God bless your awareness, your no longer being missing but actually attending to life and all its messy responsibilities. God bless your deep knowing that is always tethered to your greatest tool: choice. Look at you. You amaze me. I know how scared and uncomfortable you feel right now, yet you're still braving through it! You are claiming your motherhood. Bless you for taking the reins of responsibility back! Bless you for taking the steps you are fortunate enough to take in order to become the mother you will someday be. True, we don't know the details—when or how—but we take action where we can to support the whys that fuel our fire: the knowledge that you want to be a mother, that you are destined to be a mother. This step, while it feels lonely and unfamiliar, is the first of many deep connections you are forging between you and your children. Between you and the souls of your children.*

After my visit to the clinic, I went home that evening and opened up to the first page of a new journal and started a written diary to the sweet souls who are destined to choose me, telling them, "I know we haven't met yet, but this is how much I love you, how committed and devoted I am to you. That I am making sure, if needed, you have these healthy vessels to embody and experience life through." And there's the shift. There's my victory. In being able to *press pause* on that automatic victim playback, I harnessed the authority to change the channel through which I was living, breathing, and seeing my world.

We see the world we want to see. The victim lives in a limited world of scarcity, but the Soul swims in a limitless sea of abundance and possibility. The victim-to-victor transition is the brave journey of post-traumatic growth. It is the light-switch moment when how we see our world expands and we come to recognize that life is an offering and nothing is wasted. Not even the shit in a shitstorm. When we start to ask ourselves what we can do with it all, we move from pathology to possibility. When we start listening to that steady voice beneath the madness, beneath the wailing and crying victim, we move from "Why me?" to "Try me!" And at that point we can stand up and challenge life, daring it to "show me what you got" because we know what's beneath that is "show me what *I've* got!"

This is not a one-time exercise. My story has had multiple upgrades over the years. My wounds fueled my early story—understandably and appropriately—that I was an abuse victim. Then I became a survivor. And now I've moved to thriver. All these incarnations have a part in my evolution. The first one was the hardest to shed, but the experience of walking through those shifts and transformations over and over again had everything to do with my willingness to let go of each of these subsequent identity labels once they had served their purpose. And the practice of converting this "shit" into "fertilizer" fed my deep knowing that my graduation from or replacement of my earlier identities didn't negate their validity or my experience of them at the time. I just had to get honest with where I was choosing comfort over growth.

GIVE A SHIFT: MIRACLES EXIST

Our greatest tool for changing the world
rests in our capacity for changing
our minds about the world.

—*Unknown*

The late Stephen Covey said it best: "The way we see the problem is the problem." It is not our situations that cause our life's pain and disturbances; rather, it is our responses to these situations and the meaning we choose to ascribe to them that cause our suffering. All we need is the authority to shift our perspective, because a shift in perspective makes room for **miracles**.

So what is a miracle? Different teachings and philosophies put different language around this loaded word, but really it all comes down to this: a miracle is considered a wonder, a marvel, some extraordinary event or working of God, the Universe, or an unexplainable force. Sometimes a miracle manifests as a change in material or physical circumstances (such as physical healing), and other times, it is a psychological or emotional change. *A Course in Miracles*—an entire teaching about the subject—boils it down to this: a miracle is a shift in our perception. What that means is, more often than not, the miracle lies not in the situation or circumstance changing but our experience of it changing.

It really is about changing our mind. And we can choose to do that at any time. That thing we wince at, the one that haunts us, we can choose to see differently. It might take a miracle, but the wellspring of that miracle exists between our two ears.

My Sierra Tucson Miracle Moment

My first understanding of this shift in perspective—this miracle mind-set—happened in a recovery van. Just a few hours earlier, my shame, self-disgust, and I had boarded a plane. In total disappointment with myself and the mess I had made of my life, I was officially running from my life for my life, heading to an inpatient facility in Arizona. I was picked up at the airport with my baggage in tow (physical, mental, and emotional) and driven through the beautiful desert landscape to Sierra Tucson, the treatment center I would step into for the first five weeks of my recovery. We turned left onto the driveway, and as we pulled up to the property, I noticed a sign (God bless those signs) posted on the side of the gate that stated, "Expect a miracle."

Of course, at that time, I rolled my hurt and cynical eyes at the sight. *A miracle? What miracle? Fuck miracles.*

We made our way into the center where I would spend day after day "doing time." Yep, we weren't just passing time, wasting time, or making up for lost time. We were using every hour, every minute, of our time there each day to undo and redo whatever had been done. Day after day, session after session, there was crying and working, challenging, trying, and surrendering. And all the while, while doing time, I was looking around for that miracle. But nope. It wasn't sitting in my group therapy sessions or my one-on-ones. There wasn't a miracle to be found during equine therapy or EMDR, and I didn't spot one in our in-house twelve-step meetings, either. A week or two into my stay, perhaps from having exhausted my search, or perhaps from having exhausted myself with the level of work I was doing, I grew tired of looking and abandoned the hunt. I forgot about that message, about that sign, and stopped looking.

Until the day I was granted a temporary release. You see, when you commit to stay at the treatment center, you are literally meant to stay. As in no one leaves the premises, this womb of rehabilitation, until your treatment is complete and you've been discharged. For many that's twenty-eight days between being driven in through those entry gates and being driven out the exit. For me it was five weeks. Thirty-five days. *Except* for this one little exception: my stay at Sierra Tucson fell over the Jewish New Year, Rosh Hashanah. The facility offered to drive practicing Jews off the premises for a couple of chaperoned hours to the local temple for Rosh Hashanah services, and I, of course, wasted no time pulling out my "devout" Jew card to use as my get-out-of-jail-free card for the afternoon. *Hell yeah*, I figured. *Give me a little reprieve from this place, please!*

It had been a couple of intensive weeks since I'd first gazed cynically at the entrance gates' plea to "Expect a miracle," and now, three weeks before my scheduled release, I was being driven out the exit that Rosh Hashanah afternoon only to be surprised by another sign—clearly one I wasn't meant to see until my final departure but one I became privy to nonetheless:

"You are the miracle."

I felt tears well in my eyes as I laughed to myself. *Fuck. The miracle is* me? I'm *the fucking miracle!*

Along with a handful of other temple-bound patients, I got to see what the others wouldn't until the end of our stay. Talk about a spoiler alert. And yet it was anything but a spoiler! That sign and its message became one of my recovery catalysts. It offered me a much-needed miracle shift of perspective. It allowed me to access the foundation of all our painful steps through life recovery: gratitude. Gratitude for still being here, for being given another day, another try, another chance. Gratitude for being alive, even when it sucks. Even when it hurts. Gratitude for being given access to this place that is anything but a prison but rather a place to reprogram the painful life patterns that had kept me imprisoned. Gratitude for having the means and the support to access such a place.

Suddenly, it felt like the privilege it was. It felt like an honor to get access to tools every single human being would benefit from but cannot necessarily afford. It felt like a duty that fed a drive in me to do better, try harder, commit further. Not just for me but for all those who would give anything for this opportunity to heal, grow, and transform. I knew then that if I didn't stay committed to my recovery, I would feel guilty. Going back—to my abuser, to my old painful ways—was no longer an option. With that shift I knew I didn't get to fuck up this miracle. Not now.

The gratitude continued to overwhelm me. It was gratitude for my life (all of it, even the painful parts) that allowed me to not only read but to truly ingest, digest, and identify with the message "You are the miracle." Those words echo the voice of the Soul—of the victor—that reminds us of the monumental miracle of being alive (even when it hurts) and that our Spirit is truly stronger than anything it comes up against.

When Yogi Bhajan was asked about the subject, he said, "I don't only believe in miracles, I rely on them." I second this. But I'll add that our miracles also rely on *us* to see them. And more often than not, we are too busy focusing on what's gone missing to recognize all that is still here. It is our responsibility to perceive the miracles that surround us, to refocus what we are looking at and how. Our innate authority begs for a miracle mind-set, and that miracle mind begins when we are ready to give a shift.

MORE TO THE STORY

If you want a happy ending, that depends, of course,
on where you stop your story.

—*Orson Welles*

Now halfway through this Trauma to Dharma journey, we are probably experiencing some noticeable internal shifts. Practicing our agency by exercising our ability to choose and recognizing the power of our authority are likely fostering a deserved sense of empowerment and hope. But as we begin to rewrite our stories with confidence, it's important to remember both our humility and our humanity, because this place of possibility can be an easy trap for our ego.

What is important to understand at this stage is that while we have authority, we are not *the* authority. Life will continue to give us experiences that bring us back to our knees to remind us that we are not the ones steering the ship, so it's important that we keep our sensitive egos in check. They serve an important role in our healing, but if we allow them to dictate our course, we're bound for nowhere good. The ego can get us "there," wherever "there" may be, but it can't keep us there. To do that, we also need to recognize, respect, and allow for the greater forces that are at work in our lives.

SOUL PRESCRIPTION

Journal Question #1: Give Your Victim a Voice

The victim (ego) reacts from emotion, disconnected from choice. Write out your victim story through the lens of trauma that is fueled by the ego-driven question: "Why is this happening to me?" Blame, shame, and complain. Spell out the tragedy. Give it a voice; it deserves to be heard. It's gotten you this far, so let it speak, cry, and yell. Let it share the experience of the trauma, grief, hurt, and loss. Go to town.

Journal Question #2: Give Your Victor a Voice

The victor (Soul) responds from devotion, connected to choice. As we move from the victim's lair, we give a miracle mind shift and reclaim our stories. Write out your victor story. This is through the lens of dharma and is fueled by the Soul-inspired question: "Why is this happening for me?" There is wisdom in your wounds—but only if you're willing to let them heal rather than continuing to attach to them and use them as identity labels. So don't hold back. Claim it, own it, and change it. Give your victor a voice. This is where our tragedies can become triumphs when we're ready.

Pranayama: Self-Authority through the Neutral Mind

Once we claim our stories, we can change them. This pranayama enhances that steady, anchored seat of commitment within your Self by accessing the neutral mind—that meditative space of clarity where miracle shifts occur.

Posture: Sit in easy pose or in a chair with a straight spine. Bring your hands to the level of your heart center. Close your fingers over your thumbs into fists with the thumb tips at the base of your little fingers (if possible). Press your fists together at the first knuckles (from the tips of your fingers) in such a manner that the bases of your palms are together.

Eye Focus: Focus your eyes on the tip of your nose.

Breath: Inhale deeply through the nose. Exhale completely through the

ACCEPTANCE   AGENCY   AUTHORITY

mouth with pursed lips. Inhale smoothly through the mouth. Exhale through the nose. Breathe out the victim, blessing it for getting you this far, and invoke more of your Soul to claim penmanship of your story from "to me" to "for me."

Continue for three to eleven minutes.

Ra Ma Da Sa Meditation for Healing with Siri Gaitri Mantra

Once you've taken responsibility and recognized you have choice, you also recognize that you are an active participant in your own healing. This is the quintessential healing meditation. It holds within it eight sounds that stimulate the Kundalini flow within the central channel of the spine for healing. It brings balance into the core of our energetic body and floods it with the healing energy of the universe.

Posture: Sit in easy pose or in a chair with your feet planted firmly on the ground, your spine straight, and a light neck lock applied (chin pulled back slightly). The mudra (hand position) is most important. Your elbows are bent down by your sides and are tucked comfortably but firmly against your ribs. Your forearms are almost perpendicular to the floor with your hands extended out at a forty-five-degree angle from the center of your body. Most importantly, your palms are perfectly flat, facing up, hands bent back at the wrists. You should feel a pull in the lowest part of your forearm as you almost hyperextend your wrist to make the palms flat. (This tends to be the most challenging part of the meditation, so it is important not to let your hands relax out of the position.) Your fingers are kept side by side, except the thumb, which is spread from the other four fingers.

Eye Focus: Your eyes are closed.

Mantra: This mantra consists of eight basic sounds:

Ra Ma Da Sa, Sa Say So Hung

Translation:

Ra—Sun (energy)
Ma—Moon (receptivity)
Da—Earth (groundedness)
Sa—Impersonal infinity
Sa Say—Totality of infinity
So—Personal sense of merger and identity
Hung—The infinite, vibrating and real

This mantra taps into the energies of the sun, moon, earth, and Spirit to bring deep healing. It is important to pull the navel point powerfully on the first *Sa* and on **Hung.** Chant one complete cycle of the entire mantra with each breath and repeat. You can choose to mentally visualize the person or persons you want to heal as you send this energy to them for their well-being.

Continue chanting for eleven to thirty-one minutes.

To Finish: Inhale deeply, and hold the breath as you offer a healing prayer. Visualize the person you wish to heal as being totally healthy, radiant, and strong. See the person completely engulfed in a white light and completely healed. Then exhale and inhale deeply again, hold the breath, and offer the same prayer. Exhale. To complete, inhale deeply, stretch your arms up high, and vigorously shake out your hands and fingers for several seconds. Keep the arms up and hands shaking as you exhale. Repeat two more times and relax.

(I love Ra Ma Da Sa by Jai-Jagdeesh from *Miracles Abound.*)

Asana: Frog Pose

Frogs are my all-time favorite asana, and I call them a one-stop Kundalini transformer. Yogi Bhajan called Frog Pose an entire kriya within itself. Frogs activate the first, second, and third chakras and move that vital and healing Kundalini energy up to the higher centers. Frogs are a symbol of transformation, perfectly suited to aid our brave shift from victim to victor.

Posture: Stand up and place your heels together with your toes turned out. Squat down, raising your heels (ideally keeping them together), aligning your knees over your toes, and placing your fingertips on the floor in front of you. Inhale, raising your hips and straightening your legs (keep your fingertips on the ground, arms straight). Exhale and return to the squatting position.

Continue twenty-six times.

To Finish: Take a minute to lie down on your back. Allow the energy to move and calibrate.

Chapter Eight
ALLOWING

Any moment can be a spiritual moment, if allowed.
—Miranda J. Barrett

So we've come to understand that we have the ability to rewrite our stories, but there is also a bigger story unfolding in our lives—one we may not be completely privy to just yet. Through our agency and authority, we recognize our strength and realize, *Hell yeah*, we've got grit. But there cannot be grit without grace. We humans need both, and that grace is the **allowing** piece in this Trauma to Dharma puzzle. This journey of healing requires us to walk, crawl, fumble, and stumble with risk—that's where the courage, the grit, comes in. And it also offers us the chance to land with trust—which is the faith, the grace.

WHAT IS ALLOWING?

To allow is to give the necessary time or opportunity for something to happen. For the purposes of the Trauma to Dharma work, that "something" is all about Spirit and our individual versions of spirituality.

So this section of *allowing* is about letting go and trusting in something greater than ourselves.

Spirituality 101

The spiritual journey is individual, highly personal. It can't be organized or regulated.
It isn't true that everyone should follow one path.
Listen to your own truth.

—Ram Dass

It's said that religion is for people who are trying to stay out of hell, and spirituality is for those who've been there. Believe me: I've been there. And it's a safe assumption that anyone reading this book has been there too. So we are going to stay exclusively in the realm of spirituality here—that expansive terrain of God/Universe/Source/Higher Power/Love. We can call it whatever we want as long as we recognize that, if we're paying attention, all roads ultimately lead back to it.

This spirituality we are talking about doesn't require running off to an ashram or a monastery. It doesn't require a ten-day silent vipassana retreat. (But it could!) What it does require is us, the miracle of our aliveness, and the spirit of our breath, living and loving and failing and trying, every day. The spirituality we're talking about here is not just a ritual of church on Sunday or Shabbas on Friday evening but a practice infused into our day-to-day lives that helps us tap into the Spirit and life force within ourselves.

I often joke that I'm the Jew who found God on the yoga mat. Once I gave my wearied body and broken-down mind permission to fall flat onto my mat, I gave my Soul permission to rise. The moment I began connecting to my breath, I connected to my heart muscle that beats generously and completely for me. In the pause between exercises, I felt the prana—that magical life-force energy—pulsing in my hands, reminding me that I am bigger than myself and this instant in time. And through this practice, spirituality for me became the awareness that everything is connected.

That yoga mat hosted my God moment. My *Oh my God, all this time I've been looking anywhere and everywhere, and here you are!* moment. I was finally experiencing God as just that—an experience. No longer as a concept or story written centuries ago, but as a feeling I could access when I became present in and intimate with my own aliveness. That was when everything shifted inside me.

And once everything changed inside, well, everything changed outside. Suddenly, God was everywhere. At the Whole Foods checkout stand as the cashier laughed at the joke I'd cracked. Hidden in the sidewalk cracks when I took a face-plant and tore up my knee and elbow. (Apparently God is all He is "cracked" up to be...if we're paying attention.) Next thing I knew I experienced God while smiling at a passerby on the way into the doctor's office, while indulging in my afternoon peanut butter and dark chocolate habit, while reading a hurtful e-mail from a friend...and even while at temple during high holidays.

God wasn't "up there" but everywhere and in all the spaces between. Every day. In every way. And every when, and how, and why. God became practical—not that old, wise man with a beard peering down on us from His throne of clouds. That is what I believed growing up. And I believed He (I mean *He?* That should have been the first round of questioning!) would hear me more clearly when I paid visits to His sites—temples, synagogues, churches, and cathedrals—run by His advisory boards of rabbis, priests, and anyone dressed in a robe or standing at a pulpit.

But I awakened on the mat. And there's a reason they call awakenings rude. They leave us questioning where we've been all these years and how we happened to miss this. *This!* That God is so much more. That the religious prophets weren't tapping into something we couldn't touch or experience but rather they were passing the batons to us.

We're taught in religion to pray up to God, to search for and revere something outside of us. And that separation is what keeps us longing and suffering. Yet the moment we surrender within ourselves, to ourselves, the clearer we can see and feel that we, too, are a piece of God.

God's Hiding Place: A Fable from the Vedic Tradition

There's a Vedic fable that perfectly drives this home. Many centuries ago, God was overworked and overstretched (like most women are). And so She was looking for a place to hide. See, back in those days, God was receiving any and all who wanted to speak with Her. Her doors were open around the clock. And as was Her policy back then, She would listen to every prayer and every request: *Please God, let our next child be a girl! Dear God, we need rain for a fruitful harvest! God, can you please make the rain stop? God, I hate to bother you, but can you send money? Will you please heal my sick aunt? Can you take away this pain?* So you could imagine God and Her attendants had no time to rest. And on top of that, She never found time to tend to any other Godly business. She knew something had to change, and so She called a meeting with Her board of sages to discuss how to stem the constant flow of those looking to Her for all the answers to their problems.

The first sage suggested they build a palace at the highest point in the Himalayas. "No one has ever scaled Mount Everest—you will be undisturbed for eternity! And order will be restored."

God shook Her head and said, "No, I know my human beings. Their desire and determination will get them to the top of Everest. Before long, we'll need a different plan."

A second sage offered, "Let's build you a castle on the moon. Human beings will never get to the moon. There you will have peace and quiet, and the order of things will be restored."

God just sighed. "No, I know these human beings; they will find a way to the moon."

All the sages fell silent, discouraged and deflated.

"But wait. I have the answer," said God. "I'll put a small part of myself inside every person's heart. It will be the last place they'll look."

It really is the last place we look, isn't it? Rumi speaks to this when he muses, "You wander from room to room hunting for the diamond necklace that is already around your neck." The moment we recognize we are a piece of God, we experience the peace of God.

Our connection to Spirit starts inside our own beings, and it comes through the body and the breath. That's why I kept coming back to yoga. In feeling my body again—a place that was once a source of such pain and shame—I began experiencing an embodied spirituality I never had before. The Soul piece. The God in me. And this was validated by what I uncovered in my research. All of my study participants recounted and described how their spirituality deepened in the wake of their trauma. They found a stronger connection to their version of God and with that were able to find trust and faith again.

We aren't human beings having a spiritual experience but spiritual beings having a human experience. Yet the only way we can experience our spirituality is through our humanity. Spirit/God breathes and speaks through us—through our living and loving, our feeling, fearing, and faithing. So while it's tempting to get swept into the realm of the spiritual to skirt past the pain of our wounds, it is critical that we stay grounded in our bodies because, simply put, there is no loving and lighting this shit away.

Spiritual Bypass

For many of us, the spiritual path is a haven, a place where we find belonging and hope. But it can also be the place we escape to check out further. It is easy to use our spirituality (e.g., "I guess it was the will of God," "By the grace of Guru," and "It happened for a reason") as a sneaky way to avoid the raw and achingly human feelings we need to process in order to heal. This is what psychologist John Welwood refers to as the **spiritual bypass**.

In *Soulshaping*, Jeff Brown defined the spiritual bypass as "the tendency to jump to spirit prematurely, usually in an effort to avoid various aspects of earthly reality." The spiritual bypass is something we use to avoid being hurt or broken, so if we're not careful (i.e., conscious), we can use "God" the same way we use alcohol, food, shopping, work, and other distractions. Or the same way we use "healthy" guises such as over-exercising or restrictive eating. Yes, we can even use the things designed to help us to actually further remove us from our lives. And that begs this question: Is what you're doing helping you enter deeper into life or retreat further from it? The spiritual bypass leads us down a dead-end—as in "deadened"—road where we numb and deny ourselves an essential piece to our healing: feeling.

I've seen this happen many times but most clearly with the sweetest and kindest man I once knew. After the devastating betrayal of a loved one, he left everything behind save a suitcase of essentials and relocated to the mountains, hermit style. While there he dove deep into his spiritual practice, praying and meditating and perfecting his yoga practice. And he thought he had cleverly escaped feeling the pain, but once he returned to the real world, there it was waiting for him. We can't use our spirituality as a way to deny our humanness and its sticky emotions, nor as a box in which we place all of life's painful moments and triggers to pretend they don't exist. This path of healing is about awareness. It's meant to have us engage our witness of life, not take a seat in the VIP section in order to rise above the pain. There is no such thing. Remember: we don't rise above it; we get into it!

Spiritual enlightenment isn't measured by our height of detachment but by our depth of engagement. It is measured by our ability to be present in every aspect of our life. We can't observe our way to meaning; we must feel our way to it. And engaging our witness allows us to come to our senses (not deny them) while also expanding their horizon until we can feel what we need to while also recognizing that's not all there is. That these feelings will not steal us away from life unless we let them.

Our engagement with these feelings is what ensures our ability to live in union (or yoga) with all things. And our connection to Spirit isn't a way out of the pain but a way through it. It is meant to be a conscious antidote to life's pain, our built-in medicine cabinet that brings us back to that state of neutrality to consciously feel without being fooled by what we're feeling. It is a neutralizer, not a tranquilizer. But still, it's so hard for us to allow. Because to allow means to surrender control. To allow means to trust. And once we've been pained, we're gun-shy. Because we're afraid of being...what? Broken? But what if that wasn't the worst thing? Broken really just means open, and open is a threshold back to God.

Not Broken, Broken Open

> *God will break the heart again and again and again*
> *until it remains open.*
> —*Hazrat Inayat Khan*

In our efforts to protect and preserve our hearts, we keep clenching and closing. But have you noticed that the more we resist, the more the Universe gives us a reason to feel? To open? It's scary as hell, but the allowing piece of the Trauma to Dharma program is about letting that thing—that something greater—do its job. To trust that there is a bigger purpose to the pain we are so rigorously avoiding and trying to control. Whatever we control, we carry, and allowing is about taking that load off and setting it down. It's about actually letting it break us a little sometimes. Because I promise, if that's what we need, it's going to happen one way or another. Ernest Hemingway famously wrote: "The world breaks everyone and afterward many are strong in the broken places. But those that will not break it kills." Yes, what doesn't kill us breaks us, but those breaks make us stronger. And more tender.

As a preschool teacher (well before the yoga and Kundalini whites), I often had to manage frustrated parents during afterschool pickup, beside themselves about how bumped and bruised or stained and grimy their kids were at the end of the day. They'd exclaim, "He's filthy," or, "She smeared paint all over her new dress!" And amid their literal laundry lists, I'd have to remind them why their kids came to school in the first place and what our goal was. So I'd say, "The dirtier they come home, the harder they played and the more they learned and experienced." That dirt and grime and filth and slime were all proof that they'd held nothing back. That they gave it their all. The same philosophy applies here in our adult-sized sandbox. The more scars we have, the more we've lived and loved. The more breaks and wounds, the more we've held nothing back. So let us hope to be broken. Let us embrace and honor our cracks as badges of survival and gateways to growth.

Mark Nepo says, "It's not so much what breaks us but what that break opens us to." If we're willing to stay with it. Our greatest mistake as human beings is that when life throws us down on our knees, we are so quick to pick ourselves back up. When the world pushes us to our knees, Rumi says, we're in the perfect position to pray. So often what we actually need in those heavy moments is to stay in that state of surrender long enough to recognize that if we're in this much pain and suffering, then we have somehow convinced ourselves that we are the ones in control. And if we are indeed in charge of it all, then we must bear the burden of it all. It is in these moments, from this humble stance, that we are in the perfect place to ask for help and to open ourselves up to whatever opportunities and lessons the Universe has in store for us. Because make no mistake—there *will* be lessons.

SOUL'S CURRICULUM

What if everything that shows up in our paths is a perfectly designed message? A gift or a lesson from the Universe, tapping on our hearts to reopen and come home? An invitation for evolution and expansion? What if our challenges always unfold a deeper lesson? I had a conversation once with my teacher, Guru Singh, that went something like this:

Az: Ugh, another disappointment! If the world is my reflection, then am I just one effed-up, disappointingly challenged mess of a human being?

Guru Singh: No. Remember, it's not that the world reflects who *you are; it reflects* what *you must pass through to be* who *you are.*

He explained to me that our Soul wanted to be here, chose to be here—in this schoolhouse called planet Earth—because it knew there were lessons it needed to learn. Each of our masochistic little Souls has its own curriculum, designed specifically for our personal expansion, and no two are the same. These lessons are often hidden in setbacks, detours, and heartbreaks—in the very things that bring us to our knees in fear, desperation, and surrender—but here's where the perspective shift we tackled in the authority section can create miracles. So much of allowing happens when, instead of asking, "Why is this happening *to* me?" we start asking, "Why is this happening *for* me?" That reframe opens us to curiosity and possibility to look for the lessons the Universe provides in abundance.

If we look at the patterns of our suffering, at the areas in which we consistently struggle, we can start to see with clarity what lessons our Soul wants to experience. What it came here to learn. With this perspective, we can cultivate a new relationship to life as that of a student and seeker. No matter how much wisdom we acquire, we can still employ that open, curious mind. We can let go of our plans and expectations about why we are here and how life is supposed to look and instead open ourselves up to the reality of how and what it actually is. This is critical because how often does reality line up with our plans?

Your Plans vs. Universe's Plans

What do they always say? *You wanna make God laugh, tell Him your plans*? I present to you Exhibit A:

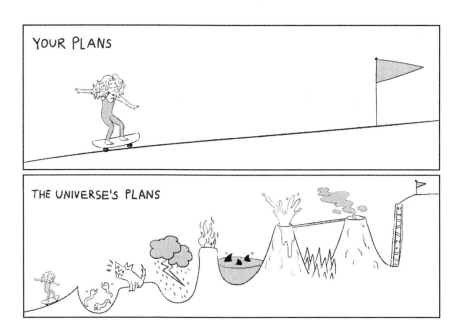

Most of us have some idea of where we want to go, how we're

going to get there, and what it's going to look like along the way. And in our mind, of course, it's smooth sailing—a clear path and sunny skies. Figure #1, if you will. And then there's what the Universe has planned for us, as illustrated by Figure #2. There are ditches and bumps in the road, mountains to climb, and moats to swim. It doesn't look pretty—in fact, it can be downright painful at times. But actually it's pretty perfect, as in perfectly designed for us. And when we recognize that our life is designed to help us grow, the path can actually feel smooth, like Figure #1, even when it looks as crazy as Figure #2—especially with the help of a spiritual somatic practice like Kundalini yoga to help our efforts feel effortless.

One of the easiest traps to fall into is comparing our personalized path to the ones of those traveling around us. Everyone's maps look different because we're all given an individualized curriculum, and it's common to perceive others' maps as easier or better in some way—or every way. This can throw us into compare and despair if we let it, or it can instead be an opportunity to recognize and embrace planet Earth as the one-room schoolhouse it is with all grades, ages, and stages crammed together with very different lessons to learn.

Hazarat Inayat Khan said, "The soul is covered by a thousand veils." Those veils are our assumptions, preconceptions, expectations, and ideas about how things are supposed to unfold. It is on us to peel them away, layer by layer, through meditation, conscious breathing, yoga, and the many tools at our disposal. The more we peel away that static and noise, the more we can trust that just maybe, if we show up, do our part, and surrender the rest, grace will meet us where we are.

The Universe Has Your Back

But that's scary, right? Because we want a guarantee bigger than the simple fact that, despite everything, we've made it this far so there must be something greater than us. So for those who wouldn't mind a little more reassurance, here's the breakdown of just how and why the Universe has your back:

1. The Universe is always conspiring in your favor.

In addition to unexpected gifts and grace, these favors include obstacles, lessons, and tests. These unplanned challenges are our personalized growth accelerators. Change, and the challenges that come with change, are the true currency of growth, and growth is painful. But the pain that comes with being stretched to new horizons can also be a stimulant, if we let it.

2. The Universe doesn't abandon you; *you* abandon you.

There's a deeper, greater wisdom always here to support, guide, and protect us. It is ever present, so if we're feeling abandoned, it's because we have abandoned ourselves. The moments when the rug is pulled from under our feet or the wool is pulled off our eyes and we think the Universe has abandoned us are actually precisely the moments when it is trying to get our attention. Awareness is giving our life our attention by being here and now. But the majority of us direct our attention to what was or what might be rather than being here now. Life can't greet us if we aren't home, and home is *now*.

3. We're constantly being guided and protected.

The signs to direct and support us along our way are everywhere. If we're not seeing them, it's because we're not paying attention. There are times these signs feel good—which is *great*—and more often they are just the message we need but have been refusing to hear. Like my dad at the airport with his Puppy Love sign. That's the perfect example of the Universe speaking to me. I needed a literal sign to get me present enough to hear the message, but signs are everywhere. The Universe never stops talking to us. We've just conveniently stepped away from the conversation. That's why we turn in to tune in, because that wisdom is always there for the taking.

IF YOU ARE
WAITING
FOR A SIGN,
THIS IS IT.

4. The Universe is generous. And hella funny.

The Universe will always give us what we need in abundance. It just may not look how we imagined because the Universe has a sick sense of humor. (I often imagine my spirit guides sitting with a bucket of popcorn, having a giggle at my expense: "Oh, look at her, getting all dressed up for her pity party. Wait till she sees what's just around the corner.") And because of its generous nature, the Universe will keep giving us opportunities to get things right. So many opportunities, in fact, that you may feel like you accidentally ordered up a dozen versions of the same situation. *(This again? Anyone ever felt like that before?)* That's how it works. These things are thrown down until we get them right, creating a growth process I refer to as the **spiral staircase**.

Falling Down and Failing Upward

We've all felt and lamented it—that moment when we wind up in what appears to be the *same* relationship, the *same* fight, the *same* circumstance, the *same* mess...and we find ourselves asking, "Why and how is this happening to me *again*? Haven't I figured this out already?" Nothing goes away until it teaches us what we need to learn. The Universe will continue to give us what we need until we finally get it, until we have undone the parts that need undoing and healed the parts that still need healing.

For those who aren't paying attention, that repetitious spin of again and again will leave us feeling like we're exactly where we've always been with no movement or progress. But this is where we can call upon our awareness to see the truth of the experience. Yes, life is knocking, kicking, pushing, and poking, but it's important to look at where it might be kicking us *up* the spiral staircase of our life lessons. Up another step, another rung, another floor. We beat ourselves up, thinking we've once again landed in the same situation we always find ourselves in, but it's critical to examine where it might be different. Or how might *we* be different? Where have we perhaps grown in the way we are responding to it? Where is our recovery time quicker? Where can we give ourselves a little credit in how we are handling it or how it's triggering us less (or differently)?

It can feel like a great cosmic joke. But with a different perspective, these landmarks that we keep coming back to—each time from a higher step or vantage point—serve as a better point of reference for our own growth and progress than almost any new situation we might encounter. In mythology, stairs frequently symbolize a breakthrough to a higher level of consciousness, and in our steady climb up the staircase of our being, we will come face-to-face with the same old demons. But as we ascend, we get to do so with greater awareness, clearer eyes, wiser ways, and more effective tools. We can learn how to navigate through them in a healthy, conscious, and responsible way, healing with every step.

I'll give you a personal example. My first effed-up relationship—you know, the one that jump-started this dharma business—well, it took me six years to figure out that it wasn't working for me. Six years! And then there was the next guy, and the guy after him, who were by no means abusive but still totally unavailable. Coming out of that initial relationship with no sensitivity, respect, love, or trust, it only makes sense that I stepped out of the gate right where I left off—wiser and more equipped but still attracting exactly what I needed in order to learn, grow, and replace old patterns. And so I dated many different versions of ghosts from boyfriends past, and whether they lasted two years or six months or three dates, each of them kept offering me the same dynamic and, hence, the same lesson. I was habitually choosing emotionally unavailable men whose treatment was not as monstrous and extreme but who demonstrated subtle and insidious behaviors that still corroborated my beliefs that men are unavailable, that I am unworthy of respect and love, and that I will always wind up being disappointed and let down.

But the important thing to note is that in each round, my time spent was less. My learning and recovery were still painful, but they were also faster. And at the end of the day, the big lesson with each of these players in my patterned life was that I was continuing to choose unavailable men because *I* was the one who was afraid to commit. Choosing these partners saved me the trouble of having to stretch myself into the terrifying territory of true intimacy. And if it weren't for these steps along the staircase of my learning and growth, I never would've gotten to this challengingly vulnerable place of true commitment with my husband.

Life loves to give us situations to show us what we haven't fully healed. If we can think of these as additional opportunities to let go of toxic patterns that we are still subconsciously carrying, we will be way ahead of the game. Because we fall down, but we fail upward. The spiral staircase of growth and learning comes down to this: embrace it or reface it. What is not owned and integrated is repeated, and it will continue to recur until we get it right.

FAITH AND TRUST

Facing the patterns that are no longer serving us is scary stuff. We don't want to let go of these ingrained ways because, as far as we're concerned, they've kept us safe. Perhaps they were a necessity at one time, a way to survive and cope. But they are no longer working; this is where we must fall into the faith that we're ready for a new, updated, or upgraded way.

    With authority, we learned to trust ourselves once again. With allowing, we humbly recognize the spirited piece that has our back and knows more than we do. Allowing is really about our version of faith and getting comfortable with not knowing what that thing is or how it works. Paul Tillich spoke of this. The opposite of faith isn't doubt; it's certainty. So it's time to get comfortable with doubt. The moment we stop resisting life's waves and surrender, we uncover the current that carries us through it all. *That's* the faith piece. So much of our pain results from relying solely on our own strength, as if we are the ones in control. And therein lies the struggle. We are so afraid to let go, yet *sometimes we need to let go to hold on.* Faith, then, is learning to swim in the sea of life's ambiguity.

Living the Questions

> *Don't search for the answers, which could not be given*
> *to you now, because you would not be able to live them.*
> *And the point is to live everything. Live the questions*
> *now. Perhaps then, someday far in the future,*
> *you will gradually, without even noticing it,*
> *live your way into the answer.*
> —*Rainer Maria Rilke*

I cannot tell you how often I turn to this quote. When Rilke implores us to "live the questions now," he is inviting us to reshape our relationship to the unknown. He is giving us permission to give our weary heads a rest. Our minds will do anything to try to bypass the pain and discomfort that come from wrestling with the unknown. And so we sabotage living and loving the questions by trying to control the search, by working to unearth premature answers that will reveal themselves only when we are ready to receive them.

The key to living the questions is softening our grip on needing to know or control the answers and instead embracing the mystery of life. It's funny; I was using my iPhone to take notes a while ago after another heartbreak where I was convinced he was "the one" and now had to get myself back out there. I was typing away, spilling and spewing my way through that miserable moment of not knowing, that terrifying time of doubt. And as I continued to type out my mind chatter of worries, the moment I typed out the word *misery*, God bless iPhone's autocorrect, it changed the word *misery* to *mystery*.

Talk about signs. Talk about the sneaky ways the Universe will speak to us. It really allowed me that pause to regroup, reframe, and reconsider. It allowed me a moment of reprieve from the head—where misery lives (a by-product of the fear-fueled stories that consume us)—and back into the heart. That's where mystery lives. Misery is all head; mystery is all heart. My iPhone's autocorrect gave me the greatest gift during that time of transition: it allowed me to see where our experience of misery is just mystery having a panic attack!

Wordsworth said, "The mystery of life isn't a problem to be solved but a reality to experience." Easier said than done when we've got brains hardwired to solve problems. (And of course, when there aren't any problems to solve, they will happily conjure something up!) But now we are being called to abort the head trip called misery and instead bring a little more heart to mind. Because the heart is a romantic, it loves mystery. And the heart is faithful; it trusts what the mystery has in store. It transforms that ego-driven head trip of misery into its very own

"Magical Mystery Tour," where we surrender our need for immediate answers and flirt with the possibilities. Where we live and love the questions until the answers trust *us* enough to reveal themselves. That's right—part of the mystery is learning to trust that the answers will reach us when we're ready for them. Because the truth is, if we're not ready, we won't recognize them anyway.

Ready or Not

The process of writing this book offers a perfect example of this. For years—decades, really, of research and preliminary writing—I knew the Trauma to Dharma program had to be turned into a book, but I didn't know how it would get there, or when, or *who* would help it get first into book form and then out into the world. I grappled with all these unanswered questions and worries, but they didn't keep me from writing and editing and bringing to life what I could, because I knew quite simply that this book couldn't be completed until *it* was ready. So I lived in the questions as I quietly—and sometimes not so quietly—did my work.

And then, one day, I received the answer (well, one answer) in the form of an editor. Except she wasn't one yet. Monica was a yoga student, client, and friend I had known for more than a year. I knew she was a writer in her own right and that her voice resonated with me, but she didn't become "the answer" to my book question until I was ready to see and receive it. I finally hit a dead end with the project, having gone as far as I could on my own, and we had one conversation that turned into a meeting that turned into a work session that turned into a two-year process of sculpting and honing all the work I had done before Monica showed up into the book you are holding in your hand right now.

The answers don't always just show up and we see them. Sometimes they do. Sometimes we need to refine the questions we're asking. And sometimes these things simply aren't the answers we need until we're ready for them. Which brings us to the wisdom of "not today's problem." When we really, truly need an answer, it will be aligned for us to receive it, so our job is to just keep doing the work before us, trusting that we will be given what we need when we need it. And trusting that if we don't have an answer, it means we don't need one yet.

But there's one more piece to this. We also have to be honest with ourselves about where the answers we so desperately need might be ripe and ready, right smack in front of our faces, though we're refusing to see them. The same way we can't force an answer if it ain't ready, we also can't deny an answer simply because it's not the answer we're hoping for or envisioning.

There's a famous parable about a man trapped in his house during a flood. He began praying for God to rescue him and had a vision in his head of God's hand reaching down from heaven and lifting him to safety. As the water started to rise in his house, the man's neighbor urged him to leave and offered him a ride to safety, but the man yelled back, "I am waiting for God to save me!" so the neighbor drove off in his truck.

The man continued to pray and hold on to his vision, and as the water rose, he had to climb up to the roof of his house. A boat came by with some people heading for safe ground. They yelled at the man to join them, but he said he was waiting for God to save him, so they moved on.

The man continued to pray, believing with all his heart that he would be saved by God. The waters continued to rise, and a helicopter flew by, lowering a ladder to take him off the roof. The man waved the helicopter away, shouting back that God would save him. The helicopter left, and the water came over the roof and swept the man away, and he drowned.

When he reached heaven, God greeted the man, and the man asked, "God, why did you not save me? I believed in you with all my heart. Why did you let me drown?" God replied, "I sent you a truck, a boat, and a helicopter, and you refused all of them. What else could I possibly have done for you?"

Letting go of the timing of these answers and our ideas of what they're supposed to look like is a big part of our work. When we can get out of our heads and instead come back to what these things are meant to *feel like* in our hearts, we will be able to see them much more clearly for what they truly are.

When the Answer Is Right in Front of Your Nose

In the summer of 2015, I was preparing to make my annual trek to our Kundalini Summer Solstice Sadhana retreat up at Guru Ram Das Puri in New Mexico, where a sea of two to three thousand Kundalini yogis gather to meditate, chant, practice yoga, and commune under the stars. For many—myself included—the main draw of this retreat is the three days of White Tantric Yoga. This has nothing do with sex or Sting or the kind of tantric you may be imagining; rather, it is a beautiful yet wildly uncomfortable practice of sitting across from a meditation partner and staring into his or her eyes for eight hours a day while doing meditations that can include chanting and poses.

This was the first summer in years that I didn't have my trusty tantric partner, Lisa, with me. (Remember that flight home from JFK and the awful fight we had? Yeah, that happened just before this retreat, and well, Lisa was still ice-cold and thawing.) So here I was, en route and partnerless; I surrendered, allowing my Kundalini tribe to find me someone.

Enter Ricardo.

We met just minutes before three full eight-hour days of meditating and staring into each other's eyes, and upon introduction, I thought...nothing. Sweet guy, sure. Great sense of humor. But not *my* guy. We had a natural chemistry, and I felt a comfort and ease in his presence—which was noteworthy, considering at times we had our arms up for sixty-two minutes straight! But no, I was confident that this definitely wasn't my guy.

And that's the cosmic joke of jokes. God placed the man I had been praying for directly in front of my eyes, and I still refused to see him! And let's be clear: I saw him, but I refused to *see* him because it terrified me. His adoring attention and available presence felt foreign to me. His respectful gaze and thoughtful gestures were a shock to my system because I wasn't used to them. I wondered why the hell he was so kind to me and assumed there must be something wrong with him. I refused to see what I was praying for because I had come face-to-face with another old, stale belief: that I wasn't deserving of it. Oftentimes the thing we are longing and hunting for the most terrifies us when it shows up. But if we're living in awareness, we're able to see beyond the fear to recognize what's there. We're able to lean into the discomfort and trust what's been delivered to us. Ricardo proposed exactly a year after our destined meeting. We got married three months later.

The answers to our prayers show up when we are ready and

present, but our readiness and presence require work. That's our recovery, our commitment to growth. It takes a lot to stand still at the center of our life. I didn't meet my husband online or at one of the many parties I rolled my eyes about but still attended, yet all those steps readied me for meeting him and for recognizing him (with a little help) when I did. So living the questions is about learning to have a loving courtship with the unknown. It is letting go of our need to wrestle with it and instead patiently resting within it. It is trusting that, despite our discomfort, we will be held through our fear and uncertainty. And it is surrendering to what the Universe gifts us when we do.

Surrender and Attraction

So much of allowing is about letting go of our need to control how and when "it" will all turn out. It is true surrender. And true surrender or allowing is not about becoming a complacent lazy-ass, but it's also not about handing a shopping list to God filled with specifics about exactly what we want and when we want it with the expectation that God will fulfill all our desires. The Law of Attraction implies that we know what's best for us and that God and the Universe don't...which is a lot of ego in action. But what if the point isn't actually to get what our ego wants but to allow the Universe to give our Soul what it needs? Because it, with all its infinite wisdom, can do it far better than we ever could with our limited human minds.

This doesn't mean we can't get what we want in life. We just need to shift our source of desire. Ultimately, we want to be manifesting from the Soul, not the ego. And it's easy to tell when we're doing this because manifesting from the ego feels like an effortful forcing of something that just isn't fitting, while manifesting from the Soul is still work but an effortless kind where serendipities and synchronicities abound. The ego knows what it wants, but the Soul knows what it needs—which is to thrive and live out its dharma. Remember, the ego comes from the head while the Soul comes from the heart, so the key is to let our core desire be a feeling. Because underneath it all, that's really what we are seeking—to feel a certain way.

What *The Secret* misses in teaching us the power of manifestation is yes, we ask, believe, and receive, but we also need to *feel* it. What is it going to feel like to receive what we've been praying for? When we do all the vision-board exercises, the power doesn't exist so much in the images we're pinning up but in the feeling and vibration those images ignite in us. Our emotional vibrations are transmitted into the universe, and that vibration is what creates attraction. And while that may sound like metaphysical nonsense, there's legitimate science behind it. In his book *Power vs. Force*, Dr. David R. Hawkins explains how different human emotions calibrate at different vibrational levels. Emotions such as shame, guilt, and fear rest at the bottom of the vibrational scale, while emotions such as peace, love, and joy sit at the top. So that person you meet who's got that "good vibe"? She's vibing high on gratitude or love.

Since the cosmos is also made up of vibrations and can be changed just by our attention, the vibration of our thoughts and emotions has the power to affect and attract. You've heard the saying "like attracts like," right? The world we create or attract is the one that most closely aligns with our vibration of thinking and feeling. So having a higher vibration increases our manifesting power. Because gratitude and joy/happiness (the results of gratitude) are emotional vibrations that make it easier for us to attract what we want.

So yes, we can ask for "it," believe in "it," and be open to receiving "it." But also—most importantly—we must get clear in our bodies about what we want to feel when "it" is delivered. And it's not a bad idea to surround ourselves with people, things, and activities that make us feel good or vibe high. When we do that, we can let the Universe take care of the details because, per the Rolling Stones, "You can't always get what you want." I used to hate that song because of its bitter truth, but that's also the allowing in action. It's trusting that while we don't always get exactly what we want, the Universe will more often than not deliver what we need. That answer we've been seeking may not look at all like we had imagined, but we can trust that it is designed for our highest good—which is really just code for our highest growth.

The Perfect Amount of Soon

I'm a sucker for spiritual modalities. Be it a healer, intuitive, guide, or medium, you name it and I'm in. So when a dear friend gifted me an angel-reading session a few years ago, I was game—just as long as I could bring my inner skeptic along with me. (I am also a scientist, after all.)

For the uninitiated, this spiritual angel-reading medium essentially meets with you, asks to be invited into your space, and then proceeds to check in with your angels or spirit guides. While I've always felt a deep connection to the Universe and a supportive presence of guides cheering me on, I am also always curious to learn more, so with an open invitation, the medium stepped into the cosmic threshold of my world, and the session began.

My spirit guides quickly began to advise her that in order to deeply connect to them in the future, it would be helpful for me to light three separate candles. Easy enough. And then, after a slight pause, in which she was clearly interpreting another message from my guides, the medium said, "Huh, this is clearly specific to you. They are also asking you to offer up a feather."

A feather? That got my attention. I love everything feathers. But still I kept my skeptic close. We carried on to learn that my spirit guides were quite happy with me, calling me responsible and downright fun to be with. I smiled to myself. *Well, I'm glad* someone's *having a fun time in my growth and evolution...*

Having squared away all introductions, it was time to get to business. "So what's the one burning question you are wanting to ask your guides?" I cracked a nervous smile and mustered the nerve to ask the question that had burned its way through quite a number of almost-but-not-quite relationships. I felt my face redden, embarrassed by my willingness to vulnerably lay it on the line, and I said, "I have spent quite some time readying myself for my husband and the father of my children, and well...what I want to know...what I am burning to know... is whether he's, like, stuck under some heavy piece of furniture or if he is truly on his way to me."

I had barely gotten all my words out when, eyes closed, she started nodding and interrupting me with a "Yes, yes, he is on his way." She went on to assure me that my spirit guides insisted I place no energy worrying or concerning myself about this.

Now while that may have been enough of an answer for some, I was not about to leave it at that. She asked if I felt complete with that response, and I most certainly did not. I felt the urgent fire of impatience burn out another question: "So they say he's on his way, but do you mind asking them *when*?"

She looked at me and smiled a wide, empathic smile. "Of course. Oftentimes your guides will offer up greater detail. Let me ask."

So there I sat, watching and waiting as she asked and listened. I was eager to hear something finite and tangible I could wrap my doubting and fear-filled arms around, waiting for something certain—a day or month—to hold on to. She looked smug and amused as she prepared to gift me with my spirit guides' answer to my lifelong burning question. *Come on now! When will he arrive?*

Their answer? "In the perfect amount of soon."

I stopped. *The perfect amount of soon.* There was something about that response that softened my impatiently fearful grip on the need for certainty. There was something about that response that humbled me into a state of grace. I realized my spirit guides weren't Google. They couldn't (or wouldn't) tell me exactly where, when, and how to get what I want. And furthermore, who am I to speed up God's plan? Who am I to question the grander intelligence that weaves this story together? And so I let go.

When the session was over, I left with my thoughts of feathers and husbands and perfect amounts of soon in tow. And as always, I immediately called my best friend to relay the news. While chatting with her on my afternoon walk with Bailey, I filled her in on every detail. Or should I say, my skeptic did. "Yeah, yeah, she mentioned him getting here in the perfect amount of soon. Yeah, right. And she insisted I offer my spirit guides a feather on my altar. Okay, lady."

But just then, as I continued walking and doubting and disputing everything I'd heard, I looked down, *and there it was.* One of the largest feathers I'd ever seen, just lying there in the middle of the sidewalk.

Okay. Got it. Heard you loud and clear.

I let go of the skeptic and picked up the feather, which found a home on the altar in my bedroom...that I now share with my husband.

Slow Your Roll and Let the Universe Play Its Role

Do you ever feel like we're stuck on a crazy train of go, go, go to get, get, get? Waking up with an irrational urgency to catch up to a day that hasn't even started yet? It's like we're racing around in our very own emergency vehicles, traveling through delusional war zones in our heads. But where are we rushing to? What are we racing for? When did everything in our lives become so *urgent?*

I was meeting with an acquaintance recently, and as he walked up to greet me, his face was buried in his phone. Without even looking up, he apologized but said he just needed to finish an "urgent text." I caught a glimpse of his screen as he typed away, and you know what this urgent response was? A smile emoji.

When he finally stopped to talk, I asked him how he was doing, and he answered, "Ah, man, I'm getting by." Getting by? What does that even mean? If we're talking definitions, it means surviving and making ends meet. And I thought, *Well, yeah, if sending that text felt like life or death, then I can only imagine what happens when life really sucker punches you.*

And make no mistake: I'm guilty of this too. We all are. And that's not to minimize the significance of our contributions to this world or the importance of that insistent and persistent something inside that wants us to be and have all that we desire and deserve. But when that urgency turns into depleting haste, we start to miss the point. Where exactly are we rushing? What are we constantly trying to catch up to?

I started to think about why I do this—why and where I'm trying to catch up to some crazy ticking clock that makes me feel late to my own life—and as the fates would have it, I came across an old journal from my college days. In it I found predictions from my nineteen-year-old self, including one that I'd be married with four kids by twenty-four or twenty-five. Ha! No wonder I always feel like I'm catching up! I have this old, uninformed impression from my past hiding out and wreaking havoc on the present. Most of us probably have some version of this, so of course we feel this urgency. No wonder we feel like we're just getting by. But when we catch ourselves singing that "getting by" tune, it's time to start getting *real*. Yes, there is work to be done, and there are purposes to be lived, but what good is life if we're too busy managing it to experience it?

I was contemplating all this on a walk with Bailey before he passed. He was older, walking slowly with his arthritic hips, and sniffing all the fresh grass and, yes, even the shit. My unconscious undercurrent of impatience ticking away, I started rushing him. But then I caught myself. I stopped and took a breath, and when I looked up I noticed a new sign that had been put up in our neighborhood:

EXPECT DELAYS, WORK AHEAD.

We all know how much I love a sign. And what I came to realize in that moment is these delays in our life are not denials; they are simply the Universe's way of saying, "Slow your roll. I've got this." There is work to be done. Take a moment to pause and breathe. We have to be here in order to get there. And while things may not be happening on our time, I promise you they will be right *on* time. This is where we must stop *trying* harder and instead start *trusting* harder. While we play a co-creative part in our life's plan, we must also have faith in its greater unfolding. We have to trust and allow the deeper wisdom that is working with us and for us. And the best way to tap into that is by pressing pause.

God Is in the Pause

In the work I do I am often asked, "But where is God?" He can't possibly be in this excruciating pain, or that senseless violent act, or those heartless crimes. And I get it. As an abuse survivor, for years I was haunted by the same doubt-fueled question. I was screaming and searching for God, Universe, Spirit, for any semblance of peace. And it took my having to fall to pieces to uncover where peace was. After hearing the life-changing voice proclaim on my yoga mat, "When you feel there is something missing in your life, it's probably you," I had to redirect my search inward. Connecting to my breath, getting still and silent, and taking the time to really pause reconnected me to that essential part of myself that *is* God.

Often it's in our most desperate and despairing moments that we finally give ourselves permission to experience God. And the moment we recognize we are a piece of God, we can experience the peace of God. So when I get asked, "Where is God in all this?" my answer is God is everywhere and in all of it, especially when it hurts. We just need to pause to experience it.

In Hebrew, the words for *God* and *breath* are the same. God becomes accessible to us from the flash of grace we are granted when we take a *pause* to take a *breath*.

Catch your breath > pause > flash of grace > God

God is in the pause, and we can use our breath to experience the flash of grace that visits us in the God pause. This is not always easy, but that's why it's called a practice. It's commonly said within the recovery community that for every year we stay committed to recovering, we are granted another second of pause between any given thought, feeling, or occurrence and our response to it. That pause is all God, and if that's not incentive to keep at it, I don't know what is.

Woe Is Me

I like to call myself a recovering intensity addict. A drama junkie. A younger version of me loved wallowing in my pain so much that I would create anything I could to get back there. And even with all my growth and recovery, I'm not immune from falling prey to that old pattern from time to time. Because even though it makes me miserable, that misery sometimes still masquerades as safety, as the only thing in my life that will corroborate my sad stories. And remember, we'd rather be right (sad as shit but still right) than happy. I'll give you an example.

A while back I was invited to a book launch. On a weeknight. Allllll the way in Hollywood. After a full day of clients, the last place I wanted to be was sitting in a fancy hotel with a bunch of people who were surely cooler than me. And did I mention it was all the way in Hollywood? But despite my resistance, I got a case of the shoulds: *You should go, Az. You've been home all week. You've got to make more of an effort to get out there. You might meet someone there. You're not gonna find your partner sitting at home in your sweats, hair in a bun, watching episodes of Oprah's* Super Soul Sunday...

Ugh. I knew that bitch was right. Discouraged but determined, I got myself all dressed up, drove through rush-hour traffic and into the valet, walked into the swanky lobby lounge, and asked to be directed to the launch party. After receiving an "I don't know what event you're talking about, ma'am" response from the bellman and the concierge, I discovered I had screwed up the dates. The book launch was the following month.

So there I was, dolled up in the W Hotel in Hollywood, all by myself. I began scrolling down my list of favorites on my phone, wondering who I could call to come meet me. Who'd be up for joining? I reached out to two different friends with no response and then looked at the rest of my list. Everyone was at home with their spouses or partners; their kids and families; and their happy and perfect, cozied-up-together lives. And here I was. *All by myself.*

Are we cueing Celine Dion yet? Because this is right about the time the violinists enter, cued up to one of my favorite go-to playlists titled Pity Party from my life soundtrack: *Woe Is Me*. This is my go-to reaction.

I shamefully walked back to the valet and got into my car after a sympathetic, "Awww, you're leaving already?" But I didn't drive off until I had scrolled through my music and picked out the saddest, most melodramatic shoot-me-now song I could find and proceeded to blast it. I mean, hi, intensity addict. Hi, drama junkie.

Yet as I began going to my habitual comfort zone of a pity party that sings out the lyrics to my old done-me-wrong song, I paused the music and just noticed...*What are you doing, Az? Why do you keep replaying this same telenovela of your life? You just got yourself a free night—what do you want to do with it?*

Yep, while driving down that shady alley, having accepted that pity party invitation, I literally hit pause. And God is in the pause. I knew in that moment I had a choice, and while I didn't deny the part of me that was genuinely disappointed and lonely (i.e., that triggered junior high girl who was convinced she was all alone with no friends), I didn't allow her to sabotage my night either. In that moment of grace, I decided that whatever happened, I'd be okay. Hell, I'd be more than okay. And spoiler alert: I was.

PRAYER

> *Grace meets us where we are*
> *but never leaves us where it found us.*
> —*Mark Nepo*

We can't talk about spirituality and allowing Spirit to have its way without diving into prayer. Prayer is the start of the most meaningful and sacred conversation we will ever have. It's also one of the greatest things to do once we've learned to pause. The whole point of the God pause is to build in a window for prayer (which is simply talking to God) and meditation (which is when God talks back). Prayer is surrendering our own plans and ideas and instead welcoming a deeper wisdom from within...and without. It's where we engage in talking, asking, confessing, and expressing ourselves to the Infinite.

Yogi Bhajan often said there is no power in the human but the power of prayer. But it can be hard to envision and embrace prayer as empowering, because falling into prayer requires acknowledging the pain and fear associated with the challenges we're facing. It involves admitting to not having all the answers and, in fact, needing help. And it's painful to admit we're scared and don't know where to go from here. But the moment we surrender to prayer, we give ourselves permission to let go of the pieces of our lives we cannot control. The ego (a.k.a. our control freak) sees this as a sign of weakness, as giving up, when actually it's truly a giving in—to faith. And there is nothing stronger than faith.

Prayer comes from the Soul. Yogi Bhajan said we must align our mind, body, and Soul in yoga—in union—to come to a place of stillness and clarity, because prayer is not delivered from the mind, where there is a circus of thoughts and ideas trying to influence our direction. When prayer comes from the chaos of the mind, we end up hearing the warning: "Be careful what you wish for! It may just come true!" So instead we must tap into our Soul to speak from that space of grace. And if we wonder what exactly we are supposed to do with it, *A Course in Miracles* offers this simple and profound directive: "God, where would you have me go? What would you have me do? What would you have me say and to whom?"

And that's not to say we can't also pray for the things we want, just as long as we understand that the answers don't always come quickly and aren't always what we want them to be. It's said that God answers our prayers in three ways:

1. Yes.
2. Not yet.
3. No, I have something better in mind.

That first one we all understand. The second—well...sometimes our prayers take time to reach us. (Sometimes they take the perfect amount of soon.) Saying a prayer is like baking a cake—they take time to cook. All we can do is our due diligence—preheat the oven, mix the ingredients, and pour it into our nonstick pan. But once we've placed that sucker in the oven, we've got to give it time to bake. If we impatiently open the oven door to see if it's ready, it never gets a chance to bake. Every time we do that, we prolong its completion; the more we try to force it, the longer it takes. This is where letting go and letting God comes in. We need to do our part and then let the Universe do the rest, trusting that our prayers take time to reach us.

And what about when they don't reach us? In other words, number three. Ahh, number three...which can be so heartbreaking and frustrating at times. Still, that one is my favorite. So many times number three has saved my sorry ass. As they say, life's rejection is God's protection. Or redirection to something so much better than we could've imagined for ourselves. So often when we look back on things that didn't go our way, we can see that our unanswered prayers actually were exactly the answer we needed.

Prayer is the epitome of allowing, and the great truth is that prayer is less about who we are praying to, or what for, and more about the act of humbling ourselves. Dutch philosopher Søren Kierkegaard said, "The function of prayer is not to influence God, but rather to change the nature of the one who prays." The intention of prayer isn't to change *things* but to change *us*. To soften us and unclench our stronghold on all we think we can control. Our ego's attachment to control creates blocks, and prayer creates openings. In us and around us. And God loves open spaces. The Universe sees a vacuum and moves to fill it with joy and peace and all the things our Soul desires. So yes, we can pray for a miracle, but let's not discredit that the miracle *is* the prayer. It brings us to the clear channel that allows us to tune into our knowing within the unknown. This is what the Aquarian sutra "vibrate the cosmos, and the cosmos will clear the path" is talking about. That vibration begins with us and with our simple, intention-fueled prayer.

Pillars of Prayer

We can pray in so many ways – there are endless texts and teachings that will outline how. But at the end of the day, life is complicated as it is, your prayers don't have to be.

These are the two pillars of prayer that I lean on:

1. Surrender

Most people don't pray until they're in crisis and this is it. Our SOS moment. Life can be a shit show. Can we admit that we can't do it by ourselves and need help? Can we acknowledge that we're fallible, flawed, and in charge of so little? And can we humble ourselves to accept aid from whatever human or divine source might offer it? Can we humble ourselves and simply ask, "Dear God, please guide me to my next right step"?

2. Gratitude

And yet prayer is more than just a cry for help in our desperate times of need. It can also be an expression of our gratitude. Meister Ekhart said it simply and perfectly: "If the only prayer we ever say is thank you, that will be enough." Gratitude will shift our perspective (hi, miracle!) and our vibration (hi, magnetism!) every single time.

And of course, there's always the perfect prayer that uses no words at all, that is the simple and total surrendering of our own ideas and welcoming in the wisdom from within. *Dear God, Please let me trust what I cannot see.*

IF YOU DON'T SEE GOD IN ALL, YOU DON'T SEE GOD AT ALL

In our journey from Trauma to Dharma, we have come into acceptance with our flawed and fallible humanness/mess and fallen into a place of reconnecting with ourselves—with the "me" that has been missing. And through that me we are able to connect to the Spirit that surges through all of us. Once we have experienced that presence of God within ourselves, we are able to embrace the God in everyone else. Because it *is* there. That spirited pulse is an empathic thread that weaves us all together into this human fabric, and the simple awareness we are working toward is if you don't see God in all, you don't see God at all.

To further our healing and growth, we must surround ourselves with people who get us, because while we have come to understand that we need a "God," it's time to recognize that God—in addition to being that knowing voice within us—is also experienced through other people. And we need other people and their support. We cannot do this alone— whatever alone looks like to us—because life here on planet Earth is not a do-it-yourself network.

SOUL PRESCRIPTION

Journal Question #1: Spirituality

What does your experience of spirituality (connection to Spirit, God, Universe) look and feel like in your life? When do you feel most at peace? When do you touch or taste those moments of grace?

Journal Question #2: Spiral Staircase

Our healing through this messy life is like a spiral staircase. What's been your "spiral staircase" of development? What patterns have been playing on repeat? What lesson keeps knocking you on your ass and/or kicking you up the stairs? Can you see where you're moving up? Having a faster response? And if not, where might you have to start looking for that?

Journal Question #3: Your Soul's Lessons

Our challenges always unfold a deeper lesson. In this one-room schoolhouse called Earth, what have been your greatest lessons so far? Go back. Think of a painful disruption, crisis, or challenging situation in your life (past or present). What were the lessons in that experience? What was it there to teach you? What buried strength or trait did it help you uncover in yourself? What gift did it uncover in your life?

Pranayama: Ego Eradicator

If the Soul is covered by a thousand veils, then this is your veil buster. This powerful pranayama strengthens our magnetic field by breaking through the layers of egoic noise that often keep us from listening to the Soul. And it's also an effective way to enter that God pause.

Posture: Sit in easy pose or in a chair with a straight spine. Raise your arms up to a sixty-degree angle. Curl your fingertips onto the pads of your palms at the base of the fingers. Thumbs are stretched back, pointing toward each other above the head.

Eye Focus: Your eyes are closed, focused on the Third Eye point.

Breath: Begin Breath of Fire, rapidly and rhythmically inhaling and exhaling through your nose.

Continue for one to three minutes.

To Finish: Inhale deeply and bring your arms overhead with your thumb tips touching. Exhale and relax your arms down.

Ardas Bhaee Meditation as Prayer

Yogi Bhajan explains this mantra and meditation best: "Ardas Bahee is a mantra prayer. If you sing it, your mind, body, and Soul automatically combine and without saying what you want, the need of the life is adjusted." This is a way of calling upon Guru Amar Das and Guru Ram Das (who represent the Hope of the Hopeless and the Lord of Miracles), and it is the mantra of answered prayers, moving beyond difficult situations, and gracefully letting go.

Posture: Sit in easy pose with a straight spine or sit in a chair with your feet flat on the floor. Relax your upper arms by your sides, and bring your hands up to the level of your heart. Interlace your fingers and create a little steeple at your heart.

Eye Focus: With your eyes closed, gaze down at the tip of your nose.

Mantra: ***Ardas Bhaee Amar Das Guru***
                 Amar Das Guru, Ardas Bhaee,
                 Ram Das Guru, Ram Das Guru
                 Ram Das Guru, Sachee Sahee

(The mantra recording I use in class is "Ardas Bhaee" by Nirinjan Kaur from *From Within*, if you would like one to chant along to.)

Continue for seven to eleven minutes.

To Finish: Take a deep inhale, and as you exhale, release your hands.

Adi Mantra Laya Style: The Quintessential Faith Pill

>>>—— ACCEPTANCE   AGENCY   AUTHORITY

I often tell my students, "When in doubt, chant it out." My go-to "leap and the net will appear" mantra is the Adi Mantra Laya Style. This mantra calls on us to open and receive our own internal wisdom, to adjust ourselves on a Soul level, and to listen to our inner guidance. By chanting this mantra, we lean toward dissolving the "Self" as a human who has an ego so we can allow the flow of the universal consciousness to come through us as we practice.

Posture: Sit in easy pose or in a chair with a straight spine. Bring both palms in front of your heart center, facing upward. Touch the sides of your palms along your little fingers and the sides of your hands, in a position to receive. Form Gyan Mudra (thumb and index finger touching) in each hand.

Eye Focus: With your eyes closed, gaze down at the tip of your nose.

Breath and Mantra: Chant the entire mantra three to five times in one breath.

Ong Namo Guru Dev Namo
Guru Dev Namo, Guru Deva

(If I'm not chanting this mantra on my own, I love chanting along with Guru Singh's soul-lifting version on his *Naad Mantra* album or White Sun's beautiful version on their self-titled album.)

Continue for five to eleven minutes.

Asana: Tree Pose for Auric Balance

This grounding pose builds nerve strength by rooting us into the earth. Our Spirit needs to root in order to rise and experience all it is destined for. It also helps to develop patience, persistence, humility, and humor as we fall and fumble and try again in our spirited attempts to find balance. All part of our Soul's curriculum.

Posture: Begin by standing and balancing on your left leg. Lift your right heel up to your groin (either bring your left leg into lotus pose or press the sole of your foot along your inner thigh with your toes facing the floor.) Drop your shoulders back, slightly lift your chest, and pull your chin into neck lock. Stretch your arms out to your sides with your left palm facing down and your right palm facing up.

Eye Focus: Either focus at the Third Eye point or pick a steady point before you and gaze beyond it.

Breath: Breathe long and deep.

Continue for three minutes and then switch sides.

Chapter Nine
APPRECIATION

I will always appreciate those who made me go
through rough times because without those,
I wouldn't have the wisdom and power
that lies within me now.

—*Gugu Mona*

The most important relationship we ever have is with ourselves. And in order to appreciate anything in our lives, we must begin by connecting to ourselves—to our Soul. Once we've done that, we can experience the spirited presence that is pulsing within and around us at all times and slowly uncover the thread that connects us to one another in the web of humanity. We can begin to look beyond the human mistakes and earthly stories to see Soul to Soul. In fact, once we've connected to the God in ourselves, we can't *not* see the God in others. Ken Wilber called man "the mask of God," and I love that. Beneath the skin, beneath the superficial differences and illusion of separation, there we all are, made up of the same stardust. And when we see this, we can fall deeply into a space of **appreciation** for our people and community. Our tribes. And we can humbly recognize that we weren't designed to do this life thing alone.

WHAT IS APPRECIATION?

Appreciation is a full understanding of a situation; for the purpose of Trauma to Dharma, it means to step into a situation without prior assumptions or preconceptions—without an opinion or story about it. Which allows us to understand it fully. Appreciation is dropping our masks and finally opening up to and embracing the potential for intimate connection with others. It's recognizing that, while it can be scary as hell, life happens through that spark of connection. Appreciation opens us to braving into shared spaces of vulnerability and me-too moments.

White Tantric Yoga

> *Could a greater miracle take place than for us to look*
> *through each other's eyes for an instant?*
> *—Henry David Thoreau*

One of the greatest examples of a shared space of vulnerability I can think of is White Tantric Yoga—that practice of meditating for eight hours straight with a partner. (The one where I met my husband, Ricardo.) Through this practice of sitting across from another human being for a series of sixty-two-minute meditative chunks and staring into each other's eyes, we break through the subconscious blocks, stale beliefs, heavy judgments, and identity labels that attempt to separate us. It's incredibly powerful. Most people couldn't last five seconds. Think about it: When was the last time you stared into another's eyes? And I'm talking locked eyes, not a one-second glance. Go ahead—try it for five seconds. It will probably feel like an eternity. So now imagine the discomfort and resistance one must move through to settle into that space with another person. Face-to-face. Eye to eye. Holding an asana while breathing powerfully or chanting. It'll break down some barriers, all right. And of all the mantras we've chanted throughout my years of this practice, one in particular has left its vibrational imprint with me: "I am you. You are me. There is no difference."

Staring into the eyes of another, we are invited back into that timeless space where we once again recognize our infinity and affinity toward all beings. We humbly experience the first of Yogi Bhajan's Five Sutras of the Aquarian Age: recognize that the other person is you.

Even though we all long for deep connection, we rarely allow ourselves to really look into another's eyes. We are afraid of that transparency and the emotions that come with it. Yet beneath the ego's fog of separation and our surface-level differences, there lies a truth that we need each other in order to experience the connection of all things. When we get past our insecurities around being seen, we can fall into this shared space where we see our Self reflected in the other and uncover our common ground. Rumi alluded to this when he said, "Why struggle to open a door between us when the whole wall is an illusion?" I am you. You are me. There is no difference. We can only truly see our Selves reflected in another person. And we can experience that most fully in a space of relationship.

RELATIONSHIPS

Now that we recognize life is constantly assigning us lessons perfectly designed for our growth, it's time to embrace that our relationships are our greatest teachers. And yes, they are often the ones whose classes we wish we could skip. Our relationships—that is, the state of being in relation to someone else—are where the rubber meets the road of our life laboratory. And the principle of appreciation is all about diving into our relationships. We are all teachers *and* students, givers *and* receivers. Each of us is a mirror for those in our lives, reflecting the parts that need growth, the parts we are ready to unearth, face, and embrace in order to step into more of who we truly are. I'll say it again because it's so important: we need community and connection because we need each other to know ourselves.

Connection, Vulnerability, and Intimacy

Life and growth are all about **connection**, and I'm sorry to say it, guys, but connection—real, life-giving, life-affirming connection—comes only through **vulnerability**. Through our willingness to put some skin into the game, to be present, and to feel. Together. The more we are willing to expose our humanness, the more we create those courageous moments of vulnerability to connect to one another.

God bless Brené Brown for reminding us that vulnerability is the human way and the path of the brave. Our willingness to be seen and heard is our greatest strength, and the more we stand out, the more outstanding we will be. Our greatest defense is an open heart. Remember Officer Intimidation at the Immigration Office? Remember our me-too moment? None of that would have been possible if I hadn't been willing to get emotionally naked before her and allow my human "mess" to show through. And not only did that miracle me-too moment feed me through the connection we shared, but it moved me. It propelled me onward. Our relationships provide this sacred space for us; we just have to claim our place to open up and be fully seen.

Now a note of caution: Our greatest defense is an open heart, but our greatest tool is our intuition. Vulnerability is inherently risky—it simply doesn't exist without the possibility of danger. Our intuition assesses risk and allows us to discern who is appropriate to practice this with. And it's critical that we not be reckless and throw our vulnerability out to the proverbial wolves, because that's likely to result in deeper, more painful wounds. But when we find safe and healthy mirrors to be in relationships and practice vulnerability with, we must be brave enough to let them see *all* of us, including our imperfections and flawed and fallible ways. Because, as Brené Brown teaches, vulnerability is the glue that holds intimate relationships together. And that's where this is all going—**intimacy.**

Ahh, intimacy...is there a more perfect play on words? INTO-ME-SEE. Vulnerability is the space we enter in order to be intimate, and intimacy is little more than sustained vulnerability. Vulnerability requires faith, and intimacy requires trust. It's uncomfortable, to be sure, and terrifying at times, but the reward of intimate relationships is that there is nothing better, more powerful, or more healing than being fully seen, accepted, and loved for everything that we are and are not. Our human longing to belong rests in the mutual acceptance of intimate relationships.

Rumi says, "The wound is the place where the Light enters you." When our wounds are exposed within the safety of intimacy, and they are *loved*...my God, you find me a better medicine than that. This light of love can train our eyes to see what we couldn't see before—that our wounds can be tender openings that invite us into the most beautiful parts of ourselves. And they also allow us to see, feel, and understand the pain of others. It is through our broken open vulnerability that we redirect our attention from what is missing to what is always there—our indomitable Spirit that connects us to every beating, pulsing, human heart and Soul in our lives. And it is in this connection that we uncover the strength to endure the trials before us—together.

Going to the Movies: A Metaphor

Our relationships are our greatest teachers and mirrors, and *we* are the common denominator in our relationships. So if we keep coming up against the same thing, if we continue to play out the same scenes with new actors and a new audience, whose fault do we think that is? Wherever you go, there you are, after all. And one of my favorite ways to explain this idea is with a metaphor.

Let's say we're ready to go to a movie we've wanted to see for a while, and it's playing at the local theater. So we purchase our ticket and head on over to the Cineplex. Large popcorn and bottle of water in tow, we settle into our seat as the trailers finish. The movie begins, and about twenty minutes in, we start to get antsy. Despite our expectations (or maybe because of them), we're just not enjoying it. If anything, it's feeling a bit offensive. ("Ugh, this is *so* not for me!") So we get up, leave the theater, walk back to our car, and drive out of the parking lot. Victory, right? Well, maybe not so fast. Because then we continue driving across town until we get to a different theater where we proceed to park, stand in line, and buy a ticket for the same movie. Different theater, same movie. New space, same old story. And yet there we sit, expecting an entirely different experience. Now, we'd never actually do this, so why do we do it with our relationships?

We are human projectors, and our relationships are the perfect screen to play out our assumptions, preconceptions, and expectations. Not everything that happens in our relationships is our fault, but a good part of it is. So if we're noticing the same old, unhealthy patterns, we can't just change the space we're in. We must reevaluate our place in it. Remember the spiral staircase? We have to own it and embrace it so we don't have to reface it. The sooner we claim and reframe our story, the less we'll put our eager yet tender heart through the ringer of the "same old, same old." And the less overly salted, stale popcorn we'll have to consume.

Helping Each Other Unpack

We've all got our baggage: the emotional triggers, musty resentments, outdated "how to get what I want" guides, and those bubble-wrapped wounds with fluorescent "fragile: handle with care" stickers. But do we really handle with care? We all long for connection, so what do we do? We tirelessly work to improve ourselves, to polish and perfect our outsides in order to board the RelationShip. We pack up and stow away our baggage, flawlessly dress to impress, and show up with our best foot forward. And then we wonder why we're always waiting for the other shoe to drop? Well, that other shoe would be the one connected to our *real* foot. Not our *best* foot but the one that regrounds us after said "ship" has left the dock, the oxytocin-induced "Baby, I love everything about you" texts start to dwindle, and the real work begins: the work of unpacking. And make no mistake: relationship is the art of unpacking.

We've all got junk in the trunk, and relationships are messy and imperfect—just like our baggage. Unpacking requires courage to air it

all out and commitment to see it all through. It begs for our compassion
to feel each other's fear and have each other's backs as we take turns
letting go of the old moth-eaten parts that no longer serve us. And lastly,
it pleads for our patience because those bags don't empty themselves
overnight. The key is to find the people who love us enough to help us
unpack. The ones who will call us out on our shit and still stay, who will
call us out *and* see us through. But in order to find those people, we
must be willing to show up as one of them. With our real foot forward.
Courageous, committed, compassionate, patient, and ready to handle
with care.

A Blessing or A Lesson

When it comes to this important work of unpacking, there are two types
of Souls that help with the heavy lifting. There are the **angels** in our
lives who we recognize immediately. The ones who are always front
and center, rooting us on, lifting us up, and gently holding our most
fragile and delicate pieces. And then there are the **assholes**—and we
all have them. The ones who've pushed, poked, challenged, and hurt us.
And believe it or not, the assholes play an equally important role in our
journeys.

I'll never forget my own introduction to the power of this notion.
I was sitting with my teacher, Guru Singh, one afternoon, having one of
our weekly exchanges, this time over lunch. And just as we sat down for
our meal, we did what we always do and blessed the food. Only this time
he had a greater blessing in mind. We sat there, hand in hand, and Guru
Singh began to get nostalgic on me. "Take a moment and look at where
we are today, my dear. And honor how far you've come. We have so

much to be grateful for." And then he proceeded down a gratitude track.

Thank you for this food.
Thank you for this day.
Thank you for our families and our friends we call family.
Thank you for...and then he went on to name my abuser.

It's a good thing this was during grace and not after, because I would have definitely choked on my quinoa. I was taken aback (to say the least), and I interjected, "Why in the hell would I be grateful for that asshole?"

Guru Singh just stared back at me with his piercingly blue eyes and a sliver of a smile and said, "Because if it wasn't for him, Az, you wouldn't be here."

And then it hit me as those liberating moments of epiphany do, when something just opens and the world around us brightens. Yes, he had everything to do with why I was there. And the truth is, if it hadn't been him, it would have been someone or something else. But it *was* him. And my escape from him was my ticket back to me. He left me so empty, so starved, and that hunger eventually led me down this path to feed my Soul and the Souls of those I am blessed to touch. It was true—I was grateful. And still angry. I was grateful and still hurting. I was grateful and still healing.

My experience of his darkness catalyzed my need for my own light. The greatest side effect of this painful past was my commitment to no longer dimming myself. My trauma thrust upon me via this Soul— this asshole kind of Soul—broke me open and helped me uncover my dharma. My purpose. My I-know-why-I-am-here-and-what-I-need-to-do drive.

That moment of gratitude over lunch nourished me in a way no meal could. And one thing was getting clearer to me with every passing day in my recovery: What looks like the worst thing for us can sometimes end up being the best. Not always, but sometimes. Our tribes are filled with angels. And yeah, some of those angels are disguised as assholes. Some of them stick around for the duration, while others come in for a fleeting stretch of growth, but all of them have different reasons and seasons, and all of them are perfect pieces to our life puzzle.

We've all got that thing that got us here and got us clear. That thing that got us willing and ready to take the reins of our life back. And that "thing" most certainly does not have to be a person—it could be an injury, illness, or loss, just to name a few. Cancer, a divorce, or a tsunami—real or metaphorical—are all examples of "assholes" in our lives that we have to have a relationship with. And as a friend said to me years ago, after yet another painful breakup: "Relationships are either a blessing or a lesson." But at the time, even in the rawness of my wounded heart, I countered with: "Well, isn't the lesson the blessing? So...isn't it all a blessing?"

I shocked myself when I said that. *Me.* Still healing, still triggered, still carrying wounds of an abusive ex. Yet it was clear. Somewhere amid the struggle and surrender, I experienced the shift. I was able to see that glitch in my life differently. Viewing it now through the eyes of the Soul and its limitless purpose and possibility, it was clear just how much my pained past was becoming more and more purposeful with every step and stumble in my recovery.

If the Universe sends us nothing but angels (some disguised as assholes) to teach us the lessons we need, then what if those who hurt us most are the Souls who loved us enough to play that villainous role in our learning? I know it's a stretch. I know the protective resistance that comes up at the thought of forgiving someone or something that pained us at our core and ripped the life from us. But I also know that by the time I had that moment with Guru Singh, I had slept and wept and lived with my pain long enough to be willing to loosen my grip. Because the truth is it never had a hold on me; *I* had a hold on *it*.

And that's grace. The soft surrender. The experiencing Spirit within the brokenness. It doesn't diminish the magnitude of our pain or right the wrongs. It just gives us the right to gently scrape our hearts off the floor and move on. It gives us the chance to open our eyes within the darkness long enough to find that flicker of value in our beaten but still beating aliveness.

WE THRIVE IN TRIBES

Be with those who help your being.

—*Rumi*

Our traumas and pain can leave us feeling so alone and isolated, and in our culture, we're raised to believe we can do it all, including tending to our wounds. And the truth is we can. It's important to know we can handle any situation life throws at us. We have the tools within us to take care of ourselves. We just can't do it alone. There's a reason there are seven billion people on this planet. But our do-it-yourself society has collapsed **codependence** (which is an unhealthy reliance on others or enabling others' dysfunctional behaviors) and **interdependence** (which is not unhealthy at all). We've stopped giving much of ourselves to others or allowing others to give to us, because we don't want to enable or seem needy. We've come to think of needing others as a negative thing, but that is a misguided and dangerous goal of total independence and self-sufficiency. People love and want to feel needed. We need to feel valued, connected, cared for, and respected. And the fact is, doing it alone—not asking for and relying on others for support—actually goes against our nature.

There's an African proverb that says, "The reason that two antelopes walk together is so that one can blow the dust from the other's eyes." I don't think I realized how much we need our people and tribes until I learned about the antelopes. Leave it to our animal friends to remind us of our own humanity. We see clearer together. Our well-being is dependent on one another. When I have a weakened moment, when I can't see, you can see for me. You can help me see.

We are each fumbling through our own daily dust storms, doing our best to navigate the mental and emotional gusts that obstruct our view. We all have blind spots—our stories, assumptions, and fear-filled dust bunnies. And our fellow travelers are the ultimate dust busters. We need each other to know ourselves, which is just another way of saying we need each other to see what we are not able or willing to see, and to help us see beyond the dust we have collected along the way.

To stand by and blow dust from another's eyes is not to spoon-feed them our version of vision; nor is it telling them which path is theirs to walk. Rather, it is seeing the world through their eyes instead of our own and, from that space of understanding, leading them back to their own internal GPS. Because the greatest dust busters simply guide us back to *our* way. They hold space for more openings, which enables more shifts.

Antelopes are herd animals, and so are we. We are born for each other and of each other. Which reminds me of the African concept of Ubuntu. *Ubuntu*, which translates to *humanity*, literally means humanness or the quality of being human, and it stems from an African phrase that says, "A person is a person through other people," or "I am, because of you." People are not people without other people. We need a community to be human, to live out our humanity. *Humanity*, after all, is just another word for kindness, benevolence, compassion, and understanding—things that can't be expressed or inhabited by oneself. Humanity is a communal thing. We belong to each other, and we are worth more together than we are alone.

The Difference between Heaven and Hell

Imagine this picture of hell: We are escorted down a grand corridor and into a majestic banquet hall. The long, candlelit tables are lavishly decorated with the finest china and adorned with an abundant feast of the most delicious food. There is an orchestra playing, and everyone is dressed to the nines. This is the kind of party people dream of attending! Yet as we step closer toward this magnificent feast for the senses, we begin to notice something haunting. The guests look miserable. Their faces are gaunt and creased with frustration. Each person holds a utensil—but these utensils are three feet long! They are so long that while the people in hell can reach the food on their platters, they cannot get any of it back into their mouths. In spite of the abundance before them, they are starving to death. It's awful.

Now let's shift things up. Cut to heaven. We are escorted down that same grand corridor and walk into the same majestic banquet hall.

We notice the same long, candlelit tables piled high with that lavish feast. Here again, we see the party guests seated around the tables with their same three-foot-long utensils. But this time, instead of moaning with hunger, the people here are all vibrant and vital. They are full of life and laughter, joyously celebrating. All with the same three-foot-long utensils. So how are they not starving? We take a closer look and cannot help but smile as we realize that while they still cannot feed themselves, they have learned how to feed each other.

Heaven and hell...it is neither the qualities of the place nor the abundance of resources but the way we come to treat each other. We thrive in tribes. And we need each other to feed each other. But how many of us are still starving? For connection, relatedness, and a sense of belonging. No human being is alone, and no man is an island, so if we feel as though we are living alone, we need to look at what beliefs we have about ourselves and the world that keep us from asking for a helping hand, an empathetic ear, or a soft shoulder to cry on. What beliefs rest behind our resistance to expressing our needs and asking for attention? Some of those beliefs might be that we're not worthy of asking for help, that we don't want to burden and impose on others, that we feel we are not deserving, and that we're afraid to admit we can't do it alone.

By expressing our needs, we open ourselves up. Yes, we expose our fears and our weaknesses, but as scary as that is, there is a gift in that expression. Not only are we offering ourselves the opportunity to show up in courage, but we are also giving those around us an opportunity to show up in the way that we as humans are meant to—for each other. If we put trust in those around us, we will never go hungry.

As human beings we hunger for connection to feed and sustain us the same way we hunger for food. Every one of us longs to know we are not alone. And when we have the awareness to understand this, it is on us to be courageous enough to express it. That's how me-too moments are born. Our sense of belonging is realized through our acts of kindness and compassion, so we must acknowledge and appreciate all those who have and continue to walk alongside us, blowing the dust from our eyes. These are the members of our tribe.

And a note of caution: Not everyone is meant to travel with us for our entire journey. The more we commit to transforming our inner landscape, the more we must be prepared for the change in scenery along the way. In other words, not everyone is gonna stick around for our transformation party. Our growth and commitment to our healing can threaten those who aren't ready or willing to do the same. Some people will be disappointed in us for having changed. Those people in our lives mean well, but they would much prefer we stay small, fit into the box they have us in, and not disrupt their status quo. Because they're scared. That's all that is.

Our recovery will threaten those who aren't ready to grow because one way of blowing the dust from others' eyes is by showing that change is possible, and not everyone is ready to see that. Our growth won't include everyone, and that's okay. Be prepared: Some people may feel let down or abandoned by our evolution, and if that's the case, the Trauma to Dharma journey might also include some side trips known as guilt trips. These can be both self-driven and also from people who miss the older version of us that served them but no longer served us. And when that happens, we get to experience the often unimaginable yet life-changing process of forgiveness.

FORGIVENESS

Your forgiveness speaks of you, not of them.
                                    —*Najwa Zebian*

The more we're able to see through the eyes of the Soul, the more we're able to experience the sting of life's lessons as blessings. If life is one big schoolhouse and our relationships are teachers, then **forgiveness** is part of graduating to the next level. And forgiveness doesn't mean we condone hurtful behavior or deny its existence; it simply means we stop carrying pain from the past and allowing it to control us. It is one of the hardest feats we will ever accomplish, but it is among the most significant, because when we don't, we just end up punishing ourselves. To not forgive is to believe the past is all we have.

All sustained relationships depend, to some extent, on forgiveness. People hurt one another no matter how much love they share, and it's true that the greatest hurts are usually from the ones closest to us. No relationship—friendship, marriage, family, or otherwise—can last without forgiveness, because without forgiveness, there is no allowance for human frailty. And look, this is one of the hardest things we come up against in moving from Trauma to Dharma. The act of forgiving is oftentimes more painful than the thing we are actually forgiving. But our capacity to forgive reveals a great deal about our Selves. It is a measure of our ability to recognize the humanity in someone who has hurt us and to tolerate the disappointment that others won't always be what we need them to be.

And this sensibility applies to our view of ourselves too. Because forgiving others is nothing but the mirror image of forgiving oneself. It's a softening of our hearts and an unclenching of our fists so we can be open to receiving new life, new experiences, and new opportunities that wish to enter. We truly heal through forgiveness. And we forgive in order to release and move toward inner peace, to untie the knot that binds us to our pain. As Lewis B. Smedes wrote in his book about forgiveness, "To forgive is to set a prisoner free and discover that the prisoner was you."

The Forgiveness Process

Forgiveness is a natural and organic process that cannot be forced upon us. We cannot do it prematurely for the sake of getting it over with (remember, we don't get over things; we get through them), and that means forgiveness happens only when we are brave enough to feel our way through the hurts of our humanness. There is no right or wrong way to forgive. It's usually not a wake-up-one-morning-and-decide "I'm forgiving him completely; all is done!" kind of thing. Although it can be. Perhaps it's loud. Perhaps it's quiet. Maybe it's face-to-face, or maybe it's simply Spirit-to-Spirit. It can be spoken or written, sudden or gradual. Sometimes it happens in ritual or ceremony, with intention and conviction. And sometimes forgiveness happens when we're just braving onward, choosing to live our life until one day we run into that person or think about that awful time, and we realize we aren't as shaken up by it as we used to be—that, in fact, we're not really feeling…anything.

Forgiveness can happen in any of these or countless other ways, but there is one constant. Remember the three facets of the mind: positive, negative, and neutral? Well, forgiveness happens in the neutral mind territory. The neutral mind is where we access the Soul. No charge, no problem, just progress. Once we engage the neutral mind, we can start to see the lesson and move from "they did this to me" to "they made it possible for me to grow." This opens us up to compassion—to seeing that we are all doing the best we can and everyone's fighting a secret battle—which begins the process of forgiveness. Forgiveness is our way of remembering. Forgiving our humanity—and the humanity of everyone else around us—is our only way back to connecting to our Souls and the light that fills and fuels us. And yes, sometimes forgiveness is less about forgiving *them* and more about forgiving *their humanity*.

Yogi Bhajan, in all his wisdom, gave us a list of five things to forgive:

1. ***Forgive God that He separated you from Himself and created you as a creature.***
   Forgive God that He separated you from Him—*and* that he separated you from You. Forgive Him that He created us as these human beings dealing with the longing for sacred God moments that we can experience only by connecting with our spirited travelers.

2. ***Forgive your destiny that it is as it is and that you have to achieve it.***
   Yeah, we kinda signed up for this. I know...it sucks. And it hurts. Keep going.

3. ***Forgive the distance and the environments that are always challenging and the cause and effect that are happening.***

In other words, all those crappy circumstances.

4. ***Forgive your capacity, your ability, your duality, and your divinity.***
Forgive yourself for what you have been capable and incapable of, for where you've hurt and let down yourself and others. And forgive yourself for what you didn't know before you knew it. Let this be permission for all of us to stop "shoulding" all over ourselves.

5. ***Forgive yourself that you have to go through it.***
Forgive yourself for having been a Soul that chose to experience itself so fully. And while we're at it, forgive each other's flawed and fallible humanity, because forgiveness is a way of remembering who we are and recognizing each other beneath all the human-mess.

And to this divine list I would add just one more:

Forgive yourself for doing what you had to survive.

All the coping mechanisms and strategies in all their many and varied forms—forgive yourself for those too. Because we have just been doing the very best we could.

Asking for Forgiveness

And what about when we're not the ones being asked to forgive but the ones asking for forgiveness? When we are forced to acknowledge our own mistakes and failings? That, too, can be profoundly painful. (And it can make us all the more appreciative of those in our tribes who are living in conscious and compassionate awareness.) I recently had an experience with this when I learned that a dear friend was deeply hurt during my wedding, feeling left out from the proceedings. It was an unintended oversight on my part, and the minute I received his almost-but-not-quite Dear John e-mail, I was heartbroken. And excruciatingly uncomfortable.

My biggest fear as a friend is that I'm going to let people down, and it will result in me being unloved. We always try to do the right thing, but even with pure-hearted intentions, we can still come up short and hurt the ones we love. Relationships are about intention, not perfection, but even though I preach and teach all day that there's no such thing as perfection, I was beside myself. I had that horrible pit in my stomach that I'd potentially broken trust or lost a friendship or...or...or...

That innate fear of being abandoned, discarded, irrelevant, and not loved when we've inadvertently hurt someone is primal, and the first thing we want to do is fix it. React immediately and take action because it's so uncomfortable. But the one thing we actually need to do is *feel* all of it. And by feeling it, I don't mean stewing in it—we're not soup. I mean staying with it in a period of nonreactive, uncomfortable-as-hell silence to move through the layers of emotions and injuries that typically follow a standard pattern.

First we face *panic* and *fear* over not being able to handle someone we love being disappointed in us. We want to fix it. This rudely awakens our inner child, the elementary school student who was afraid she would be left out, ganged up on, and ignored. It's at this point where we have to question how much we want to tend to the other person's hurt and how much we want to tend to our own aching discomfort because he's hurting, *because we hurt him*. Because, my God, we can't stand that someone dislikes us or thinks poorly of us.

Shortly after, we move into *defensive anger*, placing blame somewhere else or trying to hand that discomfort over to someone else by coming up with excuses. (This wasn't *my* fault!) But the fact remains that we can build a mile-high pile of excuses and explanations, but all that's doing is creating a greater divisive wall between us and the person we hurt.

So then we settle into *guilt*, because now we've turned that anger and blame inward. The regret and remorse for our wrongdoings, the wishing we could go back, the disappointing and shaming ourselves for knowing better and not doing better not only builds a wall between us and our loved one but now builds a wall within ourselves. All of which is separating us from the truth that lies further beneath: *hurt*. The deep, guttural kind of pain because (1) we are feeling our friend's hurt, and (2) we are hurting for ourselves and our torn friendship. To surrender to this raw and honest layer is so scary but so necessary because once we fall beneath it all, we land on the truth: *I love you, and I'm sorry*.

Ho'oponopono

And this is the perfect time to bring in **Ho'oponopono,** the ancient Hawaiian practice of reconciliation and forgiveness. *Ho'oponopono* translates to *make it right* and is based on four key phrases that also happen to be four of the hardest, most vulnerable phrases we struggle to say.

I'm sorry. I stand here responsible and accountable, a perfectly imperfect, flawed, and fallible human-mess in progress.

Please forgive me. Please forgive my humbly human ways, what I've said or done, and most especially how I've made you feel.

Thank you. For your compassion, for listening, and for holding this space and standing with me in this discomfort. And thank you for loving me the way you have, of which the depth of your hurt is proof.

I love you. This discomfort I feel is birthed out of my deep fear of losing you and your love. But even if I did, I would still continue to love you.

There are specific cultural rituals around Ho'oponopono, but it is a beautiful concept that can be adapted and adopted into our everyday practices, either in direct apologies or meditation. Yogi Bhajan prescribed a happy, healthy, holy way of life through his 3HO organization, but I don't believe we can live a happy, healthy, and holy life unless we practice *my* version of 3HO, which is **honesty, humility, and humanity**. That's where our Spirit speaks through our human-mess, and that is where forgiveness is born. And just like Kundalini, forgiveness is a practice. We return to the yoga mat to remind us of just that—that we too are a work in progress. It's called a yoga practice, not a yoga perfect. And so it is on our mats that we can exercise our imperfections, work through our fears, and continue to show up and try.

Fear-Buster Kit

None of this is easy. Nothing worth having ever is. So we simply keep going, anticipating that there will be blows along the way and accepting that fear is going to be a traveling companion. When fear rears its head, we need our tribe the most, and because that can also be when it's hardest to reach out, I created a three-step strategy for getting back to our true Selves when that fear monster creeps up.

Trauma to Dharma Fear-Buster Calling Plan

1. Call time.

Go ahead and call that timeout. Because fear is trying to steal us away from the only time we've got: now. So take a God pause, breathe deeply, and ask, "Where are my feet?" Realize they are planted right here on the ground, not racing back to yesterday or future-tripping into tomorrow. *Connect back to Now.*

2. Call it out.

Call uncle. Call a truce. Call it what you will, but just don't fight, deny, or resist it because whatever we resist persists. Fear is just doing its job, trying to keep us safe, and it simply wants to be acknowledged and heard, so go ahead and give it a voice. Ask, "What am I afraid of?" Name it, claim it, and face it. It's okay to be afraid; it means we're alive and we care. *Connect back to You.*

3. Call 'em in.

The first place fear will take us is down the dark and dangerous alley of our minds that no one should walk alone, so now is the time to call in our peeps. We're not wired to manage this on our own. Pick a trusted member of the tribe—one who gets you even when you don't—and send out a smoke signal. Nothing busts fear like compassion, and another word for compassion is humanity, so it's time to connect to that. *Connect back to Us.*

Calling Plan

It was a couple of weeks before my forty-first birthday, and my friends had started their "What do you want to do?" texts and e-mail chains. The previous year I had celebrated my fortieth with a big get-together on the victorious heels of freezing my eggs. And 365 days later, here I was. On my own. By myself. Again. Still. Now with eggs in the freezer. So instead of responding to the messages from friends wanting to celebrate, I turned my attention to the self-pitying symphony beginning its sound check on my mind's stage: *Testing, testing...you're still alone—poor, pitiful you. Testing, testing...you're not getting any younger. Your eggs may be frozen, but you're not.*

I was falling into that reactive space because when fear strikes, I head straight for my comfort zone of self-pity. But here's the beauty and magic of awareness: because I have learned to connect to my breath and engage the witness, I was able, once again, to pause. (Hi, God!) And after I **called time**, I was able to **call it out**. I noticed that insidious fear enticing me down that dark alley and was able to take a beat to trace where that feeling was coming from. In that beat, I was able to see the source and witness her. And if I'm able to witness her, then (halle-fucking-lujah!) I am not her. She is not me. Or at least not *all* of me. So I knew what had to be done. I had to **call 'em in** to keep me from following this dark, shady part of my psyche down the rabbit hole. I used my lifeline and called Shelby: "Hey, it's happening again. She's back. And it's gettin' real dark up in here. I've started the pity party."

She heard me and held me in that space of compassion. Not judging or trying to fix me, she was able to just be there while I felt and expressed my sadness, disappointment, and fear. She just listened, and that's all I needed. The simple act of calling out fear—first to myself and then to someone in my tribe—allowed it to dissipate. It just wanted to be acknowledged. That's all. It didn't need to be fixed; it just wanted to be felt.

And right then and there, while talking to my best friend a couple of weeks out from my birthday, I gave a shift. I canceled my pity party and decided to throw one huge dance party. And that's exactly what I did. I surrounded myself with my friends, and we danced and danced.

THERE'S NO PLACE LIKE HOME

None of this would have happened without the God pause, which time and time again creates that space of grace for us to be able to give a shift. That is the gift of living in awareness, and the way to awareness is by practicing acceptance, harnessing our agency and authority, humbly allowing, and now learning to appreciate the company we need to keep us here. These tools—the pranayamas, asanas, writing exercises, and commitment to our daily practices—are all strengthening our awareness muscle, which gives us the steadiness and strength to stand in the center of our storms and find our way home.

Ram Dass said we're all just walking each other home, and I couldn't agree more. That is why we need each other. Once my study participants had committed to their Kundalini practice and were learning to be more present in their lives, they began to experience a shift around how they understood and made meaning of their life disruptions

ALLOWING   APPRECIATION   AUTHENTICITY ⟶

and pains. As a result, they began to soften around the people in their lives and started noticing how they were cultivating deeper intimacy with their tribes. They were risking being more vulnerable and showing up more authentically. That authenticity is where we are going. That authenticity is home. And home isn't as far away as we might think.

SOUL PRESCRIPTION

Journal Question #1: Angels and Assholes

Who do you appreciate? Who's your tribe? Those who help you thrive and support your being and growth. Those you've been vulnerable with. That includes both angels and assholes—all who've helped give you the lessons you needed. If you could thank them today, what would you thank them for? Begin to write your very own gratitude sentiments to those fellow Soul mates who fall into your tribe of appreciation.

Journal Question #2: Fear-Buster Calling Plan

Who's on your calling plan? Who are your go-to people when fear comes knocking? The people who have helped show you your Self and your truth by blowing the dust from your eyes? Who are your antelopes?

Journal Question #3: Forgiveness

Let your Soul speak. Who and/or what do you need to forgive? Who and/or what are you willing to forgive? Where are you willing to let go? Where are you willing to offer compassion and empathy to your Self, another person, or a situation? And where might you need to be asking for forgiveness?

Pranayama for Forgiveness and Letting Go of Past Emotions

By slowing down the breath, we slow down the mind, and this pranayama helps train you to move from sixteen breaths a minute (which is common) to four breaths a minute. This powerful pranayama also activates the pituitary and pineal glands, which support one's experience of the state of Shuniya, from which you can clear and release; forgive; and be at peace with what was, what is, and what will be.

Posture: Sit in easy pose or on a chair with the spine straight. Bring your hands in front of your heart center. Touch the tips of each finger together (i.e., index finger with index finger, ring finger with ring finger, thumb with thumb, and so on). Your fingers will be pointing up, thumbs pointing toward your chest, creating a steeple at your heart center.

Eye Focus: With your eyes one-tenth open, gaze down at the tip of your nose.

Breath: Inhale for five seconds, hold the breath for five seconds, and exhale for five seconds.

Continue for three to five minutes.

Meditation for a Calm Heart

They say a few minutes of mirror-gazing can reduce stress and increase self-compassion. Loving and appreciating ourselves is the foundation for loving and appreciating others. Take a moment and wade in your very own reservoir of appreciation for all that you are and all that it's taken to get you here—the good, the bad, and the ugly. Physically, this meditation strengthens the lungs and heart. Emotionally, it adds clear perception to your relationships with yourself and others.

Posture: Sit comfortably, with a straight spine, in front of a mirror. Place your left palm on your heart center. Bend your right arm, resting your elbow against the side of your body, and hold your right hand in gyan mudra (thumb and index finger meeting with the other fingers extended) at the level of your shoulder.

Eye Focus: Gaze directly at the mirror into your very own eyes. Give yourself your full, uninterrupted attention. Acknowledge yourself for where you've been and how far you've come. (If that's too much for you, this meditation can also be done without the mirror and with your eyes closed.)

Breath: Inhale deeply into your heart, and retain the breath as long as you comfortably can. Then exhale slowly and hold the breath out as long as you comfortably can. This activates the calming parasympathetic nervous system and can calm a panic attack after a minute.

Continue for three to five minutes.

Asana: Bow Pose

Bow Pose is a powerful spine strengthener, navel activator, and heart opener. Coupled with breath of fire, it stimulates the movement of energy straight to the heart. The stronger the spine, the more supported the heart. The more the navel point (your power center) is activated, the more confident you'll feel, and the more trusting the heart will be to remain open and willing to vulnerably connect.

Posture: Lie on your stomach, bend your knees, and reach back with your hands to grab your ankles. Press your hips into the ground. Use the strength of your legs pressing into your hands to pull your upper body off the ground, and then lift your legs off the ground so you are balancing on your navel point.

Breath: Begin breath of fire.

Continue for one to three minutes.

To Finish: Relax on your stomach with your head to one side.

ALLOWING   APPRECIATION   AUTHENTICITY ⟶

Chapter Ten
A U T H E N T I C I T Y

Authenticity is not something we have or don't have.
It's a practice—a conscious choice of how we want to
live. Authenticity is a collection of choices that we have
to make every day. It's about the choice to show
up and be real. The choice to be honest.
The choice to let ourselves be seen.

—*Brené Brown*

I call Trauma to Dharma a journey home because that is what living in awareness does: it brings us home. And this last principle of that journey involves finally giving ourselves permission to live authentically. If awareness is healing, and healing is integrating all of who we are into one perfectly imperfect Self, then living in awareness requires nothing less than living in **authenticity**.

WHAT IS AUTHENTICITY?

Authenticity is our genuine, most truthful way of being. It is embracing all of who we are and what we have been through in order to be real with ourselves and the world. And to be authentic means to be *fully* real, not half-assed or piecemeal by presenting just the parts of ourselves that are convenient, or comfortable, or what we think other people want to see. It is to show up completely and unapologetically.

Our Soul's expression comes through *all* of us—every perfectly imperfect piece—and yet we think of the proclamation "you're so full of yourself!" as an insult, an assault on the ego. That's because our society tends to confuse fullness of self with narcissism or self-absorption without taking into account that humans depleted from fear, shame, and dulling their shine to fit in cannot exist to their Soul's fullest extent. This isn't about feeding the ego; it's about feeding ourselves so we can be whole and abundant enough to feed others. And nobody is responsible for our wholeness and completeness but us. In the past, when someone would accuse me of being full of myself, I would cower in shame. But now, after all I've done to find and embody who I truly am, if someone says I'm full of myself, I can't help but smile and say, "*Thank you. I've healed and worked really hard for that!*"

Carl Jung said, "The privilege of a lifetime is to become who you truly are." After living a lie, blanketed in shame for most of my twenties, I now have a deep-seated allergy to anything other than real, and that is where authenticity comes into play. This isn't about airing our dirty laundry but about sharing the raw and messy reality of our humanity. It's not always pretty, but this is where authentic connection happens— in letting go of who we think we're supposed to be and embracing who we actually are.

PERFECTLY IMPERFECT AKA CRYING BROKEN PEOPLE

I experienced my greatest lesson of "realness" in the raw grit of residential treatment for my abusive relationship. One of the first questions a fellow resident will ask upon meeting a newbie "inside" is "What are you in for?" Talk about the no-bullshit, shit-getting-real approach. We wasted no time with the surface-level stuff and met right in the tender heart of the matter. And it freed us.

Think about it. When we show up to a treatment facility, twelve-step meeting, or support group, we are showing up broken and open. Vulnerable. Bruises, scabs, secrets, and scars exposed. There's no more hiding the pain, shame, or struggle. Ideally we're entering a safe, accepting, and non-judging meeting place—a land of "me-too." Which, as far as I'm concerned, is the happiest place on Earth. (Sorry, Disney.) So while I was uncomfortable as hell in my skin, my life, and everything that had brought me to that treatment center to begin with, I found deep comfort in others not trying to fix my pain or, worse, trying to fix *their discomfort* around my pain. It was one of the great, unexpected gifts of treatment that no one criticized, compared, or competed with one another's pain. We simply connected through our suffering and supported one another in that warm womb of wounds.

Do you remember that R.E.M. song, "Shiny Happy People"? This was the fucking opposite of that. And thank God, because I *hated* that song. It would come on the radio (back when we actually listened to the radio), and I'd literally yell out, "Fuck you, R.E.M.!" I was angrier back then, yes. But I also didn't need to be reminded of that plastic, mask-like version of happiness they were ironically bashing. Because don't get me wrong: I am all about happy and shiny, but only the kind of happy and shiny that's a brilliantly bright result of our slimy and grimy authenticity. And that's what I found in treatment. We showed up in all our perfectly imperfect glory, and by fully exposing our pain and the not-so-healthy ways we used to manage it, we inspired one another to come back to life in a healthier, brighter way. We dropped the "fine" masks that we wore for the outside world, and in exchange, we got to be real.

Fine

I think we all know what I mean when I refer to the "fine" mask, right? We all have one, and we've all used it. While running through town doing errands or hobnobbing at a holiday party, we bump into one of the parents from our children's school or an old friend we haven't seen in a while, and the conversation usually goes something like this:

"Hi! Oh my God, it's so good to see you! How are you?"

"Me? Oh, I'm *fine*. We're *fine*. Everything's *fine*. Joey is top of his class. And little Sarah is already walking! Oh, and Derek and I are crazy *fine*. Going out of town for a little getaway next week."

Do we all smell that? Lean in a little closer. More often than not we feed each other a load of bullshit. Maybe there are a select few who we happen to meet while in a "good place," but most of us have *something* going on that we're quick to cover up with a big, heaping load of *fine*.

On my second day in treatment, during our group check-in, we went around the room, taking turns sharing our "core feelings." ("Today I'm feeling sad/hopeful/scared/angry/frustrated/etc.") When it came to me, I went straight for my go-to answer: "I'm fine." Cue the record scratch. Big mistake. *Huge.* I was immediately shot down by one of the head counselors, who asked me if "fine" was a feeling and instructed me to tell everyone what it felt like. I was dumbfounded and embarrassed, and as I sat there in silence, he schooled me on what "fine" actually meant:

Fucked-up, **I**nsecure, **N**eurotic, and **E**motional

And you know what? That's exactly how I was feeling. But I'd been trained on the outside to never share my insides. This was the first time it felt like I was given permission to take off my perfectly put-together display and just be me: authentically fucked-up, insecure, neurotic, and emotional me. And I'm here to pass on that permission. To anyone who might not have heard this yet, I want to personally tell you: It's okay to take off the mask.

It's gonna be necessary, actually. Wearing the inauthentic and protective "fine" serves only to protect and separate us from the one thing we are most starving for: connection. So no more *fine* allowed. We're not here to get by; we're here to get real. Our willingness to expose the honest, the dark, the dismal, and the ugly—to live authentically— gives others permission to take their masks off as well and uncover the thread of humanity that connects us all. Because let's face it, people don't actually want shiny, happy people all the time. We want fucked up, insecure, neurotic, and emotional. We want the truth, even if it's messy.

Remember those tribes we thrive in? Surrounding ourselves with people who support our being allows for being exactly what and where we are in any given moment—whether that's light and hopeful or snot-nosed, bleary-eyed, and desperate. And this isn't about misery loving company. This isn't an invitation to throw a pity party; it's an invitation to throw a me-too party. Which is vulnerable and scary and an act of total faith, I know. But when we give ourselves permission to be honest, not only does that become an anchor back to our own freedom and joy, but it can also offer others a path to theirs. Love, safety, and tenderness heal, and everyone is going through something. Everyone is in the mess in some form or another.

Masks

While in treatment, I had one other major breakthrough related to both authenticity and masks, this one in the art room. Our lead therapist had given each of us a plaster mask and the task of rummaging through the wealth of craft supplies to create a personal mask that depicted the way we had been living (or barely surviving) with the pain in our lives. The artist in me loved this project and went to town, meditatively focused on crafting together my persona.

When it came time to share, the handcrafted masks were moving and heartbreaking with their artistic cracks and tearstains. Mine, however, didn't include any of those markers. I held up my mask, which looked...like me. Big smile on a freckled face, and I had even managed to find some Fraggle-like yarn that worked as hair. You know, shiny, happy Az. Except I had covered that killer smile with an X of duct tape.

Everyone took a beat, the meaning clear. I was beautiful but quiet, happy but silenced. They got it. But that wasn't all. I turned the mask over, and everyone sighed in recognition. Inside it was painted black and blue. That dichotomy best described the way I was living, hiding my shame, pain, guilt, and fear—my human-mess. The mask expressed it all: the way I kept it together on the outside, staying silent and playing nice, convincing everyone "I'm fine" and exhaustively keeping the peace while I battled a raging war inside.

But here's the secret: We're all a little black and blue inside, bumped and bruised and worse for the wear. That's what makes us human. And when we have the courage to take our masks off, turn them over, and meet each other where it hurts, that's when our pain can become a bridge to connection and healing. That was the beauty of treatment. We felt safe to open ourselves to one another without pretending and without denying the wounded and not-so-shiny parts of ourselves. There was no judgment, just acceptance. Everyone got to see my blacks and blues. And they loved me not in spite of them but because of them. That's humanity. Fuck shiny and happy. Perfectly imperfect wins every time.

HUMANITY

My authenticity depended upon turning my mask inside out. The irony is that by dropping my fake smile and false fineness and owning the bruises and scars, I actually became happier and shinier. Because all the energy I had been putting toward resisting was then able to go toward *connecting*—with myself, my Spirit, and the Souls around me. It required putting some skin into the game, but that's what authenticity does—even if that skin is black and blue.

We've all got the things we're covering with a mask—whether they're literal or metaphorical bruises. But what if—*what if!*—those things we're hiding are exactly the things someone else is looking for? And what if, by exposing them, we are able to give someone else *and* ourselves the miraculous gift of a me-too moment? The bridge to connection is authenticity, and that starts with honesty. Certainly the truth can hurt—we're all here because the truths in our lives have pained us in some way—but that same old truth will also set us free. So it's time we get comfortable and start to feel at home in our own skin.

You Be You

There's a Hasidic tale that reveals with amazing brevity both the universal tendency to want to be someone or something else and the ultimate importance of becoming one's Self and living authentically. When he was an old man, Rabbi Zusya said, "In the coming world, they will not ask me: 'Why were you not Moses?' They will ask me, 'Why were you not Zusya?'"

It takes an extraordinary amount of courage to be ourselves out loud in the world. That's why we try to be someone or something else—because being anything other than our fullest Selves simply takes less courage. The word *courage* comes from the Latin root *cour*, which means *heart*, and as Brene Brown shares in her 2010 TEDx Talk, the original definition of *courage* was "to tell the story of who you are with your whole heart." So there it is again—*whole*. Courage. Authenticity. Healing. It all goes back to wholeness. We are not here to prove anything but to improve everything. And that requires not just our real Selves but the *entirety* of our real Selves and our unique expression.

And I know it's hard. But rather than a challenge, I like to think of it as the greatest invitation of our lives. I don't care about your job title, zip code, or how many followers you have. I want to know how you feel, whether you struggle like I do sometimes, and if you'll allow me to be in my mess without trying to fix it. Can you just stand by with a fresh towel and clean clothes, because isn't that what it's all about? Isn't that all any of our Souls want underneath the chaos of earthly noise? The safe space to be seen and heard and held. If so, we must do that for each other. We must invite each other into the raw, real, and colorful conversations that—yes—might include a little black and blue.

Resistance

The minute we say yes to moving, stretching, and embracing all of who we are, watch out. Because we will come face-to-face with every reason we should continue to stay quiet and play small. Refusal will be thrown at us in every way, shape, and form. And all the naysayers will show up, kicking and screaming that we're unworthy or incapable of fulfilling this next new feat. **Resistance** is always plotting and lying and stealing us away from fully living out loud. For every dream burning inside, there's an army of resistance prepared to stop us, but what's critical to understand is that resistance serves a purpose. The more powerfully it shows up, the more important that change or path is to our healing and being.

Additionally, resistance exists to refine and strengthen our senses. It's meant to poke and provoke us. Yogi Bhajan described every teacher as one who pokes, provokes, confronts, and elevates, and we can think of resistance in exactly those terms—as a teacher. And our greatest resistance is deeply familiar, because actually, it's every thought we think. Our biggest and baddest infantry of doubters, haters, and naysayers is the one between our ears—the voices in our own head that are scheming up ways to convince us to throw in the towel.

Because of my time spent as a preschool teacher, my favorite way to explain this experience of resistance is to compare the inside of our heads to a classroom full of antagonizing preschoolers. Stuck inside on a rainy day. With instruments. Imagine dozens of dissenting voices that sound like hundreds, whining, pining, blaming, and complaining. It's pure mayhem as they bang, strum, toot, and drum. In this scenario, we are the teacher, and that dissonant band can continue to make noise, or it can instead create music. Our choice. It just needs a conductor.

The resistant army needs a commander-in-chief, and that brave leader is none other than us. We are the ones we've been waiting for. And our first step is to take one of those powerful God pauses and recognize that all those voices are not who we are; we are the one listening to them. They are just energy needing direction. And sometimes it takes everything we've got to not pick up an instrument and play right along, but remember, energy flows where our attention goes, so we are the director here. We have the opportunity to recognize and identify what we are feeling in our body (fear, overwhelm, doubt, confusion, overexcitement, etc.) and then ask ourselves: *Is there a real threat here, or is this simply the scientific equal and opposite reaction to our effort to do something different?*

If it's the latter, we can take this energy as a sign that we're on the right track and channel it accordingly. We can use it to create momentum by choosing one of our tools or practices to bring us back to a neutral state. And from there we can take the next right step. Over and over again. We can confront that self-saboteur and elevate ourselves beyond it. This step-and-repeat will carry us all the way through our inner resistance and give us the strength and confidence to stand up to any naysayers we may then encounter on the outside, be they doubters, saboteurs, or the cripplingly powerful force of other people's opinions. And we don't do this by being mean. We just stop playing nice. Playing nice is like playing safe, and we play safe only to avoid rocking the boat. Well, fuck the boat—the ship is sinking.

Nice vs. Kind

Every Martin Luther King Day, I teach a special yoga class designed around Dr. King's quote "I've decided to stick to love...Hate is too great a burden to bear." It's one of my favorite classes all year because I am all about the love, and in it I also talk about that passage from 1 Corinthians that you've probably heard recited at more weddings than you can count: "Love is patient, love is kind..." You hear that? Love is *kind*. Not nice. There is a difference.

Nice tends to be externally motivated, often at the price of remaining silent and censored in order to stay conventionally correct and socially accepted. Nice runs on the desperate fumes of our need for approval. And man, we've all got a case of what I call OPO (or Other People's Opinions). So what do we do? We dress to impress with our accessories of pleasantries. We politely please and agreeably appease. We dance around confrontation to get our fix of validation. *Nice*. But that just doesn't feel like love to me. That feels like fear.

Kind, on the other hand, is just that: the other hand. An open and honest, sincere, and helpful hand. With no interest in playing for likes or shares, or in collecting fans or followers, kind is intrinsically motivated. Kind is not afraid to respectfully speak even if others disapprove. It's got the inviting mind with an "open" sign even if others are closed. Kind has no strings attached to circumstance; it's not tethered to conditions. Except one: the human condition. And our built-in drive to live, give, love, and serve; to lift and listen; to share and care; and to earnestly speak our endangered truth. If that ain't love, I don't know what is. So screw nice when we can instead be kind. It's time to speak up and speak out, to stand up and stand out. Because it's the loving thing to do.

Part of practicing authenticity is bravely choosing being real over being liked, and that can be daunting. We're not going to pretend there isn't risk involved in putting our true Self out there, but the fact remains that there's even more risk in hiding our gifts from the world. Anne Frank said, "Look at how a single candle can both defy and define the darkness." We need each other to light each other up, to light each other's way, and to cast away the shadows of fear and doubt that attempt to keep us small and apart. What we do and say matters. But those of us wanting to change, heal, and add a little more light to this world must remember that it's gonna fucking burn sometimes.

If we really want to be the light, we can't avoid the heat of life. Martin Luther King Jr. is a prime example of that. So are Jesus Christ, Mahatma Gandhi, Malala Yousafzai—the list goes on. Throughout time, being an advocate of love and kindness, of equality and acceptance, of peace and forgiveness has always been treated as an act of rebellion. Of subversion. So know that it will not always be met kindly. It seems counterintuitive, but there are people who will not understand or support an agenda of kindness, honesty, and authenticity. This is not a reason to stop. It takes only one candle to light up the dark, and that light is contagious, so imagine what millions can do. Imagine what can happen when we use that fire as fuel to activate and advocate, to radicalize and organize, to mobilize and actualize, and *rise* and *rise* and *rise*!

HOME

I long, as does every human being, to be at home
wherever I find myself.

—*Maya Angelou*

Phenomenally, when I spoke to my study participants, they consistently used the same words to describe their healing experience and where they landed on the Kundalini mat and within themselves. Those words were, "I just felt at home. I had finally come home." And this mirrored my own trauma recovery. By incorporating this spiritual somatic practice of Kundalini yoga and applying these principles to our lives, we all felt a sense of being back home within ourselves.

As I said earlier, I call Trauma to Dharma a journey home because that is what living in awareness does—it brings us home. And home is our authentic way of being. It's settling into and getting comfortable with what happened, with what is happening, and with not having all the answers to "so what happens next?" Home is living in and claiming our authenticity by being fully and only who we are. It is recognizing that we are flawed and fallible, and that makes us perfectly ourselves. And it is seeing this not as an excuse to stay the same but to stay in the game even when we fumble, stumble, or fall.

When I think of "home," I think "walk in the door and throw down my bag of crap" kinda home. "Pull off my bra and put on my sweats" kinda home. "Tie back my hair, sink into that chair, and take that softening exhale" kinda home. When I think of home, I think cozy,

ALLOWING   APPRECIATION   AUTHENTICITY ⟶

warm, and safe—safe enough to put down my protective shield, to take off the armor and masks, because it's a nonjudging and accepting space where I can get emotionally honest and vulnerable, raw, and real. When I think of home, I think of "me too." It's where our paths connect. But only if we're fully showing up, because home is *all in*.

Go Big *and* Go Home

We've all heard the saying "go big or go home," but in the context of healing and recovering (and, frankly, living), I think it's not an *or* but an *and*. Go big *and* go home—because home *is* going big. Home is being seen. The moment we finally come to embrace our messy, complicated, whole Selves as the most honored guest within that home we call our hearts, something profound happens. And it's the same thing that happens every time we sit on that yoga mat and tune in. It's a homecoming. A reunion between us and that certain something or someone we've been longing and aching for our entire lives—our Soul.

We are all on the hunt for this missing piece/peace, and that's why I call Kundalini the yoga of the Lost and Found. Because we find ourselves here—we find our home *within ourselves* here, once again. Just as one can walk into a religious service or a twelve-step meeting in any city across the globe and be with their tribe, Kundalini is an open gate. By walking in the door and sitting on that mat, there is a collective understanding. We're here to be and feel home through connection and movement with breath, with Spirit, and with others.

Authenticity, then, is finally giving ourselves permission to be who we are and feeling at home with it. It is a coming to peace with our wounded, colorful Selves and our torn and tattered lives, and it is being at peace with not being at peace all the time. And in both my research and personal experience, that sweet spot also comes with some sweet perks.

Gratitude and Happiness

For all that has been, thanks.
For all that shall be, yes!
—Dag Hammarskjold

Having come from a disconnected and despairingly depressed state after their personal traumas, the majority of my study participants experienced an overall sense of happiness, joy, love, and/or peace as a result of their Kundalini yoga practice. And *every single one of them* connected their experience of happiness back to gratitude—specifically that they were finally, blessedly home. Yogi Bhajan said time and time again that happiness is our birthright. And as far as I'm concerned, gratitude is the gateway back to that birthright, back to what is hidden at the core of all things: joy, happiness, love.

When we talk about "happiness," to be clear, we're not alluding to some shiny, happy "fine" masks or Pollyanna versions of ourselves. My participants didn't mean they found some pot of gold at the end of the Trauma to Dharma, Kundalini-infused rainbow. Instead, their heightened sensitivity and deeper connection to their internal senses and feelings (good *and* bad) strengthened their connection to others and the Universe, which in turn reminded them that they were alive. They were happier simply because they felt more alive, and their lives were the fullest they'd ever been because they were no longer missing from them—numb or checked out, hidden or hiding. So their happiness stemmed from—*ta-da!*—living in awareness.

BE THE LIGHTHOUSE

At this point in their healing, my study participants were feeling, breathing, and connecting to their aliveness (even when it hurt), and their happiness grew from their gratitude for this aliveness and their recognition that they were too alive to be shut down. The more we commit to coming back to ourselves, the more that authentic light of our being shines. And though it might be scary or uncomfortable for a time, we have to be willing to stand out—to shine—so other people can see us, like a lighthouse. Because the more we burn and shine our light, the more it lights the way for others who've lost their way and can't find home. Simply by feeling at home—by being and radiating ourselves—we give others permission to do the same.

To live authentically is to courageously share all of who we are, and through authentic living, we begin to understand and own why we were born. And that "why"—that place where our authentic way of being meets the world's deepest need, where that uniquely missing piece in the world is one that only we can fill—that is our dharma.

SOUL PRESCRIPTION

Journal Question #1: Models of Authenticity

Who's a model of authenticity in your life? There can be more than one, and they can be people you know personally or not. Who have been your lighthouses—people who've shined their light in order to show you what is possible?

Journal Question #2: No More Fine Masks
What's beneath your "fine" mask? What are you willing to brave into embracing and sharing? What might being seen look like for you? If you didn't care so much about what other people thought, what's the first thing you'd probably do?

Journal Question #3: Home Is in the Heart

Where have you felt disconnected from your Self and your life? Where might you still be feeling the pain of that distance between where you are and who you are? What still stands in the way of you coming home to you? What are the blocks?

Journal Question #4: Principles of Awareness

What *A* principles (acceptance, agency, authority, allowing, appreciation, authenticity) are you still struggling with? Which ones can you put deeper into practice?

Meditation for Wholeness and Healing a Broken Heart

Our hearts suffer when we have disconnected from our Soul and have denied parts of our Self. This meditation is designed to heal a broken heart, and if healing means to make whole, then our greatest step toward healing is integrating and embracing all the perfectly imperfect parts of ourselves. The heart loves and gives impartially. It doesn't have favorites. Imagine if we learned to do the same—and if we started at home, where it counts the most.

Posture: Sit in easy pose or in a chair with a straight spine and a light neck lock, palms together, lightly touching in a relaxed prayer pose. The tip of your middle finger is at the level of your Third Eye point. Your forearms are horizontal to the ground, elbows high.

Eye Focus: Your eyes are closed and focused on the tip of your nose.

Breath: Breathe long and deep.

Continue for three to seven minutes.

Asana: Kundalini Triangle Pose (Downward Dog)

Embracing and exposing all the parts of ourselves is a *stretch*. Literally. Living in awareness and embracing our authentic way of being can get uncomfortable. But I'd rather lean into the discomfort that accompanies reaching my fullest potential than the discomfort of staying small and silenced. This pose teaches us to lean into the discomfort that accompanies our authentic growth stretches.

Posture: Begin on your hands and knees. Align your wrists directly under your shoulders, and knees directly under your hips. Tuck your toes under, press into your hands (fingers spread wide), and begin to lift your hips toward the ceiling. Press your hips up and back, reaching your chest toward your thighs. Lift up through your tailbone to keep your spine straight and long.

Breath: Breathe long and deep.

Hold for three minutes.

To Finish: Take a deep inhale and as you exhale, begin walking your hands back toward your feet, rising up one vertebra at a time. Keep your feet rooted in the ground and stand steady and still.

Chapter Eleven
DHARMA

*When you combine the ability to express your unique
talent with service to humanity,
then you make full use of the Law of Dharma.*
—*Deepak Chopra*

There's a story I love about a woman walking down the street who falls into a hole. Scared, she yells out, "I'm stuck down here; someone help me!" A passerby jumps down into the hole, and the woman yells at her, "What are you doing? Now we're both stuck down here!" The helper responds, "Don't worry. I've been here before, and I know the way out." This is the essence of **dharma.** Our pain can expand us and the way we come to make meaning of our lives. When we allow it to, it can give us our greatest insight into our purpose, destiny, or calling. Once we've done the work to be at home within ourselves, we can support others in being who they are. By leaving our lights on, we can help them find their way home. And that act—the special way we choose to shine our authentically and perfectly imperfect light—becomes our dharma when it is used to help others.

WHAT IS DHARMA?

Dharma is our Soul's purpose, and we can find it in the place where our authentic way of being meets the world's deepest need. Our dharma is the unique contribution we alone can make to our fellow humans as a result of all we have been through and what we have become from it. Because ultimately we are here to help one another and to be useful where we can. Where trauma is a complete disconnection from Self, Soul, life, and the world, dharma is the flipside; it is feeling the sense of connection to all that we are and to the deeper purpose of what enlivens and inspires us. It is living a life of mission and meaning, no more and no less.

As we discovered in the principle of authenticity, our first level of humanity and living our Soul's purpose is finally giving ourselves permission to be who we are. Once we've claimed that and are willing to share it, once we are letting our light shine through the cracks in our world, we are stepping into dharma territory. We are moving from light to lighthouse. And the purpose of a lighthouse is to be a beacon for guiding ships that are out to sea.

Dharma isn't about a career, degree, title, or position; nor is it about power, status, or accomplishment. It's not the what we are or do but the why behind it and how we choose to show up for it. It's about what we love and what feels easy and rewarding to us that also happens to genuinely serve others. It's how we manifest our why as an expression of the parts of ourselves that had been shut down. And it isn't about packing up and moving to live in an ashram or monastery; it's about living a life that feeds us while it also feeds others, because our dharma—whatever it may be—lights us up. It's impossible to give off light without also being lit up.

Our dharma evolves as we do, so we must continue checking in with ourselves about it, deeply reflecting on what it means to have a life of meaning: to us, to others, and to our relationship with Spirit. And the answers to this don't come from an outside voice calling us to be something we're not. It's not what we think we should want or what we've been told that we want but what we truly desire, as communicated to us from the voice inside. That deep-seated knowing calls us to be the person we were born to be and tugs at our Soul, saying, "This is the way." And there are many vehicles through which we can express that, our career being only one.

We all have a dharma, something we were brought here to do that is completely and totally ours. We all showed up here in this human-mess because we answered some personal call. These dharmas are as individual and specific as we are, and just as there is no such thing as a trauma hierarchy, there is also no dharma hierarchy. No one's purpose is better or more meaningful or important than anyone else's. We touch the lives we are meant to touch. And though it can be easy—and very human—to fall into compare and despair, those are the workings of the ego. When this happens—and it will happen, again and again—we can employ the ever-powerful God pause, breathe, give a shift, and go back to reclaiming our authority and permitting the Soul (not the ego) to pen this purposeful story of ours. Because dharma is the Soul's workplace and playground. It is both our commitment to higher consciousness and our road to it.

PAIN INTO PURPOSE

There are places in the heart that do not yet exist;
suffering has to enter in for them to come to be.

—Leon Bloy

So all this pain-to-purpose talk, it happens right around now. Once we've stopped avoiding the pain and started relating to it in a new way, once we've let the victim go and summoned the victor, we can begin moving from tragedy to triumph and uncovering the opportunity in the obstacle. This is how we transform pain into purpose. Our dharma is our way of turning coal into diamonds and "mettle" into gold.

Our Soul's purpose came into the world with us, and just as a seed is compelled to become the tree, flower, or blade of grass it was meant to be and will use every last fiber of its being to fulfill its potential, so too must we, because our dharma comes with a sense of responsibility and duty. It's not so much that we are on a journey but that life and consciousness are on a journey through us, begging for our courageous expression. Yogi Bhajan said that dharma is when one's life path is aligned with one's infinite, authentic Self, and when we are living in dharma, "we are in flow with the universe, with our spirit, and with our basic nature." So when we are living, doing, and being from a place of authenticity in connection with a higher, divine calling or purpose, we are living in dharma. And it is not always easy, but my God, is it worth it.

Pessimism to Activism

What if this darkness is not the darkness of a tomb
but the darkness of a womb.

—*Valarie Kaur*

The nature of life's polarities is that it's always darkest just before the dawn. And we can thank that darkness because we need it. It attracts the light. When the trusty rooster crows, we know the heavy darkness of night has fallen into the crack of dawn. And well...we know all about cracks! They are a portal for the light. And now they are also our rooster call to action. For those of us who are awake and alive, this is our dawning. Our rise-and-shine moment. It's okay that we may still have wells of disbelief and frustration, anger, and fear. That anger of ours is fire, and we need it. Though we must also remember that anger can either cook for us or burn our house down. We've seen that misused anger burn us, our pasts, our Earth, and humanity. *But that's not us.*

Having traveled this Trauma to Dharma journey, we are all equipped to let that anger cook for us instead of burn us down by consciously, nonviolently, and unapologetically transmuting our pessimism into activism. An activist is an alchemist. And Kundalini yoga? Pure alchemy. Together, the principles of Trauma to Dharma and the ancient science of Kundalini yoga neutralize, alchemize, and actualize. So it's not about denying our anger but using it as fuel to birth something necessary, timely, fierce, and phenomenal.

Be the Storm

The devil whispered in my ear,
'You're not strong enough to withstand this storm.'
And today I whispered back, 'I am the storm.'
—*Unknown*

We have all battled our own inner demons: those devilish voices telling us we're not good enough, strong enough, smart enough, whatever enough. But the time has come to give a shift. The time has come to harness and utilize the thing we've feared most: our own rising storm of strength and wisdom. And this fierce and forceful storm of storms isn't violent or abusive, destructive or oppressive. It may not play nice, but it is inherently kind. This storm is creative and constructive; it organizes and mobilizes. Fueled by fierce compassion, inclusion, and connection, it is done staying hidden and quiet—it is rising. It is done feigning sleep, and it is no longer afraid of the storm, because it finally understands and owns that it is the only storm that matters. And once we know that, we cannot unknow it.

This kind of realization comes with responsibility, because this gift also comes with the obligation to communicate it. We are allowed to see the truth only with the agreement that we will pass it on to others. So what we now know, we must share. We must use our voice, gently or loudly, angrily or compassionately. But we must use it. Even when it feels like a burden.

LET YOUR PURPOSE BURN BRIGTHER THAN YOUR FEAR

Just as we experienced in authenticity, the minute we come face-to-face with our mighty purpose, we will also come head-to-head with our fear. The fear monster is really going to make itself known right now, and it's going to show up in every figure and form it can. Beyond the internal and external naysayers and saboteurs that we discussed around resistance, and our crippling fear of other people's opinions, we're likely to be paid a visit from any or all of these other faces of fear:

EXCUSES: The chorus of "I'm not ready," "I don't have the time," and "Maybe someday." But when will we be ready if not now? There are seven days of the week, and someday isn't one of them. As they say, excuses are tools used to build bridges to nowhere and monuments of nothingness.

COMPARE AND DESPAIR: Iyanla Vanzant addressed this one best when she called comparison "an act of violence against the self." We are all on this planet with unique purposes, and it doesn't serve us or those we are here to help to get distracted by what others are doing and how we think we measure up against it.

IMPOSTER SYNDROME: You know that fear of being found out as a fraud? The clever little trick about this one is it's only experienced by those who are striving to become a phenomenon. We will hit this glass ceiling of fear only if we are endeavoring to get past something. So just like resistance, this is actually a good sign.

If there's one thing we've learned through every step in this process, it's that life begins at the end of our comfort zone. And you know what else begins there? Fear. So really we have only one choice if we are to live our fullest and brightest lives. We must begin to make friends with fear and get comfortable with a little discomfort. We must allow our purpose to burn brighter than our fear.

Teacher, Teach Her

I'd like to think that, after all these years, my fear and I are super tight. But we weren't always tight like, "Hey, fear, I see you. I see what you're trying to sabotage here! Thanks but no thanks—I got this!" It was more like I was tightly wrapped around its stake of resistance, falling for every reason and season behind why I had no real purpose and nothing to offer the world. Luckily for me, the Universe is very generous with opportunities to prove me wrong and impress upon me that I do, in fact, have a mighty purpose here.

It was a late Monday afternoon in early November 2009, and I had just completed my Kundalini yoga teacher training a few months prior. I was winding down my day and gearing up to go to Guru Singh's evening class—a Monday night ritual for me and so many others—when I got the call. It was Guru Singh on the line, and he sounded awful. I was certain I had misinterpreted his request between his coughing and congestion. "Hey, kid, I'm feeling pretty crappy. So I'm going to need you to sub my class for me tonight." My heart dropped, and my stomach churned like when I would unexpectedly get called on in elementary school and didn't know the answer. *Me? Sub for* him? *Is he* crazy? *I'm not a teacher! I can't do it! I'm not ready! I've barely graduated!* I responded with radio silence.

"I need you to step in," he continued, and I grappled with what to do. How could I say no to him, after all his years of guidance and support? He got me. He knew just how to bypass the resistance rally inside my head: first, by calling me at the eleventh hour so I didn't have time to conjure up excuses, and second, by pulling at my caretaking heart strings. (He's sick and needs my help!) So in spite of my fear—my terror, really—I showed up and braved my way through a sea of students who were disappointed he wouldn't be teaching and doubtful of my qualifications and credibility (myself very much included!). But I taught, and after class, I realized that while I had disappointed some, I had also pleasantly surprised many.

From that night on, I became Guru Singh's go-to sub. And every week after that, still nervous as hell with my fear in tow, I would show up to teach. I'd feel the humbling sting when some students would see me walk into the classroom, realize Guru Singh wouldn't be there, and then proceed to roll up their mats and walk out. And I'd be equally humbled when the handful of others would approach me after class and thank me for moving them through a beautiful experience.

I haven't stopped teaching since. With every step onto that teacher's bench, I felt alive and purposeful. And as dharma and destiny would have it, not long after, I was gifted the honor of permanently taking over Guru Singh's Monday night class—the same one where I first sat on a tearstained yoga mat and found that something missing and, later, where I didn't feel "ready enough" or "good enough" to teach. Who knew that so much of who I was destined to become was on the other side of what I doubted and feared the most? Apparently *someone* knew. I recently reminisced with Guru Singh about that first terrifying night of subbing and how far I'd come. I asked him if he remembered that late-afternoon call and how sick he was, and he smiled at me and responded, "Oh, I wasn't *really* sick."

Self-Doubt

One of fear's cozy bedfellows is **self-doubt**, and it can be a dream killer. Doubt means to lack confidence, to live without faith, or to be in distrust, and both doubt and fear exist in the realm of the mind. It's our overthinking that invites them into our lives, and it's helpful to remember that they exist only when we begin to believe every thought we think. Self-doubt fuels that imposter syndrome and turns life into a comparative study. So if we can catch and combat self-doubt, we can save ourselves from a lot of blocked pathways to our being.

The other thing that I love (that's right, love!) about self-doubt is that there is a silent *b* in doubt. How brilliant is that? Because that's exactly what doubt does—it tries to silence our being. It tries to sabotage our living, experiencing, trusting, and sharing, which are all ingredients to being alive. And we can't stop self-doubt, but we can stop it from stopping us. As with resistance, we can recognize self-doubt's voice as an indication that we're onto something, that we're on the brink of growing and creating, and we must keep on keeping on. After all, Yogi Bhajan taught us to keep up and we'll be kept up.

Limiting Beliefs

We are all constantly getting messages about ourselves and our capabilities from the world around us. Familial, societal, and cultural conditioning tell us what it means to be female/male/married/single/ straight/gay/rich/poor/black/white/brown/etc./etc./etc. We absorb these beliefs and images and take them on as our own, and that causes us to doubt ourselves when we don't fit the idea and ideal prescribed to us. But these concepts aren't one size fits all. Just like those T-shirts that we all know do *not* fit everyone, there is no one size fits all way of being either.

And listen, sometimes these beliefs might be accurate, but we can know that only if we filter them through our own truth. Because they start off as thoughts, and oftentimes our thinking gets in the way of our knowing. Remember, the head thinks, but the heart knows. And the heart is where our purpose burns. Our heart is our compass, not our head. So when these limiting beliefs stand in the way of our taking action, it's time to pick up any of the tools we've now collected, get out of our heads, and dive back into our bodies—the way back to our hearts.

My Heart Hijacked My Head: Trauma to Dharma is Born

The head thinks, and the heart knows, and our job is to reconcile the two. After the breakthroughs with my doctoral research and dissertation findings, I (as in my heart) knew I was onto something. My heart knew these principles I'd uncovered could be applied toward helping my clients and students heal. And so I followed that knowing and spent years witnessing triumphs and successes with the brave souls I was blessed to work with. And yet even with those triumphs, my head kept thinking I still didn't know enough, so it (my head) persuaded me to sign up for a Kundalini yoga–based recovery program to learn more.

Over a week of this training program and thousands of dollars later, I flew back to LA feeling disappointed and frustrated. There was so much missing in what they were teaching that I found myself wanting to interject and correct the teacher at every turn. (Look at that—I actually did know something!) Back at home a few days later, I got a call from the director of Yoga West, the studio where I teach. She'd heard I had done the program and wanted to get my blessing on hosting the same training here at our studio. And to this day I don't know what came over me, but without missing a beat, I said, "I have a better idea. Let me offer you guys *my* program instead." To which she responded, "How wonderful! I had no idea you had a program!"

Neither did I. Because there was no program. The Trauma to Dharma program didn't exist yet, and I couldn't believe what I'd just done. I'd sold her a program that wasn't even a program. What was I thinking? But that was it exactly: I wasn't *thinking*—I was *knowing*. My Soul-driven, purposeful, knowing heart had hijacked the conversation. It had heard the call and seized an opportunity my head would have been too afraid to embrace. And just like that, with only months to prepare, I let my purpose burn brighter than my fear. I used that fire to finally create the Trauma to Dharma program that would go on to heal and transform people's lives. If I had listened to my mind's self-doubt and limiting beliefs, these principles might still be sitting in my dissertation in a drawer somewhere, but because I did the work of healing and opening up enough to let my heart speak, my dharma was able to guide me down this purposeful path.

Turning Fear into Fuel: My Excuses for Not Writing This Book

Creating the program was an expansive and essential part of my dharma, but it wasn't the entirety of it. After teaching workshops and applying the Trauma to Dharma principles year after year, I knew what was next, and because I am deeply human, I was avoiding it. It took me a long time to finally sit down and write this book, and a lot of it was spent battling the many faces of fear.

Excuses came through first in a very rational and pragmatic sort of way: I didn't have time to write a book; I had to *work*. I had to survive, and that was the more responsible choice. Then the perfectionist came in to remind me that my research and material weren't ready yet—weren't perfect yet. And they probably never would be. And after that, the worst of them all, my inner mean girl, finally reared her head, asking who the hell I thought I was to write a book. What did *I* have to offer? She very boisterously suggested that it's already been done, and no one wanted to hear from me anyway. What did I know? I wasn't an expert—I was just an imposter! This, of course, was the same voice that had led me to continue my education and pursue a PhD. I was certain that once I got my doctorate and had all those years of research and experience behind me, she'd finally quiet down. Guess what—she didn't. She's still there, one of fear's many faces, just wanting to keep me small and safe. But how much do we compromise who we are in order to accommodate our fears?

I spent so many years staying small and quiet, pleasing and amenable, and I used to think I was compromising myself to accommodate other people's desires and plans. But really it wasn't about accommodating them at all. Through my healing and growth, I came to recognize that I was actually compromising myself to accommodate my own fear. Around disappointing them, being disapproved of, being rejected—you name it. And we all have to move through that fear of rocking the boat to do this work—because not everyone is going to agree or support it. Enter courage.

Right before big things happen in our lives, we are forced to make a choice that terrifies us. But remember, there needs to be fear for courage to appear. And we can invite it in, one breath and one step at a time. This is yet another opportunity to use our fear as fuel, harness our agency, command our authority, and tune into our allowing to pay more attention to where the Universe may have already provided the perfect support right in front of our eyes. (And for the record, this is exactly how I ended up finding my brilliant editor for this book!)

The Arrow

Now a word about all the arrows. You've probably noticed that it is the Trauma to Dharma symbol, and that runs deeper than its use as a directional sign (though we love and need those signs!). An arrow can be shot forward only by first being pulled backward. So when life has dragged us back with difficulties and challenges—which it has—that means it's also primed us to launch forward into something great, into our dharma. And the closer we get to launching, fear and resistance will pull us back further still, but that tension is nature's way of readying us to soar. This is where we can take a lesson from the archer. Like the archer, our Souls know something. They see beyond the present space and limiting thoughts to release the arrow, trusting its trajectory. My selling the Trauma to Dharma program before it was fully developed was my Soul taking the bow, and the key to success on this path is just that. Stay grounded in the present, steadily aim our focus forward on our vision, and patiently wait with the knowing that the journey will begin not by our force but with our letting go.

OUR HEALING IS DHARMA

We're not on our journey to save the world
but to save ourselves.
But in doing that you can save the world.
—Joseph Campbell

Here's some good news: the greatest gift we can offer the world is our own healing, so doing this work—healing our trauma—is part of our dharma. By picking up this book and moving through these pages and principles, you are already living in dharma! Congratulations—you're on your way! Healing ourselves and our wounds has a ripple effect that others benefit from because when we heal, the world heals.

Where Your Authentic Way of Being Meets the World's Deepest Need

Our first level of service to the world is showing up authentically. By healing, claiming ourselves, and being seen in our entirety, we give others the gift of hope and possibility. And by being who we are, we allow others to do the same. So if we do nothing more than show up fully as we are, we serve others by giving them the opportunity to see authenticity reflected back to them.

My first conscious experience of this—of being served and supported by someone living her dharma through authenticity—was with my therapist at Sierra Tucson, Carmen. Her style of being so real and transparent with me about her own experiences and what had brought her to where she was (when appropriate) was such an inspiration to me. *She* was such an inspiration to me, as someone who had been where I was and had committed to healing the pain and being of service to others. Seeing firsthand how she had turned her life around and fashioned her wounds into wisdom—wisdom from which I was reaping the benefits—informed the way I would later work with clients in my own practice, sharing my humanness, trials, and triumphs. Her deep level of authenticity and service became a touchstone for my own dharma.

In addition to guiding my practice, this authenticity is an important part of my teaching style. Multiple times a week, I sit in front of my classes and share honestly about what is going on in my life and how I use the Kundalini technology to navigate it. And the feedback I get is all the proof I need. Students frequently thank me for saying exactly what they needed to hear. They wonder how I knew and marvel that it felt like I was speaking directly to them, to which I always respond that I was actually speaking directly to *me*. And that's because I teach what I need to hear. Enough of these encounters finally helped me to understand that by simply living authentically and being vulnerably real, I was meeting other people's needs.

In his last lecture, Yogi Bhajan said, "Life is to live for each other," and isn't that really what this all comes down to? Living for each other— that's dharma. He used endless metaphors to describe just how we are meant to show up in this way, including that of a forklift. Like a forklift, we need to be able to bend and humble ourselves to meet someone where they are in order to lift and support them. And this isn't about being better or less than; rather, it's about being able to flex and bend to let others know we see them, we get them, and we're here to help where we can. To embrace our humanity is to embody humility, to be willing to bend and fall to our knees to meet another. And our greatest aid in doing that is compassion.

FIERCE COMPASSION

Our sorrows and wounds are healed
only when we touch them with compassion.
—*Buddha*

It is said that all healers must be wounded because that is where the medicine is. Medicine lives in the heart of pain, because from our suffering, compassion is birthed. Suffering reminds us of our brokenness and our humanity; it disarms us of our self-absorption and magnifies our need for one another. Our own wounds make us tender and gentle with the wounds of others, and our vulnerability connects us to theirs, uncovering the thread of humanity that weaves us all together. Our shared ache allows us to find refuge, hope, and joy even as darkness threatens to swallow us whole.

Compassion means to suffer with, and it is both tender enough to feel each other yet strong enough to carry each other. The Trauma to Dharma way summons our compassion but not just any compassion—**fierce compassion**. Strong-spined, kindhearted, feeling-the-burn kind of compassion. The ego wants to take things on, but the Soul wants to take them in. So the key to compassion—like so much of this work—is spending less time in our head and more in our heart. Our mind is where judgment, intolerance, and dogma live, all of which are fear-based. And fear wants only to attack or retreat. This creates no space for real and raw conversations or connection. Compassion, however, sees through fear by feeling others' pain and hearing humanity's cry.

And let's be clear: compassion is not a spiritual bypass. It's not a loving-and-lighting solution. It is a pausing to really listen, a widening of our lens to see and embrace many truths, and an unclenching of our fists because we can't hold each other if our hands are tied. Rather than taking things *on*—with aggression or violence—compassion takes them *in*, feeling humanity to the core of its brokenness. This is the job of compassion, and its vehicle is kindness. Every person we pass is carrying the weight of loss, disappointment, fear, and shame. So our challenge is to push ourselves to see where the pain we have experienced might be able to deepen our reservoir of compassion and open our hearts to each other to say (if even just to ourselves), "Your pain is my pain." It shifts how we treat each other. And make no mistake: we are how we treat each other and nothing more.

Compassion Needs a Container

So much of our dharma is our heightened and strengthened ability to be with, feel, and serve one another. But our compassion and empathy need a container to hold them; they need boundaries. Our greatest defense is an open heart, but an open heart isn't a bleeding heart. Compassion and empathy will leak and deplete if not given a caring, contained space to be held. Just as with the spiritual bypass, there can be too much of a good thing, so balance is critical.

A brave, generous, and fiercely compassionate heart can be open yet still protected. And in fact, it must be. We can't help anyone if we're bleeding out and running on empty, so this is where compassion and service begin at home. Just as when flying with children, we must put on our own oxygen mask before placing them on our loved ones. Remember: no me, no me too, so we need to fill up before we file out. This can be hard because once we get it, we can't wait to give it. Once we find ourselves swimming in gratitude with lessons to share and wisdom to bear, we want to go full throttle to give and serve and love. But before we race out the front door toward humanity, let's remember our boundaries and not leave home without them.

When stepping into the vulnerable space of sharing our wounds and shame, self-care must begin with getting a sense of who we are with. Because while it is true that, yes, everyone out there is fighting some sort of battle, not everyone is ready or willing to share; nor will everyone know how to hold the space for us when we do. So this requires some intuitive prowess on our end. All the tools we've been using of breath, meditation, and yoga afford us the ability to "come to our senses" to check in with how we feel around certain people. Only when we receive the signs that we are safe and supported and that it will be of mutual service to share should we then brave on.

Codependence

There's a fine line between compassionate giving and codependence, between our benevolent nature and our codependent need to fix and control what isn't ours to control. And this is where we have to put our codependent tendencies in check, because as we brave our way into feeling through our own suffering and pain, we expand our empathic bandwidth and our capacity to feel others'. But we never want to stretch ourselves too thin; we are no good to our tribe if we are exhausted, depleted, and sick. Our traumas can birth our innate need to give and serve, but dharma cannot exist at the expense of caring for ourselves and our own well-being.

If we feel responsible for other people's problems and those problems start to become our own, it's time to take a step back and reach for our tools. As a recovering codependent who would routinely lose herself in another person or relationship, this one took me a human minute to learn. But now, the way I am able to discern which side of the mental and emotional fence I am on comes down to one question: When I choose to help and support another person, am I also choosing me, or am I losing me? Or in other words, *when I say yes to them, am I saying no to myself?* Compassion doesn't kiss ass; it kicks ass—through loving ourselves as much as we love others.

Codependency is fueled out of fear, whereas compassion is fueled out of faith. And the heart of this issue lies in understanding that codependence isn't about our relationship to another person but about our relationship to our Selves. It's about recognizing where we might be allowing other people's behaviors, feelings, and opinions—and our desire to help, fix, and change them—to affect us and the way we live our lives. This is where obsessing, controlling, and caretaking can leave us bleeding out our self-worth.

Our other-centeredness is self-repression. We need to stay grounded, rooted, and centered in ourselves (hi, self-centered!) in order to bend, reach, give, and serve. Otherwise, we're falling back into our old ways of self-abandonment and going missing. I'll never forget the moment I finally started to understand this idea. I walked into a recovery meeting for codependency and written in big, chalky letters on the blackboard were the words "How empty of me to be so full of you."

SERVICE/SEVA

I slept and I dreamed that life is all joy.
I woke and I saw that life is all service.
I served and I saw that service is joy.
— *Khalil Gibran*

The bedrock of dharma is giving back. It's service, or what the yogis call **seva.** Having reverence for all beings in this world and the knowledge that we all belong to one another turns our questioning from "why did this happen?" to "what can I do with what happened?" This piece offered me the most surprising and moving finding in my research study. Every single one of my participants, after healing and recovering from their own traumas, was called to then give back in some way. It was as if their heart-wrenching life disruptions had opened them up to something bigger and awakened them to a newfound duty to serve. Each of them ended up asking in their own way what they could do with what they'd witnessed, experienced, and felt. They consciously asked how they could make purposeful meaning out of their suffering, and the resounding answer was by helping others.

The desire to be of service is an innately human trait that can get lost or covered in the wake of trauma and, well, life. But my participants proved that with the right tools and growth through our pain, we can reawaken this impulse to give back. They went from a place of feeling like they were missing in their own lives to recovering themselves so deeply and feeling so "full of themselves" that their cups ran over and they simply needed to share the abundance. And that's the funny thing about service—it's selfless yet selfish, because when we are living in our dharma and feeding others, we naturally end up feeding ourselves. So if you know something or if you have something, share it. Seva is an offering, and in giving, we receive.

Giving Is the New Getting

When we are in the role of the victim and see life solely through the eyes of the ego, we operate out of a fear of scarcity. There is not enough to go around; we are on an addictive hunt for more; and whatever we collect, we hoard and hide. But once we've started to peel away those thousand veils that separate us from the truth and have adopted the lens of the Soul, we settle into a land of abundance, where we realize there is more than enough to go around. This is the birthplace of radical generosity.

Anyone who's reading this book—anyone who's doing this work—is blessed. We are blessed with a roof, a bed, food, and water—the essential ingredients that grace our lives as ones of opportunity that many don't have. And beyond that we also have the incredible gift of awareness: awareness that we can use everything that has happened to us, that we can alchemize our pain and fear into fuel to feed others, which in turn will feed us right back. So this awareness is our call to give where we can. And we don't have to wait until the holiday season to do that. Giving is not seasonal. It is not voluntary. It is woven into our human fabric. It is how God speaks to us and through us. Giving doesn't require a season, just a reason. And that reason is we're here.

Charity is birthed out of human suffering by those who learned to heal their own broken hearts by helping to heal others. The crux of charity, thus, is transforming one's pain into purpose. Sound familiar? Charity happens when we can't take it anymore, so we decide, instead, to try giving. Wherever and however we can. Give our time. Give our money. Give our hand. Give a damn. And it is hard on this planet, so even with all our recovery, we will still experience pain. We will still be frustrated and depressed by the state of our faulty affairs. But the moment we take the gaze off our own pain, we notice how everyone else has got theirs too, and there is nothing that heals our wounds better than being of service to someone else.

Yogi Bhajan said, "When you feel miserable, find someone else more miserable and help." That is the essence of charity. So when something's gotta give, let it be *us*. Let's ask how our pain can be of service, because while we cannot help what happened, we can seek to use what happened to help both ourselves and others. We can no longer afford to spend our days lamenting whether our cup is half-empty or half-full; we are blessed to simply be holding a cup. Unlike many. So it's our duty to figure out how to fill that cup and then share it. A candle loses nothing by lighting another candle.

Pain as a Habit

We can't lend a hand if we're holding tightly to our pain, so in order to give, we have to be willing to let go of our attachment to it. I had two experiences more than a decade ago that clearly illuminated this for me. The first was during one of my regular Thursday sessions with my teacher, Guru Singh. I was having one of my helpless, woe-is-me, this-pain-is-too-heavy-to-bear moments when, all of a sudden, he got a shooting pain in his neck. Without thinking, I immediately set my kicking-and-screaming tantrum down and jumped up to tend to him. And once I did, he looked up at me with a sly smile and said, "How much of your pain and your attachment to your pain has become a habit?" He had me there.

Around this same time, I acquired a slight fear of flying. Whenever I boarded a plane, I'd break out in sweats and shallow breathing, my mind spinning with visions of the plane rolling and diving. It was awful. Until I started flying with my best friend, Shelby. Now *she* was a terrible flyer. And there was no room for both of us in our aisle to lose our shit. So being the less emotionally messy of the two (for once), I had to step up and out of my attachment to my fear in order to care for her. Simple as that. When we are required to show up for another person, we cannot be in pain. And wouldn't you know it—my sudden fear of flying dissipated.

Work as Worship

Every year I'm asked to teach a special Labor Day Kundalini class, and every year, on the heels of my commitment, I get a handful of invitations to barbecues and pool parties, which I have to respectfully decline. The overwhelming response is, "I can't believe you're working on Labor Day! Isn't the whole purpose of Labor Day to take the day off?" And every year it gets me thinking about why I do what I do. The simplest answer is that it's my duty.

Dharma is a duty; an honor; and in some ways, a form of worship and reverence. A lot of people squirm at the word **duty** because it often gets confused with **obligation,** but the difference is significant. An obligation is a requirement that's been placed upon us and is extrinsically motivated. There are everyday earthly requirements and expectations of survival from "out there." Duty, on the other hand, is sprinkled with a sense of reverence to something that further feeds our livelihood when we practice it. And in contrast to obligation, duty is intrinsically motivated. It comes from within.

This distinction really bolstered my understanding of Yogi Bhajan's intention for us all to embrace and experience our work—whatever it may be—as worship. And think about that: *work is worship.* These three words can utterly shift our experience. Work is an activity involving mental or physical effort done in order to achieve a purpose or result. We work to achieve. Degrees, promotions, and bigger paychecks. Titles and certifications. So how do we turn work to worship? Our obligations into duties? By shifting our perspective and relationship with the work we do and rewriting the very definition of work from "achieving a purpose" to "living and allowing our purpose." Which is dharma.

We can start by asking, "What is our purpose? Why are we here?" And that answer will have two essential pieces:

1. **The Universal You**. This is our humanity, which is the only way Spirit can speak through our lives to each other. This is what connects us all and makes us each a channel for affecting other humans.

2. **The Unique You.** This is our colorful, personal expression of our humanity or how we are putting our innermost being into practice.

In the Venn diagram of our lives, the overlap of the Universal You and the Unique You is where our dharma lies. So none of this means we have to quit our jobs and run off to the Peace Corps or Doctors Without Borders; nor do we have to work in a hospital or volunteer at a soup kitchen full-time. We simply have to take the answers to this question and infuse them into everything we do, because work transforms in meaning when we relate to it through the Soul as a spiritual practice. And a spiritual practice isn't reserved for churches, temples, yoga mats, or meditation cushions, after all.

All work becomes elevated and infused with a deep sense of fulfillment and satisfaction when done with the energy of love and devotion. And if our essential nature is love, then the more we align our inner being with our outer doing, the more our work becomes a labor of love and is transformed into worship. Additionally, while "work" is often thought of as an obligation to earn money, when it is combined with the aim of service to others, it is rendered sacred and becomes worship. And *whatever* we do can be of value to others once we tap into the meaning beneath what it is.

When approached from this angle, work gives a sense of purpose to the one who performs it, which takes us away from ego and into humility and connection. It's the difference between achieving a purpose and allowing a purpose to come through us. And this purpose can show up in countless ways, from the way we speak to our neighbors or treat the grocery store clerk to the way we raise our children, feed our families, or listen. If it's done with reverence, it's done as dharma.

LEGACY

What you see missing from the world is
what you're withholding from it.
—*Eckhart Tolle*

Our deepest wounds can birth our greatest gifts. That's because our wounds are where we can see just how similar we all are on the inside. Remember my mask? All black and blue and taped silent? Through this work I learned my dharma is that I can't hide or keep quiet anymore. I can't deny my truth in order to play nice. (Kind, yes. But nice? Not a chance.) Really, that's what everyone's dharma comes down to. And I'll tell you something: that makes some people uncomfortable. But the fact is that some people simply are going to be uncomfortable with our truths—no matter what those truths might be. And that doesn't mean we should shy away from expressing them.

Our dharma makes an imprint on the world, and that imprint is our **legacy**. Who we are and what we choose to do with our lives can create a ripple effect. Horace Mann said, "Be ashamed to die until you have scored some victory for humanity." Our legacy, our dharma, our truth, is that victory. The world needs each of us and our mighty purposes, so please don't cheat it. Don't cheat us. Discovering your deeper calling and the gifts you have to offer is a process you've already begun, but don't let the end of this book be the end of your journey. Living your dharma is well worth the time and effort it begs.

Most of the suffering I see in the people I work with is a result of their not seeing that process through, and you didn't get this far to only get this far. So keep going. Keep moving. Keep rising. And keep keeping each other close. Your legacy is calling, and the answer is simple: Listen better. Love deeper. Fear less. Trust more. And when it gets hard, and you're tired or lost, and you just want to melt down in a tantrum because things aren't how you imagined, take a pause and remember this: we don't ever stop kicking and screaming; we just start kicking with purpose and screaming with meaning. That's braving our way from Trauma to Dharma.

SOUL PRESCRIPTION

Journal Question #1: Seva through Purpose

You're here because you have a purpose. While some crises and pains make no sense at all and the unimaginable things you may have lived through seem senseless, they don't have to be pointless. Everything that's ever happened to you can add value to the world. What truly gives your life meaning? Reflect deep in your heart. What do you want to have contributed to the world? What can seva and service look like for you?

Journal Question #2: Legacy

Imagine long into the future, and write about how you will be remembered from the point of view of those whose lives you've touched. What is your legacy? What will people have to say about you, your life, and your dharma? How will you have left your mark? What were your gifts, and how did you contribute them to the world in your own unique way? How did it benefit others? What were the results of listening to the wisdom of your heart and living a life in harmony with your Soul?

Journal Question #3: Dharma Statement/Mighty Purpose

Whittle down the sentiments from your legacy reflection to a sentence or two to come up with your dharma statement or mighty purpose. These words should describe who you are at your core and what fuels your passion, and they should speak to why you are here and where your authentic way of being meets the world's deepest need. This is your megaphone mountaintop mission statement. Write it in present tense.

Some examples include:

I provide others with experiences that inspire them to think and grow.

I help others transform their pain into purpose and move from Trauma to Dharma.

I compassionately create me-too moments.

I feed people's Souls through their stomachs.

I remind people that laughter is the best medicine.

Journal Question #4: Thank You Note

Write a letter to your Soul from this deep-seated place of gratitude. Thank yourself, your life, and your Soul for trusting you on this journey and knowing what you needed. Look how far you've come—thank yourself for getting this far.

Pranayama: Strengthening Your Magnetic Field

Living out our dharmas can leave us feeling exhausted and hypersensitive. When that happens, it's a good indicator that your aura isn't strong enough, and a weakened or depleted aura results in your absorbing *everything*. This exercise will help you set your most effective and significant boundary—your magnetic field or aura—in place so you can hold and expand your light without it leaking or depleting.

Posture: Sit in easy pose or in a chair with spine straight, arms by your sides. Inhale and stretch your arms up, palms facing up, into prayer pose (palm to palm over your head). Exhale as you bring them back down, palms facing down.

Breath: Inhale through the nose. Exhale through the nose.

Continue a minimum of twenty-six times.

Meditation: I Am the Grace of God

When life humbles us down to the floor, sometimes it's best to stay there for a moment, if simply as a reminder that there is only one place to go from there. This meditation helps keep us tuned into that primal power within our own being that is an extension of the greater spirited fabric we are woven into. It is meant to keep the ego aligned with the intentions of the Soul and to evoke the grace and grit required for living in awareness and journeying from Trauma to Dharma.

Posture: Lie down on your back, fully relaxing your face and body.

Breath: Inhale deeply, hold the breath, and mentally repeat ten times:

> For women: "I am the Grace of God."
> For men: "I am in the Grace of God."

Tense your fingers one at a time to keep count. Exhale all the air out, hold your breath out, and repeat the mantra ten times.

Continue breathing and repeating the mantra in this manner ten times on each inhale and ten times on each exhale for a total of five inhalations and five exhalations (one hundred repetitions in total).

Asana: Archer Pose

This pose truly embodies the heart of Trauma to Dharma and symbolizes the brave warrior's stance. With focus, steadiness, patience, and strength, the archer's powerful intention is a seed for what's to come, and this is an opportunity to welcome and embrace the resistance along your path as life readies you for yet another launch toward all that you are becoming.

Posture: Bring your right foot forward so that your feet are two to three feet apart. Your right toes face forward while your left foot comes to a forty-five-degree angle with your heel back and toes forward. Your left leg stays straight and strong as your right knee bends until your thigh is almost parallel to the ground. (Do not let your knee go beyond the toes).

Tuck your tailbone. Curl the fingers of both hands into your palms, thumbs pulled back as if pulling back a bow and arrow. Lift your right arm up, extended forward and parallel to the ground over your right knee. Keep your left arm bent at the elbow, and pull back until your fist is at your left shoulder. With your chin in and chest out, feel this stretch across your chest.

Eye Focus: With your eyes open, stare beyond your thumb.

Breath: Breathe long and deep.

Hold for three minutes on each side.

CLOSING

A year after our wedding, Ricardo and I went to Italy for our honeymoon. It was his first time there and my first time back in more than two decades. I hadn't roamed those Italian streets since I was a curious and somewhat naive twenty-year-old living in Padova my junior year abroad, and as I retraced my steps with my husband, I found myself consumed with a heavy weight of grief and an acute pang of sorrow. My mind traveled back to that younger version of myself, who was determined to explore and experience the world, seeking to uncover who she really was. She was a hopeless romantic who had a literary love affair with Dante Alighieri and Boccaccio. She would take day trips down to Firenze by train just to daydream at the foot of Botticelli's *Primavera* or muse up at the magnificence that was Michelangelo's fourteen-foot *David*. She was always moved by his confident gaze and the triumphant story of that young sling-carrying shepherd boy's defeat of the bigger and stronger Goliath. I thought back to her innocence and how little she knew about what would happen shortly after she returned home from this colorful year abroad. She knew nothing of her very own Goliath she would come to face a year later, the man she would meet and the abuse she would endure for six isolated years. She knew nothing of the violence that would invade her body, mind, and soul or how life would shake and break her.

We all have our Goliaths. That six-year stint in abusive hell was mine. Yet if I could go back to that curious and carefree twenty-year-old woman and rewrite all the ways she was wronged, I wouldn't. If I could warn her to change course in order to free her from those years of pain, I wouldn't. Because our freedom lies not in avoiding our pain but in living, barely breathing, and bravely moving through our pain.

If you've been to the Accademia to visit *David*, then you've seen my favorite works of Michelangelo's: *The Prisoners*. These four powerful statues line the corridor that leads to David. The Italians call them *Il Non Finito—The Incomplete*—because you can see where Michelangelo began carving out these magnificent figures from massive blocks of marble but then left them unfinished. Yet they appear far from unfinished to my eyes. Instead, they remind me of the fullness of our pained and humbled human existence. They remind me of how we are all unfinished; we are all God's works in progress. Michelangelo believed the sculptor was an instrument of God and the sculptor's duty wasn't to create but rather to reveal the powerful figures already contained in the marble. His only task was to chip away the excess in order to free them. Life will oftentimes throw us Goliath-sized pain to shake and break us, to slowly chisel away the excess marble in order for us to break open and break free.

Trauma to Dharma was born out of what was missing from my own recovery. It started as a search to understand why Kundalini yoga had helped me to find what had been missing from my own life. But if we're really being honest here—and that *is* what we are doing— it actually started on that August day in 2002 when I simply couldn't hold it together any longer. When my sheer will, resistance, and denial buckled, and I finally hit my breaking point. When I broke down. And with that breakdown, I broke free.

There is a lesser-known Hindu goddess named Akhilandeshvari, the goddess of the Never Not Broken. This goddess embodies the ability to come together and fall apart, over and over again. She's the archetype of vicissitude and change. She must break and fall apart in order to grow back together, attaining much of her strength, fortitude, and power from her being broken, open, and in flux. Her brokenness is not a weakened or damaged state of resignation or ruin but rather a wellspring of renewal and resurgence. It is a rebirth. A dying of all things that had kept her stuck and an undying of a fierce and steady Spirit that is always present and hungry to grow. She renews and resurrects herself over and over again through her brokenness.

Like Akhilan-deshvari, our brokenness is an essential part of our evolving existence. What I didn't know back in 2002—what I am here to pass on to you—is that our Spirit lives and breathes through our brokenness and broken-openness. It relies and thrives on it. So let your brokenness be proof of your spectacular aliveness. Let it be a place to catalyze and alchemize your pain into purpose and an invitation for your Spirit to live and breathe, soar and thrive. Trauma to Dharma is for the never not broken. For each of us standing atop our own personal piles of wreckage, it is a way of life and a way of no longer denying, hiding, or avoiding our brokenness so that we can grow and thrive not in spite of it but because of it.

As I walked through my old Italian stomping grounds, I reached for my husband's hand. While I felt the grief and sorrow of the foreboding pain my twenty-something self would be forced to experience, I also felt a wellspring of joy and gratitude for all she would become not in spite of but because of that pain. That pain revealed what was always hidden beneath the excess: an empowered and liberated woman who carries a treasure trove of wisdom through her woundedness. A woman who, when faced with life's Goliath-sized pain, no longer doubts her David-like strength. And a woman who walks with grace by herself and in the company of others, having learned to embrace pain as her greatest teacher, as life's master sculptor, divinely commissioned to break her open and set her free, again and again and again.

CLOSING PRAYER

Dear God, Dear Universe,

May You guide and protect us along this journey from TRAUMA to DHARMA, helping us to continue stepping with courage and landing with trust.

May we soften into surrendered ACCEPTANCE of our pain, knowing that it is through accepting where we've been and where we are that we awaken to who we are and all that can be.

May we uncover our power of AGENCY, understanding that it is not our circumstances that define us but how we choose to respond to them.

May we responsibly step into our AUTHORITY, acknowledging ourselves for getting this far and transforming our stories from tragic to triumphant.

May we walk in a state of supported ALLOWING, falling into grace and trusting the deeper wisdom that loves us enough to give us what we need.

May we remain in awed APPRECIATION, remembering that our greatest defense is an open heart and that our courageous vulnerability will connect us to each other so we are never alone on this journey home.

May our traumas break us open to keep us open so we can show up in our perfectly imperfect AUTHENTICITY and reveal the magic in the mess.

May we live in our DHARMA, letting our purpose burn brighter than our fear and sharing our light to brighten this world.

May we find ourselves at home wherever we are and keep the light on for others who have lost their way. And may we never go stray or missing again, but if we do, may You continue to place angels before us to guide our way back.

Sat Nam.

TRAUMA TO DHARMA®
Cheat Sheet

(YOUR GPS—GOD-PAUSE STRATEGY)

ACCEPTANCE
Pause. Breathe deeply. Where are my feet? Be here now.
What do I need to accept in this moment?

AGENCY
What is a conscious choice I can make right now that serves me
and all involved? How might I respond rather than react?

AUTHORITY
Give a miracle shift. Move from victim to victor.
Ask—why is this happening _for_ me?

ALLOWING
What isn't in my control here?
What do I need to let go of and trust?

APPRECIATION
What and who can I appreciate in this current situation?

AUTHENTICITY
What does being authentically me look like here?

ACKNOWLEDGMENTS

Mom and Dad, all things begin and end with you. I would not be standing here today – a liberated and empowered woman – without your love, courage, and belief in me, and without your faithfully stepping in to carry me when I struggled to carry myself. I love you.

Ricardo, the one who holds my heart so carefully and tenderly. Thank you for arriving in the perfect amount of soon and for being a warm blanket of compassion and a steady, strong, and supportive pillar. I promise to always lean in if you're the one I get to lean on. I love you with all my heart. There's no one I'd rather unpack with.

Shahr, my partner in crime for life. Every step has felt easier with you by my side. Thank you for always reminding me of my strength when all I could focus on was my weakness, and for inspiring me every day with your generous heart and your commitment to living and loving with every part of it. Of all the gifts mom and dad gave me, you are the greatest.

Tan, you were worth the wait, Coon. Thank you for becoming my sister (finally) and for not only believing in this work but living it, every damn day. You're an inspiration.

Guru Singh & Guruperkarma, thank you for seeing the brilliance of my light and how much it mattered, even when I was too afraid to see it myself. Your steady guidance and commitment has shown me the way out of my own darkness. This whole dharma thing is feeling real good, thanks to you. Love you both.

I would be nowhere without my tribe. To my nerd herd and colorful family of friends, thank you for never giving up on this book (particularly on the days I did) and for loving and supporting all the versions of me you've had to live through, not to mention all those yet to come. You are the ultimate cheering (and appropriate jeering) squad. True friendships stick, thank you for sticking.

Valerie, David, Connie, and Cathy, my Fielding dissertation committee and original Trauma to Dharma dream team, thank you for believing in "a phenomenon" worthy of research and exploration and for supporting its greater purpose: to save and heal lives.

My research study participants, you are the true heroes of Trauma to Dharma. Thank you for sharing your stories with such honesty and transparency. It is because of your courage and strength that others now have a "me too" map for how to transform their pain into purpose.

Sada Anand, my fellow doctor, I'll never forget the very moment at one of our weekly dissertation meetings when the words Trauma to Dharma were woven together. Thank you for being a forever touchstone in my life.

Judi, Sherri, and Tamara, you each played an essential role in bringing the gifts of Trauma to Dharma to life. Thank you for leaning in to help me create a program that begged to be shared. Your hands have left an indelible imprint on this work.

Lisa, Mamini, my dear friend and creative director, you truly are my "life doula," always there to help me birth the next chapter. Thank you for always knowing just how to transform my work and my life into art. And thank you for our destined NYC fight that changed the course of my life forever. Somebody loves you, Mr. Hatch!

Shawnta, Renie, and Holly, thank you for wading through that first manuscript with such thought and care. Your precious time, wisdom, and enthusiasm helped sculpt these pages and reinforced that they were worth sharing.

Monica, the editor of my dreams, thank you for showing up exactly when you did and bravely helping me whittle 500+ pages into two dozen post-its, and then one coherent book. Thank you for always and uncannily knowing what I'm thinking and for saying it even better (and shorter) than I could. You brought Grace in where she was missing and reminded me that we are only as good as the company we keep. I am forever grateful for your company and companionship. LYSODB, Twin Star.

Bailey, you have never left my side. Not for one moment. Mama, I made it!

Yogi Bhajan, the gift of your teachings and technology saved my life and the lives of so many. By your steady grace may I continue to teach and guide others to heal themselves and transform their lives, one conscious breath at a time.

All my clients, students, and workshop participants, thank you for showing up and trusting me. Your dedication to your healing and growth inspire me and thanks to you I will remain forever in awe of the true essence of humanity: that we really are here to leave this place better than we found it.

GLOSSARY

Adi Mantra: Mantra used for "tuning in" to the divine flow and self-knowledge at the start of each Kundalini yoga class. This chant *Ong Namo Guru Dev Namo* can be translated to *I bow to the Creative Wisdom, I bow to the Divine Teacher within.*

Amygdala: A part of the brain's limbic system responsible for detecting fear and preparing for emergency events.

Aquarian Age: The window of approximately 2,150 years in which the sun resides in the zodiac sign of Aquarius. It began on November 11, 2011 (or 11/11/11) and is an age of owning our wisdom and finding unity as opposed to duality.

Asana: A physical posture or position that is designed to help create strength and endurance, improve circulation and energy flow, and/or cleanse organs and other systems.

Aura: The electromagnetic or psychic field of energy surrounding all living beings. It is associated with the health of the physical body, and all the organs impact the strength and the size of the aura.

Breath of Fire: A breathing technique used in yoga that incorporates rapid inhalation and exhalation to increase mental and physical energy. It is always practiced through the nostrils with the mouth closed, unless stated otherwise.

Broca's Area: Located in the left side of the frontal lobe, it is the part of the brain that controls the ability to produce language.

Chakra: Centers of consciousness or wheels of energy throughout the body. There are seven main chakras, which align the spine, starting from the base of the spine through to the crown of the head.

Dharma: Living a life of purpose, mission, and meaning, where your authentic way of being meets the world's deepest need.

Easy Pose: One of the most common meditation positions in which the legs are crossed comfortably at the ankles while pressing the lower spine forward to keep the back straight.

Epigenetics: The study of how the mind can reprogram our genes.

Gyan Mudra: A hand position in which the tips of the thumb and index finger come together to form a circle. It is a powerful and spiritual gesture that stimulates knowledge, wisdom, receptivity, and calmness.

Hypothalamus: A small area in the center of the brain that links the nervous system to the endocrine system via the pituitary gland. It plays an important role in hormone production and helps to stimulate many important processes in the body.

Kriya: A series of postures, breath, and sound that work toward a specific outcome. Each kriya has a different effect, but all work on all levels of your being.

Kundalini: A form of primal energy said to be located at the base of the spine.

Kundalini Yoga: A branch of yoga that combines breath, mudra, eye-focus, mantra, and postures to balance the glandular system, strengthen the nervous system, expand lung capacity, and purify the blood with the intention of bringing balance to the body, mind, and soul.

Limbic System: Portion of the brain that deals with emotions, memory, and survival.

Mantra: A word or sound repeated to aid concentration in meditation.

Meditation: A practice that supports the mind and guides the body through the use of breath, mantra, mudra, and focus. In classical and Kundalini yoga, it is a process that brings us into relationship with ourselves and helps bridge the inner and outer worlds.

Mudra: A hand gesture that focuses and directs energy in a yoga pose or meditation.

Neuroplasticity: The ability of the brain to form and reorganize synaptic connections, especially in response to learning, new situations, or changes in environment.

Post-Traumatic Growth: A psychological term that describes the positive changes occurring in an individual after they've experienced a highly stressful life event.

Post-Traumatic Stress Disorder (PTSD): A mental health condition that's triggered by experiencing or witnessing a terrifying event. Symptoms may include flashbacks, nightmares, severe anxiety, and obsessive or uncontrollable thoughts.

Prana: The energetic life force that courses through all living beings.

Pranayama: The regulation of the breath through various techniques to affect and manage different states of consciousness, relaxation, and well-being.

Sadhana: Daily spiritual practice.

Shuniya: Point of stillness and pure love, lacking any judgment, expectation, opinion, or intellectualism. It is considered one of the most elevated states of consciousness.

Somatic: Relating to the physical body, especially as distinct from the mind.

Sutras: Words or principles to live by. Yogi Bhajan's Five Sutras of the Aquarian Age are:
1. Recognize that the other person is you.
2. There is a way through every block.
3. When the time is on you, start, and the pressure will be off.
4. Understand through compassion or you will misunderstand the times.
5. Vibrate the Cosmos. The Cosmos shall clear the path.

Third Eye Point: The 6th Chakra located at the mid-brow point that provides insight and perception beyond ordinary sight.

Trauma: A highly stressful event or experience that disrupts your world and the way you have come to make meaning of it, leaving you feeling helpless, immobilized, disconnected, and stuck.

Trigger: A stimulus such as a smell, sound, or sight that provokes feelings of trauma.

Vagus Nerve: The longest of the cranial nerves, extending from the brainstem to the abdomen by way of multiple organs including the heart, esophagus, and lungs. It allows the brain to monitor and receive information about several of the body's different functions.

White Tantric Yoga®: An ancient group meditative practice that works on clearing out the deepest corridors of the subconscious mind. It is done facing a partner and following instructions for meditation given on video by the Mahan Tantric, Yogi Bhajan.

REFERENCES

Brown, B. (2012). *Daring greatly*. New York, NY: Gotham Books.

Brown, B. (2010, June). *Brene Brown: The power of vulnerability*. [Video file]. Retrieved from: https://www.ted.com/talks/brene_brown_on_vulnerability

Brown, J. (2009). *Soulshaping*. Berkeley CA: North Atlantic Books.

Calhoun, L. G., & Tedeschi, R. G. (1998). Posttraumatic growth: Future directions. In R. G. Tedeschi, C. L. Park & L. G. Calhoun (Eds.), *Posttraumatic growth: Positive changes in the aftermath of crisis* (pp. 215-238). Mahwah, N.J.: Erlbaum.

Emoto, M. (2004). *The hidden messages in water*. Hillsboro, OR: Beyond Words Publishing, Inc.

Foundation for Inner Peace, (2007). *A course in miracles*. (Third Edition). Mill Valley, CA: Foundation for Inner Peace.

Frankl, V.E. (1984). *Man's search for meaning*. New York, NY: Pocket Books.

Hawkins, D.R. (2012). *Power vs. force*. New York, NY: Hay House, Inc.

Hendrix, H. (2008). *Getting the love you want*. New York, NY: St. Martins Press.

Lazar SW and Benson H. (2002). Function brain imaging and meditation. In: *Complementary and Alternative Medicine in Rehabilitation.* Leskowitz E. (ed.), St. Louis: Elsevier Health Sciences.

Levine, P.A. (1997). *Waking the tiger: Healing trauma.* Berkeley, CA: North Atlantic Books.

Lipton, B. H. (2008). *The biology of belief.* New York, NY: Hay House, Inc.

Ogden, P., Minton, K., & Pain, C. (2006). Trauma and the body: A sensorimotor approach to psychotherapy. New York: W.W. Norton & Company.

O'Leary, V.E. and Ickovics, J.R. (1995) Resilience and thriving in response to challenge: An opportunity for a paradigm shift in women's health. *Women's Health: Research on Gender, Behavior, and Policy, 1,* 121-142.

Taylor, J.B. (2009). *My stroke of insight.* New York, NY: Penguin Books.

van der Kolk, B.A. (2014). *The Body keeps score.* New York, NY: Penguin Books.

Welwood, J. (2011, Spring). Human nature, Buddha nature. Interviewed by Tina Fossella. Retrieved from: https://tricycle.org/magazine/ human-nature-buddha-nature.

Wilber, K. (2000). *One taste.* Boston, MA: Shambhala Publications, Inc.

Zebian, N. (2017). Twitter post, October, 9, 2017 12:37pm, https:// twitter.com/najwazebian/status/917474092588109824

ABOUT THE AUTHOR

Dr. Azita Nahai is a Kundalini yogi, activist, speaker and trauma specialist. She is the founder of Trauma to Dharma® ~ an experiential method that integrates a holistic mind-body-spirit approach to healing trauma and transforming one's pain into purpose. A domestic abuse survivor-turned-thriver, Dr. Nahai experienced something missing in her own recovery, and so, she created this program to fill the void. Her decades of research support the use of Kundalini yoga and meditation as a valuable therapeutic modality in post-traumatic growth. As a change agent she is fueled by her passion to empower others to become conscious and active participants in their own healing. She hopes her work will continue to help survivors access their true power to realize their dharma and transform their pain into a purposeful and joyful life. She lives and teaches in Los Angeles, California.

You can learn more about Dr. Nahai's groundbreaking work by visiting:

azitanahai.com

Facebook.com/AzitaNahaiPhD

Instagram: @azitanahai

Twitter: @azitanahai

Made in the USA
San Bernardino, CA
23 April 2018